Young, Free and Single?

Also by Sue Heath

* SOCIAL CONCEPTIONS OF TIME: STRUCTURE AND PROCESS IN WORK AND EVERYDAY LIFE (with G. Crow)

* SOCIOLOGICAL RESEARCH METHODS IN CONTEXT (with F. Devine)

PREPARATION FOR LIFE? VOCATIONALISM AND THE EQUAL OPPORTUNITIES CHALLENGE

ACTIVE CITIZENSHIP AND THE GOVERNING OF SCHOOLS (with R. Deem and K. Brehony)

* Also published by Palgrave

Young, Free and Single?

Twenty-somethings and Household Change

Sue Heath

School of Social Sciences
University of Southampton
UK

and

Elizabeth Cleaver

National Foundation for Educational Research
UK

First published 2003 by
PALGRAVE MACMILLAN
Houndmills, Basingstoke, Hampshire RG21 6XS and
175 Fifth Avenue, New York, N.Y. 10010
Companies and representatives throughout the world

PALGRAVE MACMILLAN is the global academic imprint of the Palgrave Macmillan division of St. Martin's Press, LLC and of Palgrave Macmillan Ltd. Macmillan® is a registered trademark in the United States, United Kingdom and other countries. Palgrave is a registered trademark in the European Union and other countries.

ISBN 1–4039–0124–4 hardback

This book is printed on paper suitable for recycling and made from fully managed and sustained forest sources.

A catalogue record for this book is available from the British Library.

Library of Congress Cataloging-in-Publication Data
Heath, Sue, 1964–
    Young, free and single? : twenty-somethings and household change / Sue Heath and Elizabeth Cleaver.
        p.   cm.
    Includes bibliographical references and index.
    ISBN 1–4039–0124–4 (hardback)
    1. Young adults—Social conditions.   2. Single people.
    3. Households.   I. Cleaver, Elizabeth.   II. Title.
    HQ799.5.H43 2003
    305.242—dc21
                                                              2003053602

10   9   8   7   6   5   4   3   2   1
12   11   10   09   08   07   06   05   04   03

Printed and bound in Great Britain by
Antony Rowe Ltd, Chippenham and Eastbourne

For our parents,
Reg and Dorothy Heath & Peter and Eleanor Kenyon

Contents

Acknowledgements

This book focuses on the *Single Young Adults and Shared Household Living* project, but for both of us it is also the culmination of a number of earlier, related projects. We are both indebted to the Economic and Social Research Council (ESRC) for funding our research on shared households (award reference R000237033), whilst Liz is indebted to the University of Sunderland for funding her doctoral research on student neighbourhoods. Sue would also like to acknowledge the support of former colleagues at the University of Manchester whose ideas whilst collaborating on earlier projects have influenced her own, most notably Clare Holdsworth, Pau Miret and Angela Dale. Thanks, too, to Danny Bourne for his excellent transcription skills, and to Vicky Scott for her first-rate assistance in the final stages of the shared households project. Our biggest thank you is, of course, reserved for all the house sharers who participated in our research with such generosity, by welcoming us into their homes and telling us about their own experiences of contemporary household formation.

We would also like to thank friends at the University of Southampton for their invaluable support and encouragement in various ways over the last few years, with particular thanks to Wendy Bottero, Derek McGhee, Graham Crow, Traute Meyer, Joan Tumblety, Graham Allan (now at Keele) and Sheila Hawker. Sue would like to express her appreciation to Liz Cleaver for her hard work, enthusiasm and friendship over the last five years. She would also like to thank all her family and friends for being so supportive over the same period, with particular thanks to Fiona Devine, Gwen Crawford, Abigail Barlow, Jan Roughley, Susie Smith, Danna Malone and Mel King. Finally, we owe a huge thank you to our respective partners, Tricia Worby and Mark Cleaver.

1
The Destandardisation of Household Formation

Some people are settling down, some people are settling, and some people refuse to settle for anything less than butterflies (Carrie, *Sex and the City*)

As we move further into the new century, we are witnessing the ongoing destandardisation of household formation amongst young adults. In a relatively short space of time, and across Europe, Australia and North America, patterns of movement in and out of a variety of living arrangements have been radically transformed. It is now commonplace to refer to the risk-strewn path to adulthood faced by contemporary youth. Former certainties of more or less linear transitions into a house and family of one's own have been displaced by a fragmentation of routes and a proliferation of possibilities. By the time they hit thirty, many young adults, having initially left the parental home, will have returned at least once. Most are likely to have experienced some form of communal living: in a hostel or hall of residence, in lodgings or bedsits, in student and non-student shared households. They may have spent time living alone, and will probably have cohabited at least once, possibly with a partner of the same sex. They may have children, with or without a live-in partner. If they have experienced marriage, they are likely to have first cohabited with their current spouse, and they face a strong possibility of subsequently experiencing divorce and remarriage, if they have not done so already. And on the breakdown of their relationships, they may move back into any one of these scenarios, at least temporarily.

This marks a radical departure from the experiences of household formation amongst their parents' generation: typically, a period of parental dependency, possibly followed by a relatively short spell living in intermediate, semi-independent housing (a hall of residence or college dorm,

1

a shared house, or a bedsit, for example), followed by the formation of a family of their own. Family formation, then, is no longer a once and for all event, the end product of a linear movement towards clearly defined notions of adulthood. Instead, today's young adults are increasingly likely to find themselves moving back and forth into a variety of living arrangements over the life course, invariably linked to the creation and dissolution of household forms based on intimate relationships with parents, friends and partners. These broad patterns are by no means uniform across all ethnic groups. Nonetheless, even amongst ethnic communities where more traditional patterns of family formation are still dominant, such as the Bangladeshi and Pakistani communities in Britain, southern European immigrant groups in Australia, and the Hispanic community in the United States, there is growing evidence of a shift towards a diversification of household and family forms amongst younger generations (Goldscheider and Goldscheider, 1999; Berthoud, 2000; Hillman and Marks, 2002).

This diversification is unfolding in the shadow of what has been termed 'the second demographic transition', a term which distinguishes between the demographic shifts that took place in the first half of the twentieth century and those that have occurred since 1960 across many western industrialised nations (Scott, 1999). These shifts are often associated with the rise during this period of social movements that challenged traditional sexual and domestic relations, and they are already having far-reaching consequences for wider society. Patterns of inter- and intra-generational dependency have been transformed by young people's extended dependency on their families of origin. Single person households and shared households are both increasingly common, with many young adults remaining single for extended periods of time and developing extended friendship networks in support of their single lifestyle. Most young people are likely to have several sexual partners before entering into a long-term relationship, whilst cohabitation before marriage, until comparatively recently still stigmatised as 'living in sin', has become the norm across much of northern Europe and Australia. Gay and lesbian partnerships are also becoming more visible, particularly amongst younger generations, with growing calls for the legal recognition of such relationships. Summarising these trends, McRae (1999) notes that 'if current trends in family formation and dissolution continue, by 2016 the number of adults living in families and the number married will both have fallen substantially, while cohabitation will have continued to grow' (p. 24), concluding that 'young people today are likely to remain less oriented towards traditional family life as they age' (p. 25).

Moralists of various political and religious shades point to these trends and pessimistically proclaim the death of the traditional family and the rise of a generation of selfish, hedonistic individualists who are scared of commitment and responsibility. Other commentators are more optimistic and point to the emergence of a new honesty and egalitarianism in relationships, to the freedoms brought about by an opening up of options, particularly for women, and to the emergence of new and diverse forms of social dependency, based on 'families of choice' involving friends and ex-partners as well as blood relatives and current partners. Whilst interpretations undoubtedly differ, it remains incontrovertible that young people are at the forefront of these shifts. Surprisingly, however, relatively few youth researchers have paid serious attention to young people's changing attitudes towards and experiences of domesticity, family and 'settling down', despite their implications for wider society. For all that we now know about young adults' working lives, their educational pathways and their leisure activities, we still know relatively little about 'youthful domesticity', despite the strong links that exist between all of these spheres of experience.

This book puts the spotlight on changing patterns of household formation amongst single young adults in their twenties and early thirties. Specifically, we explore how today's young adults are experiencing and making sense of current demographic transformations. We do this by focusing on young people's experiences of different living arrangements, but also by exploring the nature of their intimate relationships with family members, friends and sexual partners, and their changing conceptualisations of 'home'. In our view, too much existing research has assumed that most single young adults are reluctant 'singletons' who, given the opportunity, would be more than happy to replicate their parents' experiences of household formation. However, we do not find such explanations adequate, nor do they tally with the stories told to us by many young people themselves. In contrast, we contend that a growing number of young people appear to be in no hurry to 'settle down' in the traditional sense. In other words, they do not necessarily regard the single state as something forced upon them by adverse circumstances, but are currently (although not indefinitely) single from choice, often because they are choosing to prioritise other areas of their lives over early family formation. Moreover, being technically single – that is, in the terms used throughout this book, neither married nor living with a partner – does not necessarily preclude the establishment of cross-household relationships, nor the fostering of close 'networks of intimacy', embracing both family members and friends.

In this book, then, we bring together existing research on changing patterns of household formation, focusing mainly on the United Kingdom, but also drawing where appropriate on relevant research from mainland Europe, North America and Australia. Whilst many striking similarities exist in relation to recent demographic shifts in each of these societies, there may nonetheless be huge differences in the underlying processes leading to these outcomes. We are conscious, then, of the need to resist the temptation to over-generalise. We are, however, in agreement with Dwyer and Wyn's (2001) view that it is equally important not to shy away from making connections where they may possibly exist: 'if there is considerable evidence available from a variety of quite independent national studies that points to similarities between the new life-patterns in their younger generations and their attitudes towards their own education and future careers, it is important to draw that evidence together for our own understandings of their lives *even within* their own national settings' (p. 3, emphasis in original).

This book also presents new empirical data from a study of the domestic and housing-related experiences of a group of relatively well-educated and affluent single young adults living in non-student shared households in the south of England in the late 1990s. Although by no means representative of all young people, the graduates and young professionals who dominated our research are arguably at the forefront of shifting attitudes and behaviours with respect to household formation. As such, their experiences shed light on processes of social change, yet they are representative of a group which has been largely neglected within existing youth research. Readers are introduced to our study, the *Young Adults and Shared Household Living* project, in this opening chapter, whilst Chapters 2 and 3 provide the broader context for our research. In Chapter 2 we consider the treatment of domesticity and household formation as themes within existing youth research, pointing to their neglect within the youth cultural studies tradition and highlighting some of the key features of the constraint model that underpins work in these areas within the youth transitions tradition. Chapter 3 outlines our own framework for considering contemporary patterns of household formation, drawing on recent writings within the sociology of youth on risk, destandardisation and individualisation, and exploring three key themes: the relationship between the single life and the demands of the labour market, the emergence of 'post-adolescence' as a distinct phase in the life course, and claims concerning the transformation of intimacy in late modernity. A further theme in this chapter is the important distinction that is increasingly drawn by youth researchers working within this framework between 'standardised biographies' on the one hand and 'choice biographies' on the other. This is a distinction which underpins the growing polarisation between patterns of household formation amongst relatively well educated young professionals and their less well qualified and/or less affluent peers.

In Chapters 4–7 the focus shifts to an examination of some of the specific living arrangements commonly adopted by single young people during their twenties – and sometimes beyond. These chapters are concerned, respectively, with young people's experiences of living in and first leaving the parental home, living in student accommodation, living in non-student shared households, and living alone in a variety of settings. Chapters 4 and 5 also highlight how leaving home in order to go away to university or to depart on a gap year prior to university has become an increasingly common and socially acceptable exit strategy, particularly amongst middle class young adults. Moreover, leaving for these reasons provides young adults with privileged access to the private rented housing sector, leaving their non-student peers with fewer possibilities of finding affordable housing on first leaving home. Chapters 6 and 7 explore the growth of shared and solo living arrangements amongst young adults, highlighting once again the degree of polarisation which exists between the experiences of these household forms amongst young adults of different social status.

Chapters 8–10 move away from a consideration of specific domestic arrangements to focus on young adults' 'networks of intimacy' and their domestic aspirations. Chapter 8 explores the role of family and friends in the lives of single young adults. In Chapter 9 we focus on young people's experiences and hopes in relation to negotiating relationships with sexual partners. Chapter 10 is concerned with conceptualisations of 'home', and young adults' understandings of what it means to 'settle down'. In the final chapter we will reflect on the themes we have raised throughout the book and ask whether current patterns do indeed represent a 'transformation of intimacy', with young people in the vanguard of change. We continue this first chapter, though, by introducing the *Young Adults and Shared Household Living* research project, providing an outline of the project's origins, its main aims, and details of its research design. Further details of the project's research design can be found in Appendix 1, whilst profiles of each individual household are contained in Appendix 2.

Researching 'youthful domesticity'

During the early to mid-1990s, both of the authors of this book were involved in researching the living arrangements of young adults. Sue

Heath had been involved in a number of research projects concerned with mapping patterns of leaving home and subsequent household formation amongst young adults in Britain and in Spain (Heath and Dale, 1994; Heath and Miret, 1996). This work informed a small-scale study of the housing careers of a group of young people who had grown up in the northwest of England and whose school to work transitions had formed the focus of Heath's doctoral research in the early 1990s (Heath, 1997). Whilst the experiences of many in this group conformed to the dominant model of constraint identified by previous research on leaving home (see Chapter 2), the experiences of some fell outside of this pattern. In particular, their transitional routes had either been relatively smooth and trouble free or, even if appearing to be largely the product of constraining circumstances, were not considered problematic by the young people themselves. This raised the question of whether new expectations of household formation were emerging amongst some young people, despite the normative expectations of their parents' generation – and, possibly, of many youth researchers. Meanwhile, Elizabeth Cleaver was conducting doctoral research on student households in the northeast of England (Kenyon, 1997, 1998, 1999), exploring students' sense of being caught between two worlds – that of their student home and of their parental home – and the implications this had for their integration into local communities and neighbourhoods.

Our respective research led us to an awareness of the relative neglect of independent living arrangements – living alone or with unrelated peers – in the existing literature on household formation. Such arrangements tended to acquire significance within the literature only in as much as they were deemed to constitute a 'buffer zone' between dependency on a family of origin and independence within a family of destination. Consequently, young people who lived in such households were seen as occupying – quite literally – a halfway house: neither fully dependent nor fully independent. Whilst Kenyon's research had indicated that in the case of most students this was a relatively accurate portrayal of their situation, there appeared to be no existing research which explored these assumptions amongst a broader non-student population, resulting in a partial and truncated picture of young people's experiences and attitudes towards household formation. It was out of such concerns that the *Young Adults and Shared Household Living* project arose, with the aim of exploring the significance of the growth of shared household living amongst non-students in the 18–35-year-old age range, and attempting to unravel the ways in which choice, constraint and shifting attitudes might be interwoven in their own accounts.

The project, funded between 1998 and 2000 by the UK's Economic and Social Research Council (ESRC), consisted of three strands. First, the socio-economic characteristics of sharers and of their households were established by means of secondary analysis of individual-level data from the 1991 Census of Population. Second, the routine operation of shared living was explored through group interviews with the members of 25 shared households. In total, these households contained 81 individuals, 77 of whom participated in the research (36 men and 41 women). The household interviews, held in a communal space in each household, explored themes such as the organisation of shared and private space and time, divisions of labour, negotiations of privacy and intimacy, and social interaction between household members, partners and friends. Each major theme was introduced by a video clip taken from popular images of shared household living (*Friends*, *This Life* and the film *Shallow Grave*). This technique worked particularly well with younger household members, many of whom had their own copies of these videos on display, and who often greeted each clip with obvious recognition. We also collected data on divisions of domestic labour in each household, and invited respondents to complete a 'housing history' form, summarising the nature and duration of their previous living arrangements and the reasons for each move.

For the third strand of the research we sought to examine sharers' routes into their current communal household. Individual interviews were conducted with 63 of the original 77 household members, based on an adaptation of biographical interviewing techniques. Using the previously completed housing history form as an *aide-memoire*, the young people were invited to narrate their housing history on their own terms. After the initial, largely unprompted narrative, respondents were invited to retell their story from a variety of different perspectives in order to explore fluctuating notions of progress, independence, choice, constraint, and shifting definitions of 'home'. Most of these interviews were conducted in pubs or cafe bars, although some were conducted in the respondents' own homes.

The individual interviews have taken on far greater importance than originally anticipated, providing us with 63 extremely detailed narrative housing histories. These histories embrace not only experiences of living in various shared households, but include detailed accounts of other forms of independent living (single person households, hostels and lodgings, work accommodation, travelling, squatting and living in an environmental protest camp) and of a variety of familial living arrangements (cohabitation, marriage, living in and returning to the parental home, living with siblings and with other relatives, including step-children). Most of the individuals in our sample were, then, experienced movers and 'serial sharers', between them having lived in 633 different households, with three-quarters of these moves occurring since the age of 16. This data has proved to be invaluable to the overall aims of the project, helping us to reflect more holistically on why certain households 'work' and others do not, and on the significance of young people's current living arrangements within the context of broader housing, domestic and employment routes. Importantly, in writing this book it has also allowed us to reflect on themes beyond the scope of our original research aims, albeit amongst a very distinct group of young adults.

The fieldwork was conducted in and around Southampton, a southern English city perhaps best known outside of the UK for being the port from which the ill-fated *Titanic* sailed on its maiden voyage. With a population of approximately 207,000 people at the time of our research, it is the biggest commercial centre in the southeast, with major sources of employment including the aforementioned commercial port and allied industries, an oil refinery, higher education institutions, and the civil service. It is by no means a wealthy city, although pockets of considerable affluence exist alongside areas of inner-city deprivation. Unemployment is slightly above the national average, whilst average full-time earnings are lower than the national average. Just under two-thirds of the city's housing stock is owner-occupied, 12 per cent is privately rented, and a quarter is in the social housing sector (mainly local authority owned). At the time of our research there were an estimated 3500 Houses in Multiple Occupation (HMOs) in Southampton, housing approximately 18,000 people (Southampton City Council, 1998). There are no exact figures on how many of these were either privately rented or owner-occupied peer-shared households, as opposed to single occupancy bedsits and converted flats, although at the time privately rented shared households accounted for a quarter of all HMOs nationally (DETR, 1999).

The shared household as a collective entity formed our initial point of contact. As noted above, our primary focus was on non-student shared households. More specifically, we sought households consisting of individuals between 18 and 35 years of age, unconnected by marriage, cohabitation or family ties (Chapter 6 contains fuller details of our working definition of 'shared household'). We conducted pilot interviews with three households, each of which had posted 'rooms to let' adverts on a noticeboard at Southampton University. The 25 households involved in the main phase of the research, however, were accessed by other means, most successfully through responding to 'rooms to let' adverts in the local press, via letting agents in the private rented sector, and through snowballing. Seven of the 25 households were all-female and five all-male. Seventeen were located in privately rented properties, six in properties being bought by one of the residents, and two in properties being bought jointly by two of the residents. Eleven households lived in terraced properties, seven in semi-detached, four in detached, and three in purpose-built flats. Of these, four terraced houses, one detached house and three semi-detached houses were owner-occupied. Household size ranged from two to six residents. Appendix 1 contains full details of the characteristics of each household.

We were initially concerned about the bias in our sample towards relatively socially cohesive households, on the assumption that households in which sharers did not get on well with each other would be unlikely to agree to take part in the research. However, whilst the majority of the 25 households were indeed relatively cohesive, our greater emphasis on the narrative interviews has minimised these concerns, as these accounts contain data on an additional 259 shared households previously lived in by our respondents, many of which were far from cohesive. Moreover, individual interviews with household members often revealed underlying tensions of varying degrees of seriousness which had not emerged in household interviews, underpinning an important distinction between collectively constructed, publicly acceptable accounts of sharing and the rather more nuanced accounts that emerged within one-to-one settings.

As for the individuals within our sample, Appendix 1 provides details such as the age, gender and economic activity of our respondents, plus information on their housing histories and reasons for moving to Southampton. We focus here on the social backgrounds of our sample members. As noted above, they were generally well qualified: 56 per cent had a highest qualification of degree level or above, including 18 per cent with Masters degrees. With the exceptions of a doctoral student and seven undergraduates (four of whom lived in a mature student household which we decided to include), all were in employment. Of these, 83 per cent were located in professional and managerial occupations, and a further 10 per cent in other non-manual occupations. Our sample is, then, biased towards well educated young professionals, a group whose experiences tend to be overlooked in much mainstream youth research, yet who are increasingly likely to remain single into their late twenties and early thirties and accordingly adopt a range of independent living arrangements during this period of their lives. The experiences of this relatively affluent group, set against those of their less advantaged peers which dominate much existing youth research, are held in tension throughout this book. Indeed, as Bynner (2001) has noted with respect to our research, 'what is becoming a normative lifestyle for that increasing section of the population that gains qualifications, becomes an 'excluded lifestyle' for those who fail to get them' (p. 54). If we are to gain a nuanced understanding of such processes of exclusion and inclusion and the differential impact of social change on young people's pathways to adulthood in the current period, then it is essential that youth research moves away from its preoccupation with youth who are either 'troubled' or '*in* trouble' (Griffin, 2001). We are, then, in sympathy with Coles' (2000) call for a more holistic approach to youth research. He argues for a principle of 'inclusiveness', thus ensuring that 'holistic research, policy and practice is concerned with the needs of *all* young people, and not just the vulnerable who may, for the moment, be of paramount concern' (p. 12).

In this chapter we have outlined the major themes of this book and have introduced the *Young Adults and Shared Household Living* project. Readers are referred to Appendix 1 for further details of the project's research design, and to Appendix 2 for a profile of each of the individual households and their members. In Chapter 2, we turn to a consideration of the treatment of domesticity and household formation as themes within existing youth research, pointing to the neglect of youthful domesticity within the youth cultural studies tradition and to the rather partial accounts of household formation which exist within the youth transitions tradition. In making these points, our aim is to highlight the need for an alternative framework for considering the current destandardisation of household formation.

2
Domesticity, Household Formation and Youth Research

Introduction

This chapter provides an overview of existing treatment of the themes of young people, domesticity and household formation. Youth research has long been dominated by two main approaches: the youth cultural studies tradition and the youth transitions tradition. There are numerous accounts within the youth literature concerning the relative strengths and weaknesses of these two approaches, and we do not intend to rehearse those arguments here (see MacDonald, 1998; Cohen and Ainley, 2000; MacDonald *et al.*, 2001; Skelton, 2002 for some recent discussions). However, for our purposes it is important to note that both have operated with clear boundaries around what is considered to be appropriate subject matter. The youth cultural studies tradition has focused on young people's leisure and subcultural affiliations in the extra-domestic sphere to the virtual exclusion of other spheres of activity, whilst the youth transitions tradition, in principle embracing employment, housing and domestic transitions, has in practice tended to prioritise school to work transitions. The latter approach has, however, begun to take domestic and housing transitions more seriously, and we end this chapter by outlining some of the defining characteristics of existing transitions-influenced work on household formation.

Youth cultures and youth lifestyles: 'have they no homes to go to?'

Youth cultural studies represents a rich tradition within youth research. Its origins lie in a series of detailed ethnographic studies of deviance conducted by the Chicago School between the 1920s and the 1960s, whilst the key influence within the British context has been the work of the Centre for Contemporary Cultural Studies (CCCS), founded at the University of Birmingham in 1964. The CCCS approach marked a radical departure from a style of youth research and theorising that had been heavily influenced by functionalism, an approach which had argued that the central function of peer group allegiance during the period known as 'youth' was the facilitation of a smooth transition from adolescence to adulthood. The exact nature of the peer group was irrelevant: 'no matter how bizarre or deviant the youth cultural activity might appear, its function was essentially adaptive' (Pilkington, 1994: 17). In contrast, CCCS researchers developed a radical Marxist perspective and argued that youth culture was not all of a piece. Rather, they argued that working class youth subcultures (in contrast to middle class counter-cultures) developed in opposition to the values of both the hegemonic middle class culture and the subordinate working class 'parent culture'. Subcultures arose, then, as attempts to solve the problem of status, and represented arenas where young people could 'win space' for themselves as a 'strategy for negotiating their collective existence' (Clarke *et al.*, 1975: 47).

The CCCS approach – and much of what has followed in the decades since – has become known for its focus on colourfully deviant working class subcultures and, to a lesser extent, middle class counter-cultures. The classic text *Resistance through Rituals* (Hall and Jefferson, 1975), for example, included chapters on Teddy Boys, Mods, Skinheads and Rastas. In reading these accounts, however, one would be forgiven for thinking that the young people in question existed largely in a vacuum from the rest of the society. As well as not appearing to have jobs, they do not appear to have homes to go to or family and friends to relate to outside of the subculture. The only groups within the collection with some form of acknowledged domestic life are Corrigan's lads who nonetheless prefer to hang out on the street rather than in the home because they know that 'nothing will happen with mum and dad in the front room' (ibid.: 104), Webster's counter-cultural commune dwellers, and McRobbie's teenage girls 'doing subculture' in the privacy of their bedrooms. Young women are, then, situated within the domestic sphere but more generally are famously absent from this collection; McRobbie's much-cited chapter is a sideswipe against the failure of her colleagues to attend to the question of gender. However, even young men who live out their leisure time in the public sphere must, at some point, return to the mundanity and routine of life at home: if only, as in the case of Hebdige's Mod, to wash his hair on a Thursday night.

Contemporary research within the youth cultural studies tradition has moved on considerably from these earlier preoccupations with class-based resistance. More recent studies draw on the language of 'scenes', 'lifestyle' and 'neo-tribalism', often eschewing the term 'subculture', yet they have in general been similarly neglectful of the domestic sphere. By foregrounding cultural allegiances, they have tended to exaggerate the amount of time and effort devoted to this particular facet of young people's lives, and have virtually ignored their parallel status as sons and daughters, brothers and sisters, flatmates and householders, partners, parents and lovers. The exceptions to this general pattern are a small number of studies which have focused on certain aspects of domesticity, but in the context of the somewhat unconventional living arrangements of those concerned: young people who have adopted travel and/or a transient housing history as a form of working class subcultural or (more usually) middle class counter-cultural expression. Following an early interest in commune dwellers (Rigby, 1974; Webster, 1975), more recent studies have focused, for example, on New Age Travellers (Hetherington, 2000), 'street punks' and 'gutter punks' (Leblanc, 1999), 'DiY cultures' such as environmental protesters (McKay, 1998) and homeless youth subcultures (Ruddick, 1996). Nonetheless, the emphasis of these studies remains once again upon exoticised subcultures, rather than the relatively ordinary domestic lives of most young adults. Despite, then, considerable elements of *dis*continuity between the CCCS's pioneering work and later work within the cultural studies tradition (Clarke, 1981; Gelder and Thornton, 1997; Cieslik, 2001), this neglect of the domestic sphere represents an important element of continuity.

Thornton has offered an explanation for this neglect:

> Those groups identified as 'subcultures' have tended to be studied apart from their families and in states of relative transience ... Subcultures are more often characterised as appropriating parts of the city for their street (rather than domestic) culture. These are some of the reasons why one hears frequently of 'youth subcultures', but seldom of 'youth communities': youth attempt to define their culture against the parental home (Thornton, 1997: 2).

In other words, subculture is all about what is done *outside* of the home. There are, however, a number of problems with this position. First, it assumes that young people live in domestic situations which do not facilitate, but rather quash, subcultural expression. As Thornton implies, this is most likely to be the case where young people still reside within the parental home. However, whilst the majority of teenagers and a sizeable proportion of young people in their early twenties continue to live with their parents, many do not, and their independent living spaces may actually provide a focus for at least some of their subcultural activities. Aggleton's sixth formers, for example, often hung out in the flats and bedsits of their peers who had already left home, 'entirely free from adult scrutiny' (Aggleton, 1987: 83), whilst the rapid expansion of higher education in recent years means that growing numbers of young adults are now living away from home as students, living either in halls of residence or in shared student houses (Rugg *et al.*, 2000). In such circumstances, it is difficult to disentangle elements of the 'student lifestyle' from their domestic living arrangements. Kenyon (1997), for example, provides evidence of some very distinct behavioural traits associated with living in a student house.

Secondly, even where young people continue to live with their parents, home space need not necessarily quash subcultural activity. Rather, it may provide an increasingly important site of subcultural expression, particularly in the relatively private space of the bedroom. We have already noted McRobbie's flagging up of the importance of the bedroom to girls' subcultures, but it may be becoming a key leisure space for *both* sexes given the huge appeal of computer games and Internet-based leisure forms (McNamee, 1998; Tapscott, 1998; Holloway and Valentine, 2002). Thirdly, however, even if one takes the view that the subcultural sphere is rightly situated outside of the home, there is still a strong argument to be made for incorporating a focus on the domestic sphere into accounts of youth subculture. Clarke, for example, has argued that,

> Even if we accept that it is possible to read youth styles as a form of resistance, the (CCCS) claims that subcultures 'operate exclusively in the leisure sphere' mean that the institutional sites of hegemony (those of school, work and home) are ignored. Surely these are the sites in which any resistance is located, and they need to be considered in order to examine the relationship between working class youth and working class culture in general (Clarke, 1981, quoted in Gelder and Thornton, 1997: 178).

In other words, in order to understand fully the significance of youth subcultures and to gain a sense of how successful young people are in developing strategies of resistance – if they do so at all – it is imperative that we look beyond the leisure sphere to these other aspects of their lives. This is a view with which Miles (2000) has some sympathy. In considering cultural studies' neglect of the day-to-day in favour of the flamboyant, he has called for a refocusing of youth research towards the everyday realities of youth lifestyles which, he argues, constitute 'the outward social expression of specific identity positions' and as such 'actively express young people's relationships with their social world' (Miles, 2000: 26). Youth lifestyles, Miles contends, have been neglected within the cultural studies tradition, yet as analytical concepts may prove to be far more useful than a focus on youth subcultures. He calls, then, for a shift in emphasis, not least because of the relatively depoliticised nature of youth culture in the current period, which has meant that contemporary forms of youth leisure are rarely resistant in the sense implied by CCCS:

> Youth lifestyles, however conservative they appear to be, do not operate independently of political and social change. The benefit of this sort of approach ... is that it is potentially less prescriptive and less politically loaded than has previously been the case when commentators have adopted a subcultural perspective (Miles, 2000: 9).

Contemporary youth, then, construct lifestyles 'that are as adaptable and as flexible as the world around them' (ibid.: 160), with their leisure-based groupings marked more by fluidity and floating membership than by coherence and fixity (Bennett, 1999). Crucially, Miles argues that these identities are largely constructed through consumption, 'the primary indicator of lifestyles in a changing world' (Miles, 2000: 160). It is, of course, hard to deny the importance of consumption in the lives of many young people. Klein (2000), for example, has provided a compelling account of the 'marketing of cool' to young people on both sides of the Atlantic. In the same year that Klein's bestseller *No Logo* was published, an event billed as 'Britain's first teen lifestyle exhibition', Pop 2000, was held at the National Exhibition Centre in Birmingham: 'Forget Generation X and Generation Y. Generation £ is selling itself and letting itself be bought' (Arlidge and Thorpe, 2000: 9). However, by claiming that consumption is the key arena in which young people play out the relationship between structure and agency, it seems that Miles is replacing a narrow focus on leisure with an even narrower focus on one particular form of leisure – and one that by no means all young people buy into, as evidenced by the emergence of 'culture jamming' and anti-capitalism movements (McKay, 1998; Klein, 2000). Moreover, his focus is on a form of consumption that occurs entirely within the leisure realm: his young people buy designer labels, but they do not appear to pay board money to their parents or rent to their landlords or landladies, let alone consume rather more mundane items such as groceries or other household goods.

Despite his welcome call, then, to redress the neglect of the everyday realities of young people's lives, Miles' account still ignores the more routine aspects of their social worlds: in particular, their home lives, and relationships with friends, family and partners. Our view is that these aspects can be equally important in the construction of a particular 'lifestyle'. However, in exploring this possibility we distance ourselves from a consumption-orientated approach to lifestyle, drawing instead on Giddens' rather broader definition of lifestyle as 'a more or less integrated set of practices which an individual embraces, not only because such practices fulfil utilitarian needs, but because they give material form to a particular narrative of self-identity' (1991: 81). Giddens' point is that 'in conditions of high modernity, we all not only follow lifestyles, but in an important sense are forced to do so – we have no choice but to choose' (ibid.), due to the current proliferation of options within a society marked by individualisation and destandardisation (these themes are discussed further in Chapter 3). He acknowledges, too, that not all lifestyles are equally available to everyone, as 'life chances condition lifestyle choices' and 'lifestyle choices are often actively used to reinforce the distribution of life chances' (ibid.: 86).

In this sense, then, the housing choices of some young people may be increasingly linked to lifestyle choices, and may serve to reinforce existing polarisation between more and less privileged groups of young people. We have already noted the link between living arrangements and the student lifestyle. In addition, terms such as 'middle youth', 'kidulthood' and 'adultescence' have recently been used to refer to the lifestyles of late twenty- and thirty-somethings ('menopausal teenagers') who are deliberately cultivating a youth-orientated lifestyle as a stage between 'youth' and 'middle age', if not hoping to avoid middle age altogether, and who often embrace the deferral of couple household formation in favour of living alone or with friends. Living alone or in a shared household can, then, be both a statement of independence and evidence of a commitment to a particular lifestyle, with a person's specific living arrangements lending support to their chosen lifestyle. These kinds of connections are currently absent from most cultural studies accounts of young people's lives, and seem to be equally absent within the alternative framework proposed by Miles.

The youth transitions tradition

We turn now to a consideration of the youth transitions approach and its contribution to an understanding of contemporary patterns of household formation. In contrast to youth cultural studies, youth transitions researchers have traditionally placed greatest emphasis on the importance of economic activity in defining young people's progression from childhood to adulthood. A primary objective has been the mapping out of the changing face of the world of work and its impact on young people's experiences of moving in and out of employment, education and training. The approach is typified by a concern with highlighting elements of both continuity and change in these areas, and with tracing the determining influence of social class, gender and ethnicity on young people's transitions. This is a tradition, then, that has emphasised the effects of structural change and social policy on young adults' experiences of transitions towards economic independence. It is also an approach which, particularly in the UK, has often benefited from large-scale research funding; for example, a focus on youth transitions lies at the heart of both of the major British youth research initiatives launched in the late 1990s, the 'Youth, Citizenship and Social Change' programme funded by the ESRC and the 'Young People in Transition' initiative of the Joseph Rowntree Foundation (JRF).

In exploring young people's engagement with the economic sphere, it has become increasingly common for youth transitions researchers to refer to three interlinked transitions to adulthood: employment transitions from school to work, domestic transitions from a family of origin to a family of destination, and housing transitions from the parental home to a home of one's own (Coles, 1995). In practice, however, much existing transitions research pays scant attention to the second and third of these transitions, despite their interconnected nature. Irwin (1995) has suggested, for example, that variables such as household type are often treated by quantitative transitions researchers as 'simply another attribute that individuals bring to the labour market' (p. 35), whilst researchers using more ethnographic approaches often fall into the same trap as youth cultural studies researchers by emphasising one particular aspect of a young person's transitional experiences – in this case, work – at the expense of other aspects of their lives. Relatively few studies that foreground the school to work transition have, then, seriously attempted to tackle the inter-relationship between employment transitions, domestic transitions and housing transitions.

There have, however, been some notable exceptions, whose primary focus on relatively disadvantaged young adults has defined the field in terms of the key themes that dominate most explorations of the linkages between the different spheres of transition (see, for example, the discussion of youth transitions in Allan and Crow, 2001). Studies by Coffield *et al.*

(1986), Wallace (1987), Hutson and Jenkins (1989), Hollands (1990) and Allatt and Yeandle (1992) have perhaps been most influential in this regard. Each of these studies explores the constraining effects of delayed transitions over the 1980s, arising from high rates of youth unemployment, job insecurity and the proliferation of youth training schemes. To varying degrees they each highlight the strains placed upon the family lives of young people under such circumstances, noting in particular young people's inability to leave home and establish independent households of their own, with or without a partner. Clare Wallace's *For Richer, For Poorer*, for example, paints a vivid picture of young people whose adult lives have effectively been put on hold by their inability to establish independent homes with their partners (Wallace, 1987).

In general, though, domestic and housing transitions still remain Cinderella perspectives within the broader transitions approach, and tend to be under-researched and conceptually under-developed in comparison with work that foregrounds the school to work transition. However, increasing numbers of British researchers are choosing to focus primarily on domestic and housing transitions, with changes in the youth labour market providing the backdrop to their research rather than the foreground. Gill Jones is undoubtedly the UK pioneer in this field, and her work in this area over nearly two decades has provided youth researchers and policy makers alike with invaluable insights into the complex nature of the interface between domestic, housing and employment transitions, and the effects of successive government policies on young people's ability to leave home and establish independent households (see, for example, Jones, 1987, 1995a,b, 2000, 2002). Irwin (1995) has similarly explored the interplay between domestic transitions and broader transitions, whilst researchers at the Centre for Housing Policy at the University of York have foregrounded the housing careers of young adults (Burrows *et al.*, 1998; Rugg, 1999a). York researchers have recently completed a longitudinal study of young people's housing careers as part of the ESRC's 'Youth, Citizenship and Social Change' research programme (Ford *et al.*, 2002), whilst domestic and housing transitions have been explored as sub-themes in several other projects included within the recent ESRC and JRF youth research initiatives (see, for example, Johnston *et al.*, 2000; Gillies *et al.*, 2001; Langford *et al.*, 2001; Hendey and Pascall, 2002; Valentine *et al.*, 2002).

This growing interest in domestic and housing transitions is to be welcomed after so many years of relative neglect. However, a major criticism often advanced against the youth transitions approach has been its tendency to overemphasise the effects of structural constraint on the lives of young adults at the expense of their own agency, and elements of this argument can be applied to much of the existing literature on domestic and housing transitions. Moreover, many of these studies have been based on samples of young adults drawn from a relatively homogeneous class background, and from within a relatively restrictive age band (typically, young people in their late teens, or in their early twenties). These factors have placed major limitations on the extent to which the findings of these studies can legitimately be generalised to broader youth populations. Consequently, it is our belief that much existing research on patterns of household formation has been underpinned by what we term a 'model of constraint', and in the remaining section of this chapter we turn to a consideration of some of the features of this model.

Models of constraint within the transitions tradition

According to Miles (2000), the youth transitions approach has 'tended to treat young people as troubled victims of economic and social restructuring without enough recourse to the active ways in which young people negotiate such circumstances in the course of their everyday life' (p. 10). In fact, rather than ignoring the classic structure–agency debate, most transitions researchers find themselves regularly engaging with this tension in their own work. Witness, for example, 'in-house' debates concerning the relative merits of models based on *youth trajectories* on the one hand (Roberts, 1993) and *youth careers* on the other (Coles, 1995). The former approach stresses the importance of socially ascribed characteristics such as class, gender, ethnicity and location in determining the transitional pathways of different groups of young adults. In contrast, the latter places greater emphasis on individual choice and decision-making, albeit within the constraints set by earlier decisions: for example, young people in work are more likely than their unemployed counterparts to be in a position to 'choose' to leave home. Nonetheless, despite the increased emphasis on some element of individual agency in the latter approach, the conceptual frameworks of both have tended to lead British researchers to place greater emphasis on constraint, rather than choice, as an explanation for changing patterns of household formation. This tendency is compounded by an empirical focus on the experiences of young people for the most part in their late teens and early twenties, a group with limited financial resources at the best of times. Consequently, changes in domestic and housing transition patterns are commonly attributed first and foremost to a series of interlinked constraining factors, which we now summarise in the UK context.

First, the social policies of successive British governments have increasingly reflected the view that the state should not have to subsidise young people who leave home. Rather, the financial support of young adults should remain the primary responsibility of parents (Bell and Jones, 1999; Coles *et al.*, 1999). This was reinforced by the removal in 1988 of the right of 16- and 17-year-olds to claim Income Support except in cases of exceptional need, based on the assumption that under-18-year-olds will usually be engaged either in education, training or employment. This policy, which remains in place under the current Labour government, has been widely implicated in the dramatic increase in homelessness amongst this age group (Centrepoint, 1996). Young people who have been able to secure a place on one of the various government work-based training schemes also remain largely dependent on their parents due to the low weekly allowance payable to trainees. For example, those with places on Modern Apprenticeship schemes for 16–19-year-olds currently receive a minimum of £40 per week, whilst a young person following the subsidised job option of the New Deal for Young People will receive a minimum allowance of £60 per week, although on both of these schemes many employers choose to supplement the basic allowance with varying degrees of generosity. Childless young people aged 18–24 who are eligible to receive Jobseekers Allowance or Income Support also receive lower levels of benefit than those aged 25 or over, currently £11 less.

Secondly, there has been a steady increase in housing costs over the last 15 years, coupled with housing benefit changes which have had the effect of cutting the levels of payment made and of placing restrictions on the type of accommodation available to claimants (Rugg, 1999b). The introduction of the single room rent in 1996 has restricted housing benefit for single under-25-year-olds to the locally assessed cost of a room in a shared household (Kemp and Rugg, 1998), and is not intended to cover the higher costs of living alone. The supply of housing for young people also remains relatively restricted, particularly for 16- and 17-year-olds. The emphasis on home ownership at the expense of public housing provision under the last Conservative government has meant that there is now relatively little social housing available to single young adults. Housing associations are generally more sympathetic to the needs of young people than local authority providers, but their properties account for a much smaller proportion of the overall social housing stock (Anderson, 1999). Consequently, the private rented sector meets the bulk of demand, mainly in bedsits and shared houses (DETR, 1999).

Students are less likely to be affected by these trends given their easier access to low-cost niche-market housing (Rhodes, 1999; Rugg *et al.*, 2000), although they were heavily hit by the 1990 axing of their right to claim Housing Benefit. Despite this, until the mid-1990s it appeared to be becoming increasingly commonplace to live away from the parental home as a student (ibid.). However, it now appears that a growing proportion of higher education students are choosing to live at home for the duration of their studies, rising from 13 per cent of students in 1996/1997 to 20 per cent in 1999/2000 (DfEE, 1998; HESA, 2001). There is some emerging evidence to suggest that this trend is most pronounced amongst groups of students from lower socio-economic backgrounds who, having been long under-represented within higher education, are now disproportionately represented within the new university sector and tend to be hit hardest by the rising costs associated with being a student (Reay *et al.*, 2001).

Thirdly, the insecurities of the youth labour market for those actually in work have also contributed to changing patterns of household formation. Many full-time jobs fail to provide either an adequate income to support independent living or the security which would allow a young person to leave the parental home with the confidence that they will not have to return. The abolition in 1993 of the Wages Councils removed the protection placed on young people's low paid work, and whilst the minimum wage introduced by New Labour should redress this loss to some extent, it has been set at a lower rate for 18–21-year-olds (from October 2003, £3.80 as opposed to £4.50) and does not apply at all to 16- and 17-year-olds who are either on training schemes or serving apprenticeships. Thus the insecurities of the youth labour market and the removal of the full benefits safety net make certain living arrangements untenable. Under such conditions, young people's options are confined to living with parents or, if independence is sought, to living in lodgings, bedsits, hostels or shared accommodation. Highly qualified young adults are not immune from these trends. With increasing numbers of young people leaving university with unprecedented levels of debt, there is a growing propensity for graduates to return to their parental home, at least in the short term, on first completing higher education (Jones, 1995a). This is set to continue. Indeed, with the proposed introduction of top-up fees at a rate of up to £3000 per annum within the English higher education system, the level of debt for some students is likely to increase considerably.

The constraint model, therefore, foregrounds the structural factors that have contributed to greater dependency on parents and to a decline in the ability to achieve smooth domestic and housing transitions in the shape of a home and family of one's own. However, some researchers have challenged the underpinnings of this model. Irwin (1995), for example, claims that much of the research on leaving home and on delayed transitions to adulthood is over-deterministic concerning the effects of recent changes in the youth labour market, particularly the consequences of youth unemployment, and has ignored the importance of more long-standing demographic shifts. As a result, 'there has been a tendency to treat life course structures as influenced by, but nevertheless independent from, more general social and economic processes' (Irwin, 1995: 3). Irwin argues that changing patterns of dependency actually predate the unemployment crisis of the late 1970s, and are linked in part to shifts in women's employment patterns, resulting in increased affluence amongst families with children approaching adult status. This, alongside an increasing gap between the earnings of young people and older workers, has altered the nature of young people's dependency on their parents. As a consequence, she contends, many young adults are now living in parental households which can afford to accommodate the low wages received by young people entering the labour market for the first time. In a recent study of young Australians in their twenties, for example, Kilmartin (2000) found that board money was paid by less than a third of those who had never left home, including only half of those who were in full-time employment. This in turn impacts upon the perceived desirability of leaving home.

Irwin's argument supports a view that continued dependency on parents is not necessarily a product solely of constraint, but of *opportunity*, reflecting either a deliberate choice or a genuine contentedness (if unable to afford an alternative) about remaining in the parental home. Researchers in the Netherlands, for example, a country which has actually experienced a decline in young adults' dependency on parents since the 1980s (European Commission, 1997), have argued that the contemporary parental home now offers more physical space for the presence of additional adults, making it both materially and physically a more viable and attractive option to stay (de Jong-Gierveld *et al.*, 1991). A similar picture is painted by Litwin (1986) in her account of privileged young Americans still living with their parents well into their twenties and beyond – 'these bright, charming middle-class aristocrats' (p. 133), enjoying the benefits of what Avery *et al.* (1992) have termed the 'feathered nest/gilded cage'. The contemporary parental home may also offer some young people considerable freedom and privacy, with the more relaxed climate in which many children are now raised encouraging them to remain there longer. Pointing to the increasing likelihood that a young person will have a room of their own within the parental home, Mitterauer (1992) notes that 'having one's own space makes it possible to develop one's own sphere of individuality...In various respects, individualisation has been achieved long before the move away from the parental home is made' (pp. 107–8). Further, there are considerable incentives to remaining within the parental home if household chores such as cooking and laundry are routinely performed on a young person's behalf, although the extent to which this occurs often depends upon the young person's gender (Wallace, 1987; Hollands, 1990).

Young people in poorer families, however, seldom enjoy the element of choice suggested by this model. Indeed, many parents are faced with the option of either supporting their adult children and risking financial difficulties, or of having to ask them to leave home in order for the remaining family to survive, particularly if the children are themselves unemployed. On the other hand, if the young person is the sole earner within their parental home they may well be experiencing pressures to stay. Nonetheless, the possibility of such an extreme polarisation of experience between the children of affluent families and those from poorer families raises an important point relating to the predominant agenda of transitions research. In the pursuit of social justice, it is perhaps understandable that greater emphasis has been given to the constraint model, as it has provided a powerful critique of the negative impact on marginalised young adults of economic crises and the policy responses of successive governments. Many of the studies within this tradition have focused on the experiences of unemployed young people and those on government training schemes, who have had little choice but to remain within the parental home, or on the experiences of homeless young adults who have left home without support. We are certainly not denying the importance of such research, but we do take issue with the skewed picture of household formation that is generated as a consequence. It remains the case, then, that we still have only a partial understanding of the context and meaning of contemporary household formation amongst young adults as a whole, given that existing research tends to overlook the experiences of young people who have relatively smooth household transitions. In particular, we know relatively little about the transitional experiences of more affluent, middle class young adults, including those who are graduates and/or young professionals. This is part of a much broader tendency within youth research to focus on the experiences of less advantaged groups within society, or on 'troublesome youth', at the expense of a more rounded approach.

We also take issue with the prioritisation of couple household formation implicit within the constraint model. Many researchers, such as
Coles (2000), rightly counsel the avoidance of linear and normative
assumptions with respect to household formation. Nonetheless, implicit
assumptions tend to be made concerning the desirability of the living
arrangements to which young people will 'naturally' progress, and patterns of early marriage and childbirth that held sway in the 1950s and
1960s 'appear to hold a sort of authenticity, to suggest a 'natural' set of
life course processes accompanying full employment' (Irwin, 1995: 66).
Couple households – particularly those formed within the context of
marriage – thus come to form the pinnacle of a hierarchy of domestic
arrangements to which all heterosexual young adults (should) aspire.
Bynner and Pan (2002) note, for example, that 'postponed partnership
experience may extend for some young people into *failure* to make the
transition to partnership and parenthood at all' (p. 23, emphasis added).
By establishing the couple household as the desirable end goal of the
transitional process, it is hard to avoid an assumption of linearity,
despite the difficulties this presents in conceptualising the experiences
of the growing numbers of young people who are choosing to form
couple households – if at all – at a later age or who, having formed a
couple household, subsequently experience its disintegration. This is not
to argue that couple relationships are unimportant to young adults, nor
that most do not attach special status to couple households: far from it.
Rather, it is to highlight the variety of interpretations that young people
attach to the concepts of adulthood and independence, and to point
out that a sense of being a fully independent adult is not necessarily
contingent on living with a partner.

A fixation on marriage as a key defining moment of adulthood also
highlights the heteronormativity that underpins much research on
household formation. Not only does this fixation deny the significance
of heterosexual cohabitation as an alternative to marriage, it also
renders invisible the experiences of gay men and lesbians. Goldscheider
and Goldscheider's impressive mapping of changing patterns of household formation in the United States, for example, is weakened in this
respect. Neither of their two recent monographs on this subject – one
revealingly entitled *Leaving Home Before Marriage* – include any reference
to the impact of sexual orientation on processes of household formation (Goldscheider and Goldscheider, 1993, 1999). Indeed, the authors
seek to explain away the 6 per cent of young people in their study who
said that they had no intention of ever marrying by questioning 'how
seriously we should treat any of the answers young people and their

parents give to hypothetical questions about events some time, possibly far, into the future' (1993: 33). To a degree this neglect reflects the limitations of the data sets with which many quantitative researchers work, with few surveys as yet explicitly including questions on sexual orientation. However, this neither excuses the failure even to acknowledge gay and lesbian experience in much existing work, nor the failure to draw upon the small but growing literature that does highlight the relevance of including sexual orientation as a variable in analysing patterns of household formation. Dixon *et al.* (1989), Ainley (1991), Valentine *et al.* (2002) and Dunne *et al.* (2002), for example, have suggested that disputes arising from coming out to parents are often a key factor in the decision of many gay and lesbian young people to leave home at a relatively early age, often resulting in homelessness, whilst Taulke-Johnson and Rivers (1999) and Prendergast *et al.* (2002) have highlighted the often negative experience of living in university accommodation as a young gay man or lesbian.

Finally, there is also an implicit danger within existing studies of household formation of presuming that *constrained* circumstances are necessarily *problematic* for those involved. A good example is provided by the response to the introduction of the single room rent, referred to above. The policy was introduced to deter unemployed young people from using Housing Benefit to finance solo living arrangements, supposedly often in better quality accommodation than their unsubsidised and employed peers, and its introduction met with widespread condemnation from housing and welfare rights lobbyists as a restriction of choice. However, an early evaluation of its impact on claimants came to the surprising conclusion that most respondents either expected or wanted to live in shared accommodation at this stage in their lives, although they were less happy about sharing with strangers: 'Both the policy assumption and the lobbyists' response to that assumption are questioned by research with young adults themselves' (Kemp and Rugg, 1998: 31).

Kemp and Rugg's evaluation, then, provides a cautionary tale for youth researchers who are tempted to interpret constraint as discontent: not all young people, however constrained, regard their living arrangements as 'a problem'. Indeed, it is one of the arguments of this book that we are currently witnessing a sea change in attitudes towards traditional forms of household and family formation. This is why it is important to explore these processes amongst relatively advantaged young people, *alongside* their less affluent peers. The former group are arguably at the forefront of changing attitudes which, in turn, may be exerting an influence on the attitudes of the broader youth population. In Chapter 3 we consider why this might be the case, developing a theoretical framework influenced in part by the writings of Ulrich Beck and, to a lesser extent, Anthony Giddens on individualisation, the transformation of intimacy, and the emergence of destandardised, reflexive 'choice biographies'. In so doing, we foreground the apparent appeal of the single life, set against a broader context of the recent expansion of higher education and the restructuring of the youth labour market, the emergence of 'post-adolescence' as a distinct phase in the life course, and new forms of social relationships. Taken together, these transformations have resulted in a generational re-evaluation of traditional forms of household and family living.

3
Risk, Individualisation and the Single Life

Introduction

> The banality of our upper-middle class lives, so gaudily stuck between the mindless drunk-driving of high school – that was meant as a metaphor only – and the death that is home owning and family-having...(Dave Eggars, *A Heartbreaking Work of Staggering Genius*, p. 168)

In this chapter, we outline the elements of an alternative framework for exploring contemporary household formation amongst young adults. In so doing, we acknowledge the importance of the constraint model, introduced in the previous chapter, in underlining the broader structural frameworks within which young people experience household formation. However, we believe that it cannot account for the choices and experiences of *all* young adults, and as such provides only a *partial* explanation of contemporary patterns of household formation, particularly amongst 'older' young people. Our alternative framework is an attempt to offer a fresh perspective on processes of household formation in the light of broader social transformation. As with the constraint model, it too cannot account for the experiences of all young people, but in seeking to gain a fuller understanding of contemporary domestic and housing transitions we believe that researchers need to explore how the two models relate to each other. Successive government policies in the sphere of education, training, employment and housing, alongside adverse economic conditions affecting many young adults, have undoubtedly acted as powerful catalysts for recent demographic trends. Nonetheless, serious consideration equally deserves to be given to broader shifts within contemporary society, particularly those relating to changes in the labour market and in the life course, as well as shifting attitudes towards the politics and dynamics of contemporary relationships.

In developing these themes, we have been particularly influenced by the writings of Ulrich Beck on risk and individualisation, and Anthony Giddens on reflexive modernisation and the transformation of intimacy. Youth researchers have been increasingly influenced by their work, albeit largely in the context of exploring fractured employment transitions. However, both writers also have much to say about changing attitudes towards the desirability and feasibility of 'settling down' and the growing importance of a variety of intimate relationships in young people's lives, issues which we believe are central to considerations of contemporary household formation. Whilst not fully agreeing with all of their arguments, we nonetheless find many of their ideas helpful as starting points for thinking about the wider impact of social transformation. In the sections that follow, we first introduce the concepts of risk society and individualisation and demonstrate their relevance to processes of household formation. We then consider evidence that the single life (or at least certain aspects of it) has an internal logic and a seemingly growing appeal amongst certain sections of the contemporary youth population. In particular, we focus on the impact of labour market transformations, the emergence of 'post-adolescence' as a distinct phase in the life course, and the development of new models for conducting a range of intimate relationships.

Household formation in late modernity

A central theme within the writings of both Beck and Giddens is the assertion that we are currently living in a period of 'late modernity', an era of historical transformation marked by increased levels of risk and uncertainty at both the macro and micro level. At the macro level, we now face risks of global proportions, such as global warming, international terrorism, nuclear, chemical and biological warfare, and large-scale environmental pollution. At the micro level, former certainties have been disrupted and replaced by the necessity of choosing from a multitude of possibilities at every turn, arising from the 'destandardisation' of society, which involves a 'setting free' from traditional social forms. This has resulted in a propensity for social agents to be increasingly self-reflexive about their 'conditions of existence', as well as increasingly reflexive concerning the social institutions that structure their lives:

Individualisation in this sense means that each person's biography is removed from given determinations and placed in his or her own hands, open and dependent on decisions. The proportion of life opportunities that are fundamentally closed to decision-making is decreasing and the proportion of the biography which is open and must be constructed personally is increasing...Decisions on education, profession, job, place of residence, spouse, number of children and so forth, *no longer can be made, they must be made* (Beck, 1992: 135 – emphasis added).

In other words, individuals in late modernity are engaged in the construction of their own biographies, in contrast to the standardised biographies of the 'old order'. Furlong and Cartmel (1997) use the metaphor of train journeys and car journeys to distinguish between standardised and reflexive biographies. The standardised biography is like a train journey, where a passenger boards a train from a given starting point and knows exactly where their journey will end. There are very few opportunities for deviation once the journey has begun, and the journey is made in common with many other passengers. In contrast, a reflexive biography is like a car journey: here, the driver is in far greater control and can make a myriad of individual choices along the way, determining factors such as the speed of the journey, the exact route to be taken and the final destination. The success of a car journey, however, is ultimately determined not by the driver but by the quality and reliability of the car they are driving, and Furlong and Cartmel use this last point to illustrate 'the epistemological fallacy' of late modernity:

although social structures continue to shape life chances, these structures tend to become increasingly obscure as collectivist traditions weaken and individualist values intensify. As a consequence of these changes, people come to regard the social world as unpredictable and filled with risks which can only be negotiated on an individual level, even though chains of human interdependence remain intact (1997: 12).

In terms of the shaping of their opportunities, then, an individual with an apparently unique reflexive biography shares much in common with individuals from similar social backgrounds, yet these commonalities are hidden by the process of individualisation. Risk, then, is not evenly distributed, but affects different social groups to varying degrees.

The poorest members of society are most vulnerable to risk and are also less able to draw upon personal resources – particularly wealth – to escape risk. However, one of the consequences of the weakening of collectivism in late modernity is that vulnerability to risk is internalised, rather than attributed to a lack of resources, which has the effect of further reinforcing the process of individualisation:

> In our 'society of individuals' all the messes into which one can get are assumed to be self-made and all the hot water into which one can fall is proclaimed to have been boiled by the hapless failures who have fallen into it. For the good and the bad that fills one's life a person has only himself or herself to thank or to blame (Bauman, 2001: 19).

Although Beck acknowledges the unequal distribution of risk, he nonetheless stands accused of downplaying the ongoing significance of social class within his account of individualisation. He refers to the dissolution of social classes within capitalism, and their replacement by 'individualised social inequality' (1992: 88). This serves to obscure broader patterns of class-based inequality and makes it difficult to predict an individual's future on the basis of their class origins alone.

However, these patterns are not as difficult to detect as he seems to suggest. Manuella du Bois-Reymond (1998), for example, highlights well the ongoing social class underpinnings of different life trajectories in distinguishing between 'normal biography' and 'choice biography'. Her conceptualisation of the normal biography has much in common with Beck's notion of standardised biography but, unlike Beck, du Bois-Reymond does not yet regard it as a relic of the past, although she does acknowledge that it is in decline. Normal biographies are gender-specific and are associated with the attainment of 'early adulthood' amongst the lower middle and working classes. They are modified versions of traditional lower middle and working class transitions, but are nonetheless still characterised by early employment and family formation relative to the transitions of young people from higher social classes. In contrast, the choice biography draws upon the notion that the life course is increasingly treated as a 'project', based on strategic life-planning and the constant need to adapt to changing circumstances (Giddens, 1991: 85), and is associated more with individuals from upper middle and upper class backgrounds. Importantly, however:

Choice biographies' are by no means based on freedom and own choice, but are determined by a paradox which is typical in modern life: although (western) societies provide more options to choose from, modern (young) people are forced to reflect on the available options and justify their decisions...It is the *tension between option/ freedom and legitimation/coercion* which marks 'choice biographies (du Bois-Reymond, 1998: 65 – emphasis in original).

Beck's individualisation thesis, then, provides the backdrop for our proposed framework for exploring contemporary household forma- tion. However, we find du Bois-Reymond's modification of the language of reflexive and standardised biography a useful tool in gaining a better understanding of the unequal distribution of risk. Her account also foregrounds the tensions between choice and constraint that are implicit within the construction of biography, and which are sometimes underplayed in Beck's own account (Furlong and Cartmel, 1997; Ahier and Moore, 1999). In contrast to the language of 'youth trajectories' (Roberts, 1993), an emphasis on the individualised construction of biography implies a less deterministic approach and gives far greater recognition to the intentionality of reflexive individ- uals. Nonetheless, it remains important to acknowledge the limits of choice that exist to a greater or lesser extent for all young adults, as well as to recognise the role of chance and 'fateful moments' (Giddens, 1991; Thomson *et al.*, 2002) with respect to the potential transformation of a normal biography into a choice biography (or, indeed, vice versa).

Late modernity, then, is marked by the emergence of multiple pathways to adulthood, strewn with risks and threats, but also with opportunities and chances. That this is reflected in young people's routes in and out of the labour market is well documented (Roberts, 1995; Bynner *et al.*, 1997; MacDonald, 1997), yet a strong sense of fragmentation has also emerged with respect to processes of household formation:

The lifelong standard family...becomes a limiting case, and the rule becomes a movement back and forth among various familial and *non-familial* forms of living together, specific to the particular phase of life in question...Marriage can be subtracted from sexuality, and that in turn from parenthood; parenthood can be multiplied by divorce; and the whole thing can be divided by living together or apart, and raised to a higher power by the possibility of multiple residences and the ever-present potentiality of taking back decisions (Beck, 1992: 114, 116 – emphasis in the original).

We could also add to this equation the creation and dissolution of new family forms based on adoption, fostering and surrogacy, and the 'families of choice' (Weston, 1991; Weeks *et al.*, 2001) of gay and lesbian individuals, including those formed through gay marriage (legal in the Netherlands since April 2001) and the civil registration of non-heterosexual partnerships in a growing number of countries. Importantly, the recognition of continual household formation and *re*formation moves away from the assumption of linear progression towards couple households that often underpins more conventional approaches to household formation amongst young adults. Such an assumption casts the currently high mean age of first marriage in the United Kingdom and other northern European countries as some-thing new and threatening, even though it is in fact the relatively low mean age of first marriage during the immediate post-war years that is historically anomalous. It also ignores the extent to which young people are involved in straight or gay cross-household relationships which stop short of cohabitation in a single household: 'transhabita-tion' (Procter and Padfield, 1998) or 'living apart together' (Murphy, 1996). Indeed, there is a growing body of evidence which suggests that many young adults now expect to settle down later, rather than sooner, after a protracted period of independence. Referring to this trend as 'a kind of moratorium between living with parents and forming a family of one's own', Bynner and Pan (2002) believe it to be 'one of the most striking lifestyle changes of the current era' (p. 25). Accordingly, we turn now to consider in greater detail the internal logic and apparent appeal of the single lifestyle amongst contemporary young adults.

The ambivalent appeal of the single lifestyle: 'Welcome to the Singles Century'

Media fascination with the single lifestyle is currently rife, from soap operas and sitcoms such as *Friends, The Secret Life of Us, Sex and the City* and *This Life* and fly-on-the-wall shows such as *Big Brother* and *Flatmates*, through to novels such as *Bridget Jones' Diary* and *High Fidelity* which have spawned a new literary genre, the 'singleton' novel. The broadsheet newspapers have also chronicled the rise of the single person, with headlines such as 'Now we are one', 'The power of one', and 'We want to be alone' (Young, 1997; Smith, 1999; Rayner, 2000). In November 2000, a special edition of the Observer newspaper's *Life* magazine was dedicated to 'the singles issue'. We quote at length the magazine's opening comments, as they encapsulate much of the rhetoric surrounding this phenomenon:

> Welcome to the Singles Century. By 2010, almost half the population will be unmarried and, according to a recent survey, half the people still getting married are thinking about getting divorced as they sidle down the aisle. The rise of the single person is the greatest social phenomenon of our time ... Everything, from the family to the high street, the tourist industry to the television, has been altered by the new demographic. In this week's magazine, we celebrate the single life. For the first time, being single is a proactive life choice, like the car you drive, the food you eat, or the books you read. People are no longer willing to settle for settling down. The single stigma has faded away (the more there are, the less likely they are to be pitied). Friends are the new family. As the tide of single statistics and soundbites grows ever greater ... there's a sense that being alone is neither second best nor a stopgap between relationships. Even the late-90s stereotypes already seem out of date. Single woman doesn't ring 1471 (á la Bridget Jones) as soon as she gets in through the door. She isn't hung up on her first love (á la Ally McBeal). And single man doesn't go through his little black book the minute he's been dumped (á la *High Fidelity*) (Observer Life magazine, 2000: 3).

In the pages that followed, the magazine included various first-hand accounts of living the single lifestyle ('from the genuinely merry widow to the gay divorcee'), a panel debate involving eight 'experts' (including an academic, a sex columnist and a life coach), a quiz asking 'Just how single are you?', an interior design article on bachelor pads, recipes for one, and an article on the new Audi TT, 'a single girl's dream car'. The cumulative effect of these articles is the fostering of the view that to be single is to be fashionable, presenting a version of the single life where everyone is young and wealthy. Indeed, the market has responded enthusiastically to the rise of the affluent singleton lifestyle, from singles nights in supermarkets selling ready meals for one, through to housing developments which factor in a ready-made social life in the shape of in-house gymnasia, restaurants and bars.

Even if somewhat overstated, the Observer was nonetheless reporting on what is a very real social phenomenon. In the United Kingdom,

29 per cent of households consisted of a single individual in Spring 2001 (Office for National Statistics, 2001a), more than two and a half times the proportion in 1961, and a figure which is projected to rise to more than one in three by 2020 (Hall *et al.*, 1999). In Australia, just under a quarter of households currently consist of one person (Wulff, 2001), whilst in the United States the biggest increase in non-family living has also come from the rise in 'solo living', rising from 17 per cent of all households in 1970 to 25.5 per cent in 2000 (Fields and Casper, 2001). With rising divorce rates, the growth of 'singlehood' is not, of course, confined exclusively to younger generations. Nonetheless, there has been a significant increase over the last two decades in the proportion of young adults in their twenties and early thirties living in single person households and in shared households with unrelated peers. Moreover, this is a trend which is most marked amongst graduates and young professionals. Rates of living alone amongst British 25–29-year-olds of professional/managerial status, for example, rose from 6.2 per cent in 1971, to 12.6 per cent in 1981, and to just under a fifth in 1991 (Hall *et al.*, 1997). This association has continued with later cohorts of young Britons: a third of all 26-year-olds living alone in 1996 had a degree-level qualification, compared with a fifth of the cohort as a whole, and half had jobs of professional/managerial status compared with only a tenth of the wider cohort (Bynner *et al.*, 1997). As for house sharers, amongst 20–29-year-olds living in shared houses in 1991, 48 per cent were located in Social Classes I and II, and 39 per cent had at least one degree-level qualification, with both of these associations strongest amongst young people in their late twenties (Heath and Kenyon, 2001).

What, though, are we to make of these trends? Simplistic media representations tend to peddle an image of the single life as a glamorous 'proactive life choice' for the twenty-first century, the ultimate lifestyle statement of the young upwardly mobile and foot-loose urbanite. Contemporary young adults are undoubtedly faced with a range of choices not available to previous generations and, for a growing number of young people, it would appear that adult self-identity is no longer necessarily rooted in their achievement of the status of 'spouse' or 'partner', but can be derived from a strong sense of independence and freedom as a single person (which does not preclude having sexual partners, but often seems to preclude living with them). In order to understand why such a lifestyle might be increasingly commonplace, if not increasingly sought, these shifts need to be placed in the context of broader societal transformations: women's greater commitment to the labour market and the demands such commitment places on their private lives; the emergence of 'post-adolescence' as a new phase of the life course; and the emergence of new models for conducting personal relationships. Taken together, these transformations amount to a dramatic shift in attitude towards the conceptualisation of adult status amongst contemporary young adults, and have resulted in a generational re-evaluation of traditional forms of household and family living.

The demands of the labour market

In recognition of the current iconic status of the single lifestyle, Beck argues that the single person is 'the basic figure of *fully developed* modernity' (Beck, 1992: 122 – emphasis in original). He attributes the growth of the single state to the conditions of risk society, highlighting how the demands of the labour market revolve around an ideal type of the detached, geographically mobile and temporally available worker, together constituting 'the fully mobile society of singles' (1992: 122). Thus, he argues, employment status increasingly structures the living arrangements of many occupational groups, particularly those in professional or managerial positions, where there is often either a high expectation of or necessity for geographical flexibility. This is further reinforced by increased competitiveness within the labour market for graduate-level occupations, given the expansion of higher education and the ability of employers to choose from an ever-expanding pool of talent. Coupled with credential inflation and the increased casualisation of the graduate labour market (Dwyer and Wyn, 2001), there is then a strong expectation – indeed, a necessity – that employees keep themselves ahead of the game: 'It is no longer a question of gaining access to a superior job, but of maintaining one's "employability"' (Brown; 1995: 35). Seeking out appropriate training and work experience is part of this process, but there is also an assumption that the archetypal young professional is unencumbered by personal commitments tied either to specific locations or time frames, and will prove his or her ongoing 'employability' by being available to serve the company's particular needs wherever and whenever their skills are required.

It is partly for these reasons that Beck has argued that the labour market is 'the driving force behind the individualisation of people's lives' (1992: 94):

Everyone must be independent, free for the demands of the market in order to guarantee his/her economic existence. The market subject is ultimately the single individual, unhindered by a relationship, marriage or family ... The form of existence of the single person is not a deviant case along the path of modernity. It is the archetype of the fully developed labour market society (Beck, 1992: 116, 123).

As a consequence, decisions to settle down, whether in terms of investing in property of one's own or choosing to live with a partner, become increasingly contentious and far-reaching in their consequences. Beck therefore stresses the deliberate decisions which people now *have* to make in their lives, and the (often detrimental) consequences of allowing decisions to lapse or be made by default. Many of these decisions, he argues, are closely related to conflicts between men and women over changing expectations concerning their respective social roles, and are particularly pertinent to the lives of educated women. With their increased educational opportunities and greater academic success over the course of the late 1980s and 1990s (Arnot *et al.*, 1999), young women now have far greater expectations of equality and partnership in both public and private spheres. However, a profound gap continues to exist between their expectations, male behaviour in both of those spheres, and the institutional structures of professional life which still presuppose the nuclear family and a traditional division of labour. For example, despite the rhetoric of women's advancement within society, recent evidence from the United Kingdom suggests that women are still expected to bear the double burden of domestic and paid work and continue to earn considerably less than men for their efforts (Dench *et al.*, 2002).

Couple relationships, then, become increasingly impossible to achieve and subsequently sustain without at least one of the partners – usually the woman in heterosexual relationships – having to make some form of compromise with respect to their career. A study by Brown and Scase (1994) of the early labour market experiences of a group of graduates in the early 1990s seems to confirm this. They found that personal relationships were particularly vulnerable to breakdown where both partners had the means to survive independently of each other. Moreover, they found that 'work has become part of a holistic lifestyle, according to which priorities and compromises must constantly be negotiated' (p. 152). Under such conditions, a great deal is potentially at stake in deciding whether or not, or when, to settle down with a partner: tensions which are further magnified when the possibility of parenthood enters the frame (Beck and Beck-Gernscheim, 1995). Both young men and women, then, may be increasingly reluctant to sacrifice their economic independence and security, virtues that are highly prized within contemporary society. Wilkinson (1994), for example, has argued that 'graduate, career-minded women are now much less likely to feel the need for a partner' (p. 20), and are instead much more committed to their engagement in the labour market.

Tensions between work and relationships seem, then, to remain firmly in place for many young people. We are certainly not arguing that couple relationships are no longer desirable under such circumstances, but that they are becoming increasingly difficult to achieve on terms acceptable to both parties:

> In the single life, the longing for the other grows just as much as the impossibility of integrating that person into the architecture of a life that now really is 'one's own'. That life was fulfilled with the non-presence of the other. Now there is no space left for him or her (Beck, 1992: 122–3).

The possibility of *living with* a partner may be particularly affected by these tensions, but more generally there is little contemporary evidence to suggest that young adults are rejecting the pursuit of partnerships *per se*. In 1998, for example, just over eight out of ten 20–24-year-old men and women reported having had at least one sexual partner in the previous year, rising to just over nine out of ten amongst 25–34-year-olds (Office for National Statistics, 2000). However, this figure can be interpreted in many ways; in particular, a sexual partnership is not necessarily synonymous with a committed relationship, as evidenced by a recent study of Scottish twenty-somethings. A sizeable minority of those who were single in the sense of not living with a partner but nonetheless involved in sexual relationships said that they neither felt any emotional ties or commitment to that person, nor did they think of that person as a partner (Jamieson *et al.*, 2003). This points to an apparent deferral of commitment in the realm of intimacy, which has been associated by many writers with a more general deferral of the status of 'adult', and we turn now to a discussion of this theme.

The emergence of post-adolescence

Given that settling down with a partner is so widely regarded as a defining feature of adult status, the apparent impossibility of forming couple relationships based on equality and mutual respect has contributed to the view of some commentators that we are currently witnessing the emergence of a 'postponed generation' (Litwin, 1986) or a 'generation on hold' (Côté and Allahar, 1994). Such terminology suggests a disruption to the progression of successive cohorts through a series of distinguishable phases – or 'life stages' – which are often characterised as forming the contemporary 'life course': moving from being a dependent child to a young adult, from thence into various stages of family life, into retirement, and finally moving into old age. Increasingly, commentators are pointing to the emergence of a new stage in the life course for many twenty- and thirty-somethings, marked by an absence of some of the defining characteristics often associated with 'adulthood' at these ages, such as the attainment of independence, responsibility and commitment in a number of spheres (Côté, 2000). Various terms have been used to describe this new life stage – late adolescence, young adulthood, youth-hood, post-adolescence – but what these terms have in common is an understanding that we are witnessing the emergence of a phase of the life course which 'drives the youth phase into the adult phase and eats away a part of life which until a few decades ago was a part of adult life for the majority of the population' (du Bois-Reymond, 1998: 64).

Demographers have provided empirical support for the consolidation of this new phase over the last three decades. Berthoud and Gershuny (2000), for example, have shown that in 1973, 46 per cent of all British young people in their twenties and 74 per cent of those in their thirties could be placed in the 'young family' life stage (being the parent of a child aged up to ten), yet by 1996 these proportions had fallen to 31 per cent and 59 per cent respectively. Significantly, the biggest change contributing to this shift has been the growth of what they term the 'independent' life stage: no children, not a student, and living apart from parents. The proportions within this category rose between 1973 and 1996 from 28 per cent of twenty-somethings and 11 per cent of thirty-somethings to 38 and 25 per cent respectively. The proportion of independent individuals who are married has also reduced substantially, from 70 per cent of the group in 1973 down to only 31 per cent in 1996 (ibid., 233). Berthoud and Gershuny's analysis, then, highlights the emergence of a new and widespread phase of independent living, difficult to define in terms of fixed age boundaries, yet which corresponds well to the postulated rise of post-adolescence. In the United States, Goldscheider and Goldscheider (1993, 1999) have charted similar processes, with non-familial living becoming increasingly common amongst younger generations prior to settling down with a partner at a later age.

Most commentators would agree that this new life phase is marked by a relative freedom from responsibilities associated with traditional family life, particularly in the form of parenthood. Du Bois-Reymond (1998) highlights a number of other features which, she argues, are intrinsic to 'post-adolescence', her preferred term for this phenomenon. Importantly, she associates post-adolescence with a specific class position, namely the growth of a cultural elite of well educated, highly aspirational young adults of both sexes, made possible by the expansion of mass education in the second half of the twentieth century and the influence of second wave feminism. She notes that a form of post-adolescence was historically associated with the upper class male of the late nineteenth and early twentieth century, who enjoyed an extended period of education and leisure as befitted a 'gentleman' of his status, before settling down with a wife and family in his late twenties or early thirties. However, du Bois-Reymond argues that this life stage is now the preserve of both men and women who have undergone extended periods of education and training. Such opportunities are being offered to a growing proportion of young Britons, with the British government aiming for a 50 per cent higher education participation rate amongst those under thirty by 2010. In turn, one might expect to see the extension of post-adolescence to a greater proportion of this age group, a theme to which we return in Chapter 5.

Secondly, du Bois-Reymond argues that post-adolescents have high expectations of their working lives. In particular, she contends that they are committed to flexible and personally fulfilling careers – often within the cultural and CIT industries – which blur the boundaries of work and play, provide opportunities to incorporate their personal lifestyles into their working lives, and which also contribute to self-development. This may well represent a rational response to the uncertain nature of the labour market for young adults. As Dwyer and Wyn (2001) note, young people increasingly are having to rethink the concept of 'career' in the face of demands for flexibility and the deregulation of labour markets. The US writer Dave Eggars sums up well the assumed attitude of his generation: 'we want to complain about jobs, but we don't really want jobs ourselves – not the kind you'd complain about.' (Eggars, 2000: 175). Post-adolescents are by no means immune to unemployment, yet periods spent outside of formal work may represent opportunities – for further education or training, for self-employment, for overseas travel – rather than threats: 'this flexible attitude amongst post-adolescents also demonstrates a certain nonchalance brought about by their social origin: they know that they are backed up by their parents' financial and cultural resources' (du Bois-Reymond, 1998: 71). For such young adults, then, there are few genuine risks involved in claiming that monetary considerations, whilst not unimportant, are not necessarily a chief priority.

Thirdly, in du Bois-Reymond's view post-adolescents have equally high expectations of the conduct and planning of their personal lives and the desired quality of relationships with friends and partners. Committed partnerships, whilst aspired to in the long term, are often put on hold in order to prioritise education and training or further career development. Allied to this, the boundaries between personal independence and various forms of dependency on parents are often blurred. Movement in and out of a variety of independent living arrangements is common, with extended periods of overseas travel and high levels of work-related geographical mobility. These particular points are, of course, central themes of this book and will be explored in greater detail in subsequent chapters.

Fourthly, du Bois-Reymond argues that post-adolescents enjoy an ongoing commitment to youth culture and style well into their late twenties and thirties, and tend to be trend*setters* rather than followers. This may be particularly so amongst those who work within the cultural industries, and who often adopt designer lifestyles to match their designer careers. Chatterton and Hollands (2002), for example, refer to the occupation of the 'urban playscape' by a 'youthful service class' of 'urban service workers, knowledge professionals and cultural intermediaries', frequenting 'niche-oriented clubs'. Bennett (1999) has also noted that many of these emergent forms of popular youth culture, particularly those linked to rave and dance culture, are also increasingly subject to a blurring of the age boundaries surrounding their participants, with styles of dress and musical preference associated predominantly with those in their late teens and early twenties not uncommonly found amongst older age groups.

Fifthly, post-adolescents are suspicious of the notion of adulthood, which they associate with 'dullness, routine work, and responsibility' (du Bois-Reymond, 1998: 76). The European Group for Integrated Social Research (2001) argues that the term '*young* adulthood' captures the ambiguous status which accompanies this reluctance to embrace an 'adult' identity, through hinting at 'the intermingling of youthful and adult structures in the biographies of young men and women' (p. 103). They identify three specific ways in which young adults might experience these conflicting roles. First, they identify *divided lives*, whereby young adults experience aspects of both 'youth' and 'adulthood' simultaneously. Secondly, *pending lives*, whereby young people have no clear self-identification with either youth or adulthood. Thirdly, *swinging lives*, referring to those who quite consciously alternate between the supposed character traits and behaviours of youth and adulthood: 'young parents who cling to their youth culture; established professionals who dance through rave nights at weekends; and those who try to create alternative trajectories by making their careers in youth-cultural contexts or the hidden economy' (ibid.: 104). 'Adult' behaviours and attitudes, linked to notions of responsibility and a lack of spontaneity, are then perceived to be the very antithesis of post-adolescence. It is, of course, the assumed rejection of these characteristics – and the implication of a generational preference for idleness and irresponsibility – that earned post-Baby Boomers in the United States the epithet (alongside 'Generation X') of the 'slacker' generation.

Finally, and seemingly paradoxically, du Bois-Reymond argues that despite their suspicions of 'adulthood' post-adolescents are nonetheless essentially *life planners*, engaged in the construction of *choice biographies*, in which the life course is increasingly treated as a 'project', based on strategic life-planning and the constant need to adapt to changing circumstances (see Giddens, 1991). A recent study of two successive cohorts of young people growing up in Scotland appears to confirm this commitment to life-planning amongst younger generations, although the authors do not regard such attitudes as the exclusive preserve of the affluent. Anderson *et al.*'s (2002) study found that in comparison to the outlook of members of an older cohort when they were in *their* twenties, members of the younger cohort of twenty-somethings were largely optimistic, exercising forethought and planning for the future, often over a long period. Moreover, they felt more in control of their lives than their older peers, and on average were no more insecure nor pessimistic about their immediate future, despite facing 'quite high levels of uncertainty' (paragraph 9.2). Dwyer and Wyn (2001) have referred to this 'degree of positivity' amongst young adults facing uncertain futures as 'a perplexing optimism' (p. 83), perhaps a consequence of their socialisation into a rhetoric of individualisation and choice. Moreover, 'where structured pathways do not exist, or are rapidly being eroded, individual agency is increasingly important in establishing patterns for themselves which give positive meaning to (young people's) lives' (ibid.: 93). Anderson *et al.* (2002) appear to concur with this possibility: 'one plausible interpretation of our data is that uncertainty has positively encouraged many young men and women to take more responsibility for their own lives' (paragraph 9.2).

Du Bois-Reymond's account of post-adolescence is essentially sympathetic, conveying a sense of intrigue about the nature of generational change during the current period and the implications such change might have for inter-generational relations within Europe. She appears to be largely agnostic on the implications for good or ill of the rise of post-adolescence, notwithstanding a desire to map out the nature of the relationship between risk and chance in the biographies of all young people, not just the post-adolescent elite. She also expresses a concern to interrogate what it is about 'adulthood' that so many young people appear to find so off-putting. Others, however, conceive of post-adolescence as a rather more disturbing and negative development, and we now consider these accounts.

In these rather more negative conceptualisations, a number of discernible discursive strands have emerged. Some commentators have focused on the continuing appeal of youth-orientated lifestyles to ever older generations and regard this as evidence of the infantilism of society more generally (Calcutt, 1998). The current nostalgia in the United Kingdom for all things pertaining to the 1970s, for example, including the ongoing appeal amongst clubbers of the 1970s-style school disco complete with school uniforms and retro sports days (Brownell, 2002), could be cited as evidence in support of this view, alongside the recent European craze for 'urban scooters' which saw tweenies and twenty-somethings alike freewheeling through city streets. The rise of the 'new lad' is a closely related phenomenon, signalling the emergence of a generation of young heterosexual men who apparently have no desire to relinquish their laddish ways in favour of 'settling down'. Whelehan (2000) has argued that 'everything about the new lad suggests anxiety about the future of the male in a world where feisty women seem to be multiplying' (p. 73). Unsurprisingly, then, the rise of the new lad has been closely followed by the rise of the 'ladette', who drinks pints, watches football and can 'out-lad' her male 'mates'. Such trends have led Wilkinson and Mulgan (1995) to claim that young women are not only increasingly masculine in their values, 'attached to risk, hedonism, and living on the edge' (p. 11), but more controversially are increasingly willing to use violence as a means of getting what they want. Such behaviours do not, however, appear to have bred happiness. Bynner *et al.* (2002), for example, argue that there has been a relative decline in the psychological health of young people, especially amongst young women, over the last 12 years.

Post-adolescents, then, tend to hold a somewhat ambiguous position within popular consciousness: whilst on the one hand they are lauded for their drive and ambition, on the other hand – particularly if they are female – they are often vilified for their self-centredness. According to one survey, for example, one in five British 18–24-year-olds prioritise having a career or gaining qualifications over family life: 'Relationships inside the family, with partners and with friends all take second best in the lives of these striving young people who want success apparently at any cost' (Boseley, 1999: 3). Young people's presumed search for autonomy is seen by some, then, as evidence of a selfish commitment to individualistic and hedonistic values, evident not only in their rejection of relationships, but also in their apparent political apathy and lack of community involvement. In the United States, Putnam (2000) has used the metaphor of 'bowling alone' to capture the decline of community involvement which is evident amongst all generations, but particularly pronounced amongst younger cohorts. Counter-claims that young people are not apathetic but are instead increasingly drawn to political causes marked by post-materialist values merely serve to reinforce the negative image of a generation that is more concerned with self-actualisation and identity politics than it is with the collectivist politics of class (McKay, 1998).

Other accounts focus on the implicit fear of adulthood, commitment and responsibility amongst post-adolescents. Litwin (1986) contends that this is a phenomenon particularly associated with young people from affluent families, whose upbringing has taught them to prize excellence and individuality. As a consequence, she argues, they are shaken when their achievements are less than perfect or when events around them – including the prospect of marriage – threaten their individuality. These 'special children of perfect parents' have 'taken a look at the grown-up world and found it scary' (Litwin, 1986: 134). It may also be the case that the emergence of post-adolescence takes on particularly worrying significance for some, precisely because of its association with young people who are the traditional inheritors of the professional and managerial classes. Heiman (2001) notes, for example, that 'the ideal-type "slacker" embodies a powerful critique of the Fordist idea of productivity ... (which) revealed an undercurrent that could have been extremely threatening to "the system" had it had the chance to flourish into an organised critique of the workings of capitalism as a whole' (p. 276). She argues that such a critique is particularly threatening because it highlights the middle class 'fear of falling' within an economy which no longer guarantees upward mobility and the reproduction of social class privilege. However, she also notes that what may appear to be a form of resistance on the part of young adults may actually be transformed into reproduction, as certain characteristics of the slacker generation have been reinterpreted as key requirements of the flexible, post-Fordist employee. Moreover, Klein (2000) has shown how these characteristics are drawn upon in the marketing of 'cool' to young adults, to the point that advertising agencies seek to employ 'cool hunters', members of the post-adolescent elite whose job it is to seek out the 'next big thing'.

James Côté's *Arrested Adulthood* (2000) is currently one of the most sustained critiques of this new life phase amongst young adults, referred to by Côté as 'youthhood'. Côté's thesis is that we are rapidly moving towards a version of Aldous Huxley's *Brave New World*, marked by a desire amongst younger generations to prioritise 'the pleasure principle', to follow 'the paths of least resistance and effort' (p. 42) and to avoid the responsibilities of adulthood for as long as possible. In a world where there are few role models for contemporary adulthood, and where the traditional markers of this life stage are no longer in place, Côté argues that adulthood has become more of a psychological state than a readily identifiable social status. However, according to Côté, most young people spurn the option of 'a life course of continual and deliberate growth' in favour of what he terms 'default individualisation':

> At one extreme, people can pursue a life course totally devoid of traditional social markers without exerting much mental effort. They can do this by simply selecting a number of 'default options' now available in the restructured consumer-corporate society and mass culture of late modernity. I refer to this type of individualisation as *default individualisation*, because it involves a life course dictated by circumstance and folly, with little agentic assertion on the part of the person (Côté, 2000: 33 – emphasis in original).

Côté draws on developmental psychology in highlighting the importance of identity formation in the successful transition to 'psychological adulthood'. He is particularly influenced by Erikson's conceptualisation of adolescence as a moratorium which, through absolving young people from community responsibilities, provides a time for 'healing old wounds, if necessary, and for building future strengths, if possible' (ibid.: 37). Côté argues that this identity moratorium can now last for many years, if not indefinitely, with crises of identity now the norm rather than the exception, and with an increasing number of young people failing to enter adulthood 'as we have known it':

> Among the young, who would otherwise be moving into an adult-hood characterised by contributions to their family and community,

a glorified identity crisis is common, wherein great pride is taken in how much experimentation is undertaken, or how many commitments are avoided or rejected as archaic or associated with one of many 'isms' (especially sexism or racism). Although there is evidence that such a period of identity formation can be developmentally useful (as a moratorium), when it takes an exaggerated form or goes on indefinitely, it is more likely that there will be casualties – both emotional and physical – identified with it (ibid.: 153–4).

Côté concedes that the demise of traditional social markers is a liberating moment for 'those whose sexual and lifestyle preferences had to be kept hidden in the past' and who consequently did not experience a 'rightness' in the world. Nonetheless, he admits to being 'not overly optimistic about the future' (p. 201). The source of his pessimism is not 'the increasing diversity of lifestyle' or 'preference-based living' *per se*, but what he perceives to be a decline in a discernible sense of connection to community amongst contemporary youth, the worst of whom are 'oblivious to, and reckless with, community cohesion and generational continuity' (ibid.: 43).

To explore these ideas further, Côté develops a fourfold typology of dispositions towards youthhood and adulthood, subdivided according to an individual's high or low orientation in relation to their level of individualisation and their commitment to community structure. Those who continue to feel a sense of loyalty to inter-generational continuity – Côté's 'traditionalists' – are, he argues, 'the dying breed of late modern society' (p. 198). Instead, youthhood is increasingly characterised by the 'normalisation of narcissism' and continual crises of identity. Increasing proportions of young adults are, then, 'other-directed': highly sensitive to other people's perceptions, constantly seeking the approval of others, and subject to the whims of fashion. Moreover, they are likely to have a greater loyalty to friends than to family. This is a trait classically associated with 'adolescence', and which is suggestive of the conformity of youth. As Lesko (2001) notes, 'to be fully under the influence of others implies that adolescents are not fully autonomous, rational or determining, all of which are valued characteristics for successful, modern adults' (p. 4). Indeed, Côté argues that the line between youth and adulthood is either invisible or irrelevant to members of this group, such that many may remain in a permanent state of youthhood. In this sense, other-directed young adults appear to share a similar outlook to du Bois-Reymond's post-adolescents who, as we have seen, are also deeply mistrustful of the concept of 'adulthood'.

Alongside 'other-directed' individuals, Côté identifies a group of 'inner-directed' young adults. Members of this group continue to operate with notions of acceptable behaviour learned within the parental home, yet still have little sense of close inter-generational linkage, partly arising from their strong career commitment and their high levels of geographical mobility. They are pragmatists, and willingly adapt the patterns set by their parents in order to fit in with their own specific circumstances and their sense of unfolding identity. Individuals within this category may exhibit some elements of narcissism, but on the whole are responsible and possess a strong sense of identity. Finally, Côté's fourth group, 'unconventional' individuals, are another ascendant group, maintaining 'pre-adult' behaviour patterns and developing a 'loose (but strained)' connection with both parents and peers alike.

Côté presents, then, a gloomy account of contemporary young adulthood, marked by the 'normalisation of narcissism', a loss of inter-generational continuity, difficulties in experiencing a sense of core identity, and the ascendency of 'other-directedness', all played out against the increasing (and increasingly manipulative) influence of the market economy. Despite a number of similarities in the behaviours and character traits identified by both writers, the tone of Côté's account provides a contrast to du Bois-Reymond's rather more upbeat portrayal of post-adolescence. Moreover, there are some key points of departure between their two accounts. In particular, where du Bois-Reymond sees evidence of the proliferation of choice biographies, marked by a widespread commitment to self-development and future planning amongst post-adolescents, Côté sees instead the proliferation of narcissism and default individualisation: a significant difference in emphasis. Importantly, it should also be noted that his account does not suggest that 'youthhood' in its more extreme forms is necessarily associated with 'a cultural elite'. On the contrary, he suggests that 'the highly educated and competent 20 per cent of the workforce' will exercise control over those who 'remain locked into youthhood' (p. 180), who presumably will form some sort of 'youthful underclass'.

Côté's account ends not in total despair, but with a vision for a future which avoids the creation of a dystopian Brave New World, based on a revival of forms of collectivism and an ethic of care (pp. 205ff) 'wherein people balance their commitment to self with commitment to others and where people accept responsibility, especially for the choices they make' (Côté, 2000: 208). This argument nonetheless assumes that these characteristics are currently absent amongst younger generations, and that the ways in which they may be choosing to conduct their intimate relationships are somehow inferior to those of older generations. These and similar assumptions have been held up to scrutiny in recent research on intimacy, and in the final section of this chapter we consider the relevance of this emerging literature to the appeal of the single life and the growth of independent living arrangements. Following Jamieson, throughout this book we use the term 'intimate relationships' to describe relationships characterised by a level of disclosure: 'an intimacy of the self rather than an intimacy of the body, although the completeness of intimacy of the self may be enhanced by bodily intimacy' (Jamieson, 1999: 1). Such relationships include those with parents and siblings, with friends, and with partners, and we use the phrase '*networks of intimacy*' to refer to the full range of intimate relationships embraced by any one person.

The transformation of intimacy?

According to Giddens, we are currently experiencing a 'transformation of intimacy', driven by a sexual revolution in which women increasingly seek equality with men in both public and private domains, 'implying a wholesale democratising of the interpersonal domain' (1992: 3). We are also witnessing the development of new sexual freedoms, linked to the rise of 'plastic sexuality': 'decentred sexuality, free from the needs of reproduction' (ibid.: 2). As a consequence, he argues, the realm of intimate relationships has become a key arena for self-reflexivity and 'reflexive control' in late modern society, resulting in a proliferation of possibilities with respect to sexual intimacy and friendship, with relationships based on ties that are 'more or less freely chosen' (Giddens, 1991: 87). This is most evident in the emergence of Giddens' much-debated 'pure relationship', 'one in which external criteria have become dissolved; the relationship exists solely for whatever rewards that relationship as such can deliver' (ibid.: 6). In other words, the relationship will only last for as long as it remains mutually beneficial to the partners involved. Some commentators would no doubt argue that this constitutes the perfect relationship paradigm for the self-obsessed post-adolescent elite. Wilkinson and Mulgan (1995), however, consider this in a more positive light, arguing that young people place high value on 'authenticity' within their sexual relationships, marked by emotional intimacy and honesty, mutual affection and sexual fulfilment.

Whilst self-disclosure and commitment are integral to the pure relationship, Giddens argues that such intimacy simultaneously requires a measure of privacy on the part of each partner, 'because a balance between autonomy and the sharing of feelings has to be obtained if personal closeness is not to be replaced by dependence' (1991: 95). For these reasons, maintaining 'intimacy at a distance' by choosing to engage in sexual relationships yet *not* choosing to live with one's sexual partner may provide the optimum setting for the pure relationship within a culture which values personal autonomy and self-development. If such a relationship subsequently fails to achieve a balance between intimacy and autonomy, or to provide the requisite authenticity, then far less is at stake than if the relationship involves a strong financial and emotional commitment in the form of living together. For broadly similar reasons, many heterosexual couples may choose cohabitation over marriage, believing that the ties are less binding and therefore more readily dissolved if necessary.

It has been suggested, however, that the pure relationship may exist more as an ideal to which partners aspire, rather than something that is achievable in practice, given that most partnerships are characterised by varying degrees of compromise and disappointment (Jamieson, 1999). Indeed, most research on young people's sexual relationships suggests that heterosexual couple relationships – regardless of whether they are based on co-residence – continue to be based on unequal power relations (Holland *et al.*, 1998), whilst Jamieson (1999) has argued that '...the creative energies of many actors are still engaged in coping with or actively sustaining old inequalities rather than transforming them' (p. 491). Nonetheless, the characteristics of the pure relationship may be increasingly aspired to amongst contemporary youth, and may shape their responses to decisions concerning whether or not to live with a partner, both in the shorter and longer term. This is a possibility that we explore further in Chapter 9.

The conditions of mutual benefit associated with the pure relationship are by no means confined to sexual relationships; indeed, platonic relationships are regarded by Giddens as the prototype of the pure relationship between sexual partners, as they are voluntarily entered into and are not reliant on forms of external criteria – certification, societal approval – for their continuation: 'A friend is defined specifically as someone with whom one has a relationship unprompted by anything other than the rewards that the relationship provides' (Giddens, 1991: 90). Various commentators have argued that friendship networks are inevitably taking on increased importance under the conditions of late modernity, with many single young adults looking to their friends rather than to sexual partners or to family members to meet their immediate need for intimacy. According to Beck, for example, the intensification of friendship networks amongst single people, based on shared interests and commitments, is not only an indispensable safeguard against the 'built-in hazards' of being single, but 'is also the pleasure offered by the single life' (1992: 122). Indeed, the pleasures inherent in close friendships have been strongly emphasised within popular culture over the last decade. Sitcoms such as *Friends*, *The Secret Life of Us* and *This Life* have become cult viewing amongst a global audience of post-adolescents, portraying groups of single twenty- and thirty-somethings socialising together, often living together, having a good time and enjoying considerable independence from traditional domestic responsibilities.

For the most part, these fictional friendship networks provide surrogate families for those involved, complete with strong emotional, social and economic attachments more usually associated with blood ties, and akin to the 'families of choice' identified in studies of the social networks of gay men and lesbians. These networks, according to Weeks *et al.* (2001: 50), provide support for Giddens view that non-heterosexuals are 'prime everyday experimenters' with respect to the transformation of intimacy, not least because their relationships exist outside of the framework of traditional expectations and legal structures which govern heterosexual relationships. As such, they argue that gay men, lesbians and bisexuals are pioneers of new ways of conducting intimate relationships which will become increasingly widespread within the heterosexual world, given the decline of many traditional markers in the realm of personal relationships, and conditions of risk within society more generally:

> 'Families of choice' and other chosen relationships – creative adaptations to rapid change based on voluntary association – are characteristic responses to a shifting society, and sociologists have seen their emergence as a significant and developing feature of the heterosexual, as well as non-heterosexual, world. In modern society, most people, whether heterosexual or homosexual, live through very similar experiences of insecurity and emotional flux at various times in their lives, and relationships based on friendships and choice often become indispensable frameworks for negotiating the hazards of everyday life (Weeks *et al.*, 2001: 20–1).

In a similar vein, Pahl has argued that friendships are 'an increasingly important form of social glue in contemporary society' (2000: 1), with younger generations continuing to rely upon their peers for support and self-identity well into their twenties and thirties. Pahl, too, regards the increased prominence of friendship as symptomatic of the risks and uncertainty of modern life:

> Parents die, children leave home, couples dissolve and reunite; the emotional traumas of contemporary life take place in different places with different key actors. Sometimes the only continuity for increasingly reflexive people is provided by their friends. Unwilling to be perceived as social chameleons flitting from one job or partner to another, men and women may come to rely on their friends to provide support and confirmation of their enduring identities (ibid.: 69).

According to Pahl, the forging and subsequent maintenance of friendship networks has become an important project in itself, not least because 'we value those friends and friend-like relations who affirm the view of ourselves that we most wish to be' (ibid.: 87). Pahl illustrates this point with the example of a woman in her mid-thirties who takes great care to work on and nurture her many and various friendships – her 'social convoy' – and who clearly derives a strong sense of self-worth from her identity as a 'good friend'.

With the ongoing expansion of higher education, Pahl notes, such social convoys are increasingly likely to include friendships formed in the crucible of university life, with all its highs and lows, and further strengthened through mutual support on leaving college and entering the world of work. Friendships formed in such a way are 'bonded with ties of gratitude and mutual experience' (ibid.: 118). Whilst the stresses of job mobility and change of residence may transform some of these friendships into 'fossil friendships' – those which acquire particular importance at a specific stage in life, yet which subsequently become peripheral to a person's active social network – such friendships nonetheless have the potential to be rekindled at any point and to become important reference points in a person's life. Other friendships remain of central importance throughout a person's life. One's social convoy exists, then, in a state of constant flux around a small core of significant others, and it 'defines us, reflects us, supports us and so much else beside' (ibid.: 167).

Côté (2000) has also noted the increased importance of friendship in young people's lives, regarding it as further evidence for the ascendancy of the other-directed modern individual who, as we noted above, is more likely to have a greater loyalty to 'a quasi-family comprising peers' than to his or her family of origin. This is problematic for Côté because he believes that peer-based social networks encourage the rise of 'parochial tribalism' rather than a sense of commitment to a wider community. As a consequence, 'people seek emotional security within their 'tribe' in moralisms and ideologies that by definition work against the formation of a cohesive community' (ibid.: 39). Côté, then, is more inclined to put a negative gloss on new forms of sociality amongst young adults.

In using the language of tribes and tribalism, Côté demonstrates the influence on his work of Maffesoli's conceptualisation of the 'neo-tribe' (Maffesoli, 1996). Maffesoli has distinguished between 'abstract, rational periods of history', marked by individualism, and 'empathetic' periods of history, which are marked by a strong sense of collective spirit and sociality. According to Maffesoli, we are currently living through an empathetic era, manifest in the emergence of 'neo-tribalism': a diversity of groupings, all of which share a commitment to 'the communal ethic', which 'has the simplest of foundations: warmth, companionship – physical contact with one another' (Maffesoli, 1996: 16). These groupings, he argues, tend to be based on networks that have developed through 'elective sociality' and which exist for their own sake, rather than on associative structures based on political or religious ideology, which usually exist to further a particular collective purpose. Maffesoli acknowledges that there are inherent dangers in this model of sociality, as it can too easily give rise to 'localism' and 'the Mafia spirit', developing the potential to be used as a means of control, of exclusion and of ostracism. At the same time, however, the tribe is 'the guarantee of solidarity', and not infrequently provides a space within which mutual support can arise:

> In some ways, such mutual aid exists by force of circumstance, not out of purely disinterested motives: the help given can always be redeemed whenever I need it. However, in so doing, we are all part of a larger process of correspondence and participation that favours the collective body (ibid.: 24).

There are shades here of the mutually beneficial pure relationship, yet the broader point is that neo-tribalism arises as a result of *proxemics*, a term which 'refers primarily to the foundation of a succession of "we's", which constitute the very essence of all sociality' (p. 139). Neo-tribes, then, may be based on groupings as diverse as regulars at the local cafe bar, co-workers, participants in internet chatrooms, fellow students, families of choice and housemates. Within these groupings, certain relationships may take on long-lasting significance, but involvement even on the fringes of the group will almost inevitably lead to the creation of 'friendship chains' based on getting to know friends of friends, and friends of friends of friends, *ad infinitum*.

Where Côté and Maffesoli appear to share common ground is in the belief that these manifestations of collective spirit and sociality are essentially *superficial*, characterised by 'fluidity, occasional gatherings and dispersal' (Maffesoli, 1996: 76), and that they have arisen largely in response to the massification of society. Nonetheless, they may both be guilty of underestimating the significance of group membership to those involved, particularly if for some individuals these are their main or only sources of sociality and collectivity. Overall, though, Maffesoli's account seems to complement a more general view of the increased importance of friendship as a protective strategy, providing support and solidarity against a backdrop of increasing levels of risk and a concomitant decline in both the possibilities for, and the appeal of, maintaining intimate couple relationships.

Conclusion

In this chapter we have outlined an alternative framework for considering contemporary patterns of household formation amongst young adults. Constraint models are only partially successful in explaining these patterns, and in our view they place an unhelpful emphasis on trying to explain 'thwarted' coupledom, rather than exploring the possibility that younger generations may instead be engaged in a renegotiation of the bounds of intimacy in a number of spheres, including parent–child relationships, sexual relationships with partners, and platonic friendships. The 'thwarted coupledom' thesis also denies young people agency in an important area of their lives. Instead, we have found it useful to consider changing patterns of household formation within the context of writings on risk, destandardisation and individualisation, with a particular emphasis on the distinction between choice versus standardised biographies. We have also outlined three other themes which we believe are important to bear in mind in examining young people's domestic and housing careers: the demands of the labour market and the particular tensions these create for young women; the emergence of post-adolescence as a new and distinct phase of the life course; and the possibility that younger generations are in the forefront of significant shifts in attitude towards the politics and dynamics of contemporary relationships. In the chapters that follow, we seek to explore these themes through bringing together existing empirical research in these areas, and through reflecting on the findings of our own research. We start by considering contemporary trends in living in and leaving the parental home.

4
Living in and Leaving the Parental Home

Introduction

I lived with my parents and my sister, younger sister, in the same house from when I was born till when I left home at the age of 18. Memories, don't know, just normal growing up memories, I guess. Nothing special. Normal house. One cat, one dog. Fairly happy. Fought all the time with my sister. Actually fought all the time with my dad until I left home. I think that's fairly normal, if you really like someone you fight with them until you leave home and then appreciate that you really like them (Ellie, aged 24, household 6).

Down-nesting: the tendency of parents to move to smaller, guest-room-free houses after the children have moved away so as to avoid children aged 20 to 30 who have boomeranged home (Douglas Coupland, 1991, *Generation X*)

Across Europe, North America and Australasia, the overwhelming majority of young people live in the parental home during their late teens, with many residing with parents well into their twenties. In 1995, 90 per cent of 15–19-year-olds growing up in European Union member states lived with their parents, along with 65 per cent of their 20–24-year-old peers (European Commission, 1997). In the United States, 56 per cent of 18–24-year-old young men and 43 per cent of their female peers lived in the parental home in 2000 (Fields and Casper, 2001), whilst in Australia in the same year, 45 per cent of 20–24-year-olds did so (Hillman and Marks, 2002). Living in the parental home in one's late teens and early twenties is, then, a common feature of growing up in western societies, but the day-to-day reality of such arrangements is something about which we know surprisingly little. Indeed, in the absence of any objective benchmark, the majority of people would probably describe their experiences of home life during this period in similar language to that used by Ellie above: 'nothing special', 'fairly happy', 'fairly normal', despite varying degrees of family tension.

This chapter explores young people's experiences of living in and first leaving the parental home, drawing a particular contrast between the experiences of those who first leave home in order to move away to university or to depart on a pre-university gap year and those who leave for other reasons. Going away to university appears to facilitate a comparatively smooth, relatively privileged and unproblematic transition out of the parental home – or as one young man put it to us, 'without making it almost a personal break from my parents'. Ellie, for instance, whose comments open this chapter, first left home at 18, on completion of her A Level (Advanced Level) studies, in order to work abroad for a year before embarking on a university degree. She had no expectation of a protracted period of dependency on her family, and managed to leave home before her relationship with her father deteriorated further: 'all of a sudden I went from this person that he didn't seem to treat as an adult to somebody he treated completely as an equal'.

In contrast, young people with no expectation of going away to study are unable to draw upon what has become – certainly in Britain, although less so in other European countries due to stronger traditions of studying locally – an increasingly socially acceptable exit strategy. Consequently, they and their parents are more likely to perceive their home-leaving as the culmination of a period of unresolved family tension, even though those tensions may not necessarily be qualitatively different to those experienced by their peers who continue into higher education. This, in turn, can make subsequent returns to the parental home particularly unpalatable. Moreover, as we shall see in greater detail in Chapter 5, leaving home to go to university also facilitates access to a relatively privileged sector of the housing market: university halls of residence and an earmarked section of the private rented sector. Whilst conditions in the latter are often poor, students are nonetheless able to access such provision with relative ease.

We start this chapter by providing a historical overview of trends in living in and leaving the parental home, followed by a summary of recent trends in Europe, Australia and North America, thereby providing the broader context for many of the themes of this book. Our account of recent trends is necessarily brief, and readers are referred to Jones

(1995a) for a detailed account of British trends, to Iacovou (1998) for more on broader European trends, to Hillman and Marks (2002) for more on Australian trends and to Goldscheider and Goldscheider (1993, 1999) for more on the US context.

Continuity and change in patterns of living in the parental home: a historical overview

In early modern England, it was not uncommon for young children to experience living away from their parents for varying periods of time, whether due to impoverishment, illness or the death of a parent. However, despite these intermittent periods spent living away, most remained within the parental home until at least the age of 14 or 15 before leaving home to enter into service – typically agriculture, domestic service, or some form of apprenticeship. In most cases, this was based on a living-in arrangement. The majority of children were already well accustomed to labouring, usually having worked for their families for several years by the time they entered service. Nonetheless, moving away from home in their mid-teens was an important milestone in young people's lives, marking the beginning of a period of relative independence prior to marriage in their mid- to late twenties (Ben-Amos, 1994). In some cases, young people left home in order to further their schooling, rather than to enter into service, and this typically occurred around the age of twelve (Mitterauer, 1992). It should be noted, however, that leaving home during this period was not an irreversible transition, whilst leaving home to enter into service was by no means a universal practice, varying according to local custom.

By the eighteenth century, young people were living within the parental home for increased periods of time, but over the course of the nineteenth and early twentieth century the mean age of leaving began to fall again. The mean age amongst men born between 1750 and 1819, for example, stood at 28, falling to 21.8 amongst those born between 1890 and 1930. Amongst women, the equivalent figures were 25.5 and 23.7 respectively (Pooley and Turnball, 1997). Marriage accounted for three-quarters of all departures amongst women in the earlier cohort, but for only half amongst the later cohort, with around one in five leaving for work. Similar proportions of men left for marriage or work in the earlier cohort (around 40 per cent in each category), but only a quarter in the later cohort left home to marry, with a further 15 per cent leaving for work and over a third leaving for war service. The pattern for sons to remain within the parental home longer than daughters was established from the late eighteenth century; sons were more likely to stay at home to follow their father's trades, whereas daughters were not only likely to marry earlier, but were also more likely to go into domestic service. Living in the parental home with one's new spouse was also not uncommon during this period.

Across the Atlantic, it was far more common for nineteenth-century young Americans to work locally and hence to remain within the parental home for extended periods of time, not least because the practice of taking in boarders was increasingly regarded as a marker of poverty, and therefore viewed as disreputable behaviour (Hine, 1999). Many parents were financially dependent on their working children, precipitating an abrupt and relatively early shift from the life of a child to that of a worker. For those living the frontier life during this period, the labour of sons and daughters was essential for physical survival, whilst adult wages in factories and mines were so low that additional income was necessary to make ends meet amongst city dwellers (indeed, it was not unusual for employers to hire entire families). By the 1920s, however, it had become increasingly common for young Americans growing up in rural areas to migrate to the cities for work, a trend further reinforced by the devastating effects of the Great Depression of the 1930s (Goldscheider and Goldscheider, 1999).

Patterns of leaving home in nineteenth-century Australia were different again (Weston *et al.*, 2001). Amongst non-indigenous populations the general pattern in the earlier part of the century was for young people of both sexes from less affluent families to leave home relatively early in order to find work, for young women from wealthier families to live at home until marriage, and for young men from such families to go away to boarding school, at the end of which time they were free to leave home. Towards the end of the century and in the first few decades of the twentieth century, increased opportunities in manufacturing, retail and service industries created greater opportunities for young adults to work locally and so remain at home until marriage. Amongst indigenous Australians, however, leaving home traditionally had a rather different meaning, as complex kinship systems rendered children the responsibility of extended family networks rather than the sole responsibility of biological parents. Weston *et al.* (2001) also note that 'given the practice, until as recently as the 1970s, of the forcible removal of children and communities (the 'stolen generations'), the term 'leaving home' is likely to be regarded as a euphemism by indigenous communities' (p. 15).

Back in England in the first half of the twentieth century, young people were now living with their parents until their early twenties.

When they eventually left they were doing so for a variety of reasons, not simply to marry (Pooley and Turnball, 1997). While this pattern of dependency continued in the period immediately following the Second World War, marriage increasingly became the overwhelming reason for first leaving home. Indeed, by the 1960s the mean age of first marriage was at its lowest recorded age, and was used as a relatively reliable proxy for the age of first leaving home (Kiernan, 1985). Similar trends were observed during this period in the United States and Canada (Ravanera *et al.*, 1995; Goldscheider and Goldscheider, 1999), as well as in most western European countries (Wallace and Kovatcheva, 1998) and in Australia (Gilding, 2001). During the 1970s, however, these trends began to go into reverse. Young people on both sides of the Atlantic became increasingly dependent upon their parents, remaining in the parental home for extended periods of time, and began once again to leave home for reasons other than just marriage. In Australia, this trend did not emerge until slightly later. Indeed, Young (1987) notes that there was actually a slight *reduction* in the median age of first leaving home amongst young people who were in their late teens in the early 1970s. Nonetheless, by the late 1970s the trend towards greater dependence upon parents was well established in Australia (Weston *et al.*, 2001).

Contemporary patterns

Who lives in the parental home?

Having provided a brief historical overview, we now focus on contemporary patterns of living in the parental home. We opened this chapter with recent data relating to Europe, the United States and Australia, and this section will focus in particular on British trends. In 1999, 56 and 38 per cent respectively of 20–24-year-old men and women were living with their parents, compared with 52 and 31 per cent in 1978 (Office for National Statistics, 2000). Only a small minority do so by their late twenties and early thirties, but, as with those in their early twenties, men are more likely to be doing so than women (24 and 11 per cent of young men aged 25–29 and 30–34, compared with figures of 11 and 4 per cent for women in these age groups). Even amongst older groups, though, this is a growing minority. Amongst 30-year-olds, for example, 10 per cent of men and 4 per cent of women lived with their parents in 1981 (Kiernan, 1986), rising to 15 per cent and 6 per cent respectively by 1991 (Heath and Miret, 1996). Recent data on ethnic differences on living in the parental home is scant, but evidence from the 1991 Census suggests that black young men are less likely than their Asian or white peers to be living with their parents in their late teens, and that white young women are more likely than their Asian or black peers to be living away from their parents in their early to mid-twenties (Heath and Dale, 1994).

Cross-sectional data does not, however, distinguish between individuals who may have already left home at least once and those who have never left home. In order to capture the dynamic nature of the leaving home process, and to draw comparisons between successive cohorts, longitudinal data sources are essential, and in recent years British demographers have made particularly extensive use of the National Child Development Study (NCDS) and the British Household Panel Survey (BHPS). The NCDS is a longitudinal cohort study of people born in the same week in 1958. All members of the cohort turned 18 in 1976, and for the most part left home over the course of the late 1970s and early 1980s. The BHPS is based on a nationally representative sample of around 5500 households and over 10,000 individuals. Core members of the sample have been interviewed annually since 1991, providing a unique opportunity to explore young people's movement in and out of the parental home over the course of the 1990s.

Analysis of the BHPS suggests that, on average, 12.7 per cent of men and 17.5 per cent of women aged 16–30 currently leave the parental home each year, with the annual rate of departure increasing with age (Ermisch and Francesconi, 2000). The median age of first leaving amongst members of the 1958 cohort (now in their mid-forties) stood at 20 years and nine months for women, and 22 years and 11 months for men (Ermisch *et al.*, 1995). By comparison, analysis of younger cohorts drawn from the BHPS suggests that the median age of first leaving amongst men remained relatively static between 1976–85 and 1991–97, whilst amongst young women it increased by about one year (Ermisch and Francesconi, 2000). In other words, women born in the late 1960s and the early 1970s are staying in the parental home for a year longer than women born in the late 1950s. Sons still tend to live with their parents for slightly longer than daughters, but the gap has narrowed to only one year.

In addition to gender, there are other variables which exert an influence on the length of time young people remain in the parental home before first leaving. For example, the children of middle class families tend to remain at home for shorter periods of time than those from working class background due, to a large extent, to the increased prospect of first leaving home in order to attend university. However, middle class children are also more likely subsequently to return home, particularly after completing their studies (Jones, 1987). In contrast, their working class counterparts tend to leave later, but with no intention of a return, highlighting the ongoing significance of Leonard's (1980) distinction between 'living away from home' and 'leaving home'. Urbanites tend to live with their parents for longer periods of time than young people growing up in rural areas, with the latter leaving earlier in order to migrate to towns and cities for work and study (Jones, 1992; Burrows *et al.*, 1998). Nonetheless, non-migrant rural dwellers tend to stay in the parental home for longer and until they form a family unit of their own, living locally with a partner and/or a child (Jones, 2001). Other differences revolve around the nature of a young person's family of origin: those living with both their natural parents remain in the parental home for longer periods than do those who live with a step-parent (Kiernan, 1992), whilst the fewer siblings a young person has, the longer they live with their parents (Kiernan, 1985).

Bynner *et al.*'s (1997) analysis of the 1970 British Cohort Study (BCS70) provides a revealing picture of the characteristics of cohort members who were living with their parents in 1996, aged 26. Similar in design to the 1958 NCDS, BCS70 has followed a group of individuals all born in the same week in 1970. Now that the sample members are in their early thirties, data from BCS70 is increasingly being analysed by researchers interested in processes of household formation. Bynner *et al.*'s analysis of data from the 1996 sweep found that single young people living in the parental home were more likely than their peers living alone or in shared accommodation to come from relatively disadvantaged social class backgrounds. They had fewer qualifications than other single young adults, had a relatively weak economic position in terms of their labour market involvement, and were disproportionately located in semi or unskilled jobs. The researchers concluded that 'for many of these young adults, lack of qualifications and consequent employment prospects had constrained their progress towards independent living' (Bynner *et al.*, 1997: 75). However, it is worth noting that this research does not distinguish between young people who had never left home and those who had returned after having left at least once.

Indeed, there is an increased likelihood that a young person will return to the parental home at least once after having left for the first time. We have already noted the likelihood of graduates returning home on completion of their studies. This is by no means a new phenomenon, as students were found to be over-represented amongst the one-fifth of leavers in the 1958 NCDS cohort who had returned to the parental home at least once before the age of 33 (Ermisch *et al.*, 1995). However, the likelihood of a return is now even higher, and it is estimated that 28 per cent of men and 21 per cent of women who currently leave home at the age of 21 will return at least once before their thirtieth birthday (Ermisch and Francesconi, 2000). Young people who leave home before the age of 21 are even more likely to return home at least once (Jones, 1995a). As with first home leaving, certain groups of young adults are more likely to return home than others. In particular, single young adults – and single young men more so than single young women – are more likely to return than those who have been living with a partner (Ermisch and Francesconi, 2000). Research commissioned by the UK's Social Market Foundation found, amongst a sample of one thousand 20–30-year-olds, that one in four had returned home on two or more occasions since first leaving, with one in eight having returned at least three times (Social Market Foundation, 2002). The main reasons given for returning home were linked to the expense of living away from home, relationship difficulties, a new work location, and needing a stopgap between jobs.

Reasons for first leaving home

Young people's reasons for first leaving the parental home have also changed considerably in recent years. Traditionally, the primary reasons for leaving home within most European societies have been to marry and to find work. However, the relationship between leaving home and marriage has been gradually eroded in Britain and much of Northern Europe since the 1960s, with an overall decline in marriage rates (Ermisch and Francesconi, 2000; European Commission, 2000) and an increase in the median age of first marriage. Between 1971 and 2001, the median age of first marriage increased amongst British women from 21 years of age to 28.4, and amongst men from 23 years of age to 30.6 (Bynner *et al.*, 1997; Office for National Statistics, 2003). It might be assumed that the increased popularity of cohabitation as a precursor to marriage amongst young heterosexual adults accounts for these 'gap years'. However, the proportion of young people leaving home in order to form a couple household through either marriage *or* cohabitation is actually in decline. Amongst the NCDS cohort, for example, 60 per cent of women and 55 per cent of men first left home to live with a partner, compared with only 43 and 38 per cent respectively amongst leavers in the early 1990s (Ermisch *et al.*, 1995).

In place of partnership formation, new reasons for leaving home have emerged. With the expansion of higher education in the United Kingdom, increasing numbers of young people now leave home for the first time in order to attend university, notwithstanding the gradual increase in the proportion of students – albeit still a minority – who remain within the parental home throughout their studies. The majority of British students move into communal living arrangements, either residing in a hall of residence (particularly in their first year of study) or in a shared student house, usually in the private rented sector. This is a trend that is by no means universal across Europe; in Continental Europe, with a few exceptions, it is still far more common for students to attend local universities, rather than moving away from home to study (see Chapter 5 for an exploration of students' living arrangements).

There is also an increasing trend for young people to leave home primarily in order to achieve independence from the parental home. This particular reason can be hard to disentangle from leaving home in order to study or to find work, as the desire for independence may well be the driving factor behind such a decision. Indeed, as we shall see, going away to university is often described by young people who would otherwise be desperate to move out in terms of providing a socially legitimate reason for leaving home. Nonetheless, there is also a growing proportion of *non*-students who cite a desire for independence as the main reason for leaving home, often moving out of the parental home to set up a new household – alone or with friends – in the same locality (Jones, 1995a). A desire for independence may be driven by all kinds of reasons: a desire to come and go as one pleases and without being accountable to parents, to express one's identity outside of the restrictions of the parental home (to come out as gay or lesbian, for example, or to live outside of particular cultural and/or religious expectations), to travel, to move to a new location, to live with friends, or simply a desire to go it alone.

Above and beyond these mainly positive reasons for leaving – to form a couple household, to study, or to gain independence – many young people still leave home because they are effectively forced to do so (Jones, 1995a). Push factors in these instances may include abusive relationships and family conflict, parental hostility to a young person's sexual orientation, the inability or unwillingness of parents to support their children financially, or a lack of local employment opportunities. Depending on the specific circumstances, leaving home may occur in an unplanned, unsupported and hurried manner, leaving the young person particularly vulnerable to youth homelessness (Hutson and Liddiard, 1994; Carlen, 1996). Leaving home under such conditions is particularly associated with 'early' leavers (those who leave home in their teen years), a category which includes young people leaving care (Coles, 1995, 2000).

Comparative trends: Europe, Australia and North America

These general patterns are by no means unique to Britain. Across both Northern and Southern Europe, there has been a trend towards remaining in the parental home for longer periods of time (European Commission, 1997), with the Netherlands being the only significant exception. Even in Southern European countries, where living in the parental home for extended periods of time is a well-established pattern, there have been significant increases in the proportions remaining at home into their late twenties. In Portugal, for example, the proportion of 20–24-year-olds living with their parents rose from 75 to 82 per cent between 1987 and 1995, and amongst 25–29-year-olds, from 39 to 49 per cent. Similar trends are evident in Italy (Baizan and Lo Conte, 1995) and in Spain (Heath and Miret, 1996; Holdsworth, 2000). Elsewhere in Europe, young adults in former Eastern bloc countries have also become increasingly dependent on their parents following the collapse of Communism in the late 1980s (Wallace, 1995; Wallace and Kovatcheva, 1998).

In Australia and the United States, similar patterns have emerged. Ellis (1996) has reported Australian trends in terms of 'leaving the nest, NOT!' Whilst there is a general trend amongst young Australians towards extended dependency on parents, important differences again exist, particularly in relation to the experiences of young people from the different ethnic communities which make up the country's increasingly multicultural population. Hillman and Marks (2002) note, for example, that young people whose parents were born in non-English speaking countries tend to remain dependent on their families for longer than those whose parents were born in Australia. This is supported by Baldasser (1999), who notes the tendency amongst young Italo-Australians to leave home at a later age than their white Australian peers with British or Irish roots, and to do so in order to marry, reflecting the ongoing influence upon immigrant communities of cultural patterns linked to their respective countries of origin. Moreover, patterns of leaving home within Australia's indigenous Aboriginal communities are different again, with indigenous young Australians being more likely than white Australians to live with their parents following the completion of their education or to be living with extended family members (Australian Bureau of Statistics, 1997a). In the United States, after a low in the 1960s and early 1970s, growing proportions of young people are now once again living with their parents: around 53 per cent of 18–24-year-olds in 1994 compared with around 42 per cent in the 1960s (Goldscheider and Goldscheider, 1999). Cultural differences are similarly important; for example, non-Hispanic whites leave home much more rapidly than other ethnic groups, whilst young people from Catholic families remain at home for longer periods of time than young people from other religious backgrounds.

In both Australia and the United States, the currently high rates of return to the parental home have attracted particular attention in recent years. Writing of the US context, Goldscheider and Goldscheider (1999) note that,

> [Returning home] has gone from a relatively rare event to one experienced by nearly half of all those leaving home (and by their parents). The leaving home transition has become more renewable, less a one-way street, and more like circular migration. Not only can young adults return home, it has increasingly become normative to do so (p. 54)

Indeed, much has been made in both popular and academic discourse of 'the returning young adult syndrome', 'the cluttered nest' or 'the crowded nest syndrome', terms coined to describe the growing pressures on families to support their 'incompletely launched' children – or their 'boomerang kids' – into their mid-twenties and often beyond. Whilst in the Australian context returning home has been associated with relationship breakdown, single status and financial insecurity (Kilmartin, 2000), in the United States there has been a widespread popular assumption that young adults from the most comfortable family backgrounds are most likely to return (the 'feathered nest syndrome'). Certainly, most of the young people interviewed by Litwin (1986) in her study of 'the postponed generation' were college-educated and appeared to hail from affluent family backgrounds. Goldscheider and Goldscheider (1999) have provided evidence that this assumption is actually incorrect, but it nonetheless highlights an assumption that the middle class family home provides a qualitatively different environment for young adults moving towards independence. In the sections that follow, we consider the validity of this assumption in the light of both the existing research on youthful domesticity and the experiences of the young adults involved in our own research. We argue that one of the key differences relates to the greater probability amongst young people from middle class backgrounds of being able to anticipate and engineer a smooth and socially legitimated departure from the parental home linked to participation in higher education. In contrast, living in the parental home may be perceived in a very different light by young people who are not able to draw on this resource.

'Youthful domesticity' prior to leaving the parental home

Although most young Europeans, Americans and Australians live with their parents in their late teens, with many continuing to do so in their early twenties, the home lives of this age group remain surprisingly under-researched. As we noted in Chapter 2, despite a plethora of studies of young people's working lives and leisure activities, there are relatively few studies of what we might term 'youthful domesticity'. Such research, as there is, has focused largely on young people from relatively disadvantaged backgrounds and/or those who have been constrained to remain within the parental home due to financial constraint arising from unemployment and participation in training schemes (see, for example, Coffield *et al.*, 1986; Wallace, 1987; Hutson and Jenkins, 1989; British studies by Allatt and Yeandle, 1992). Each of these studies has made important contributions to an understanding of the lives of these particular groups of young people, yet we know relatively little about the domestic lives of young people who are following relatively 'privileged' trajectories: those who continue to follow an academic route at 16 and who subsequently continue into higher education.

We have already noted the increased propensity for young people to leave the parental home for the first time in order to study. With the growth of mass higher education in the United Kingdom, this, alongside the associated 'gap year', has become an increasingly legitimate reason for leaving the parental home. Despite the intention of widening access to groups traditionally under-represented within the university sector, participation amongst young people from working class backgrounds has, however, remained low. Consequently, there is a particularly strong normative expectation amongst young people from middle class family backgrounds of leaving home for the first time around the age of 18 or 19 in order to move away to study. Other reasons for leaving home at a roughly similar age – with the exception, perhaps, of leaving for work-related reasons – tend not to enjoy the same legitimacy, particularly in middle class families. Indeed, university-related reasons aside, leaving home in one's late teens is often referred to in terms of leaving home *early*, implying a normative expectation of when one *ought* to leave the parental home (Jones, 1995a).

Aggleton's (1987) study of a group of sixth form students is an exception in exploring not just their educational experiences, but also their leisure activities and their home lives. Whilst his particular sample focused on a group of students who were not necessarily planning to go to university, his sample was nonetheless drawn from a very distinct section of the middle classes: over half of the parents belonged to the teaching profession, and just under a fifth worked as actors, artists or designers. These are groups which Bernstein (1978) included in his categorisation of the new middle classes, themselves the sponsors and products of post-war educational expansion. Aggleton provides a fascinating account of family life in these homes: streams of visitors sharing gossip and earnest political debate in equal measure whilst sitting around scrubbed kitchen tables; the home used as the meeting place for various community self-help and pressure groups; spare rooms made available to various waifs and strays from less advantaged families; overt displays of cultural capital in the form of prominently displayed posters from art exhibitions in high profile galleries, postcards from exotic locations and artefacts from foreign holidays. These homes were marked by a high degree of openness between teenagers and their parents, and a weakening of the distinction between adult and child practices. Young people were allowed to stay out late and determine for themselves how they spent their spare time, with parents merely emphasising the importance of 'being responsible' and 'being sensible'. This openness was most marked with regard to parents' relaxed attitudes towards drug-taking and sexual behaviour, with parents allowing, and sometimes encouraging, their children to experiment within the relative safety of the home.

Aggleton's account is by no means typical of all, or even most, middle class families. Indeed, as the middle classes expand and become less homogeneous, it becomes increasingly difficult to generalise about middle class lifestyles. Distinctions such as those drawn by Bernstein (1978) between the old and new middle classes, for example, or by Savage *et al.* (1992) between the petite bourgeoisie, managers and professionals take on increased importance. Nonetheless, some of the characteristics of middle class life captured by Aggleton can also be found – albeit in diluted form – in Allatt's (1993) study of young people from three different middle class positions: an established and secure middle class family, a downwardly mobile middle class family, and an upwardly mobile middle class family from upper working class and lower middle class origins. Crucially, the teenage children in each of these families were all encouraged to take control of their own lives, with parents – especially mothers – on hand as general advisors to their offspring.

This emphasis on a greater degree of parent–child interaction appears to correspond to what is often construed as a loss of parental authority in modern societies, with parents from *all* social class backgrounds increasingly reduced to bargaining and negotiating with their children (Jamieson, 1999). Giddens (1992) prefers to regard this as evidence of a new 'democratic' basis for parent–child relationships, underpinned by negotiated trust and commitment. However, given the profound imbalance of power between the parties involved, he does not suggest that this new form of parent–child relationship should be viewed as a variant of the pure relationship. Solomon *et al.* (2002), for example, argue that the maintenance of parents' own distinct identity is often achieved at the expense of the child's emergent adult identity through the obtaining of information about their children which is not then reciprocated by similar disclosures of information on the part of parents (p. 981). Gillies *et al.* (2001) similarly point to an inherent tension within family life between children's rights to privacy, secrecy and trust, and parental responsibility to protect their children from potential harm. Giddens (1991) does nonetheless contend that the *desire* for openness and democracy within parent–child relationships has arisen out of some of the same influences that have generated the pure relationship and that 'in conditions of modernity, the more a child moves towards adulthood and autonomy, the more elements of the pure relationship tend to come into play' (p. 98).

Although the extent to which such a relationship can truly be achieved is debatable, this apparent shift towards new patterns of parenting might explain de Jong-Gierveld *et al.*'s (1991) contention – briefly explored in Chapter 3 – that the contemporary parental home now offers a more liberal atmosphere for children in their late teens and twenties. Accordingly, alongside access to increased physical space (given the trend towards smaller families), the parental home may increasingly offer greater freedom and privacy than in the past. In the United States, for example, new homes are almost 1.5 times larger today than in the 1970s, yet on average now contain fewer residents (Population Reference Bureau, 2003). Remaining in the parental home for longer periods of time may in such circumstances become an attractive option. Such perceptions proved to be commonplace amongst many of the young people involved in our own research, and were particularly commonplace amongst those who first left the parental home in order to go away to university or to depart on a gap year. This group accounted for just over two-thirds of our sample, and the majority of this group spoke of growing up in environments very similar to those described by both Aggleton (1987) and Allatt (1993), marked by a strong emphasis on independence, responsibility and achievement, and an expectation on the part of parents that their children would continue into higher education (in many cases following in their own footsteps).

Many of those who first left home for university or to depart on a gap year spoke of their gradual awareness of an increasing sense of independence and autonomy from their parents, most notably in the period immediately following the end of compulsory schooling. For some, their increased sense of independence was linked to their entry into various forms of part-time employment, whilst others highlighted the significance of holidays and field trips away from home. Learning to drive the family car at 17, and in some cases having a car bought for them, was another significant development for many of the graduate group, particularly those growing up in rural areas and living at some distance from their friends. Holly (household 13), for example, described her feelings on no longer being dependent on her parents for lifts into the nearest town:

> So I got my car and that was just, like, 'I'm out of here'. That was when I started staying over in town. That was a real growing independence. I'd spend most weekends kind of either staying in town or rolling in at about seven in the morning just as my parents were having breakfast and they were really quite liberal with me like that...it caused quite a lot of conflicts about 'we don't know if you're home for dinner', and stuff like that. But after a while they just said, 'let us know if you're eating or not, and we'll see you whenever' for the rest of it. So I did have a lot of independence when I was still living at my parents.

Indeed, a minority of the group argued that these steps forward were far more significant to them in terms of gaining independence than the point at which they first left home.

Around a third of those who had first left the parental home to go to university claimed not to have experienced any significant tensions in the run-up to leaving home. Many had only positive memories of living with their parents, with some – mainly young women – stating that they would have been happy to have continued living with their parents if they had not gone away to study. As Jules (household 1) put it, 'it was never a trauma living with my mum and dad, I always really enjoyed it.'

In other cases, the stability of home life was characterised by a reassuring mundanity, marked by its ordinariness and a lack of conflict. The following comments reflect this viewpoint well:

> There's nothing at all unusual or interesting from (my) background point of view. I didn't seem to have the teenage thing with my parents at all. I never sat down and had heart-to-hearts or what have you, but there was none of the sort of kicking and screaming tantrums and huge depressing sulk kind of things that are supposed to be traditional. I saw those – my sister had those, I didn't...Never argued with them. If anybody asked me whether I got on with them, I would have been stumped for an answer...I never fell out with them at all, there was never any of this big argument thing, I never sort of sat down and had a discussion about anything, cos I never felt that I had any of these teenage angsty problems to talk about (Steve, household 14).

Nonetheless, even though very few graduates reported out-and-out conflict within their families, the majority made reference to aspects of living in the parental home which became increasingly problematic the longer they remained there. Key tensions emerged around three general themes: a resentment of perceived dependency on parents (the frustration of being reliant on parents for lifts, for example); problems arising from what was perceived to be unreasonable behaviour on the part of parents (favouring younger siblings, for example); and tensions over the negotiation of space and freedom within the parental home (having to account for their whereabouts, for example, or partners being prohibited from staying overnight in their own rooms). However, most of these young people had grown up with the assumption that they would continue their studies to degree level, and were confident that they would leave home in their late-teens. This provided an important safety valve, and represented a socially sanctioned route to independence which was not an option for the non-graduates included in the research.

In contrast, these same issues had the potential to become major flashpoints amongst those who were not anticipating a university-related departure. Whilst by no means all non-graduates left home under a cloud, they were far more likely to have done so than their graduate counterparts, with many describing their reasons for first leaving home in terms of their need to get away from strained family relationships, even though in many respects their accounts of family life were not markedly different from those of the young people who had left home in order to start at university. However, as a consequence of not being able to draw upon the more socially acceptable exit strategy of going away to university, the point at which they had first left home was invariably experienced as a crisis point: as a negative rejection of home life rather than a positive step towards greater independence. In comparison with those who left to go to university or on a pre-university gap year, young people in this latter group often found it harder to negotiate a new, 'adult' way of relating to their parents having left home, and in some cases relationships with parents remained precarious. Nick and Jimmy, for example, two brothers who lived in household 18 with a mutual friend, had had no contact with their father in five years, and rarely saw their mother. Viv (household 17) had also fallen out with her mother who, as a strict Jehovah's Witness, had disapproved of Viv's drinking and choice of friends. Viv now barely spoke to her; indeed, she got on better with her grandfather.

For the non-graduates, the ability to spend time away from the parental home in the run-up to leaving home, particularly with friends and partners, often took on particular significance. Angie, for example, would spend every weekend at her boyfriend's house, and during the week would spend as little time at home as possible, returning only to sleep. Others sought to create their own havens from the pressures of family life. Jackie, for example, grew up in an overcrowded council house in rural Wales with parents who, she felt, only stayed together for her benefit, yet constantly argued. She spoke of the way in which having her own car took on great significance in her life:

> And I mean certainly when I was 15 I was driving illegally and as soon as I was old enough I always had a car, so I know it sounds really stupid, but like my car was my home. Because I don't do this at all now to my cars, but I'd make sure it had decent mats in, seat covers, I had a blanket, I had a fur rug, you know, a few personal bits and pieces and, you know, ornaments and nodding dogs and things. And I suppose my car was my haven, if you like. And once you've got a car you've got independence, you can drive to the beach and read or drive into the country or drive and see friends. You know, like my cars were much more personal in those days (Jackie, household 2).

For Jackie, friends who were able to leave home in their late teens through joining the armed forces or through getting married were the subjects of considerable envy. Indeed, she judged her own departure from the parental home at 21 as late in comparison to many of her peers ('in effect I was like there three years longer than I should have been'), a departure precipitated by a move to Plymouth to live in a shared house with a boyfriend who had joined the Royal Navy. Leaving for reasons of partnership formation was, however, confined to just three young women in our sample. In each of these cases the decision to move in with a partner was as much about a desire to get away from their parents as it was about a positive desire to cohabit, and in one case the relationship had collapsed within three months of moving in together.

Conclusion

In this chapter we have provided a summary of current trends in living in and leaving the parental home and have considered the impact of student status as a key marker of difference in determining the nature of young people's first departure from the parental home. In particular, the expansion of higher education has provided increased numbers of young people with access to a comparatively smooth, relatively privileged and unproblematic transition out of the parental home. In contrast to most other reasons for leaving home in one's late teens, which may be regarded as a negative endorsement of the home environment and of the state of a young person's relationship with their parents, it is a route which provides young people with a socially legitimate reason for leaving. The anticipation of a move away to university means that many of the everyday tensions associated with family life, which for non-students may precipitate an early departure from the parental home, can be seen as having an identifiable end point, thus rendering them rather more bearable (for parents as well as their children). This confers particular advantages on young people who feel heavily constrained by living in the parental home, yet who are able to anticipate a planned move at the age of 18 or 19. Prendergast *et al.* (2002), for example, contrast the experiences of young lesbians and gay men who have been able to leave home in order to attend university with the experiences of those who have not had this opportunity. In the latter case, most of their informants had been able to establish independent lives away from the gaze of their parents, who either did not know about their child's sexual orientation or had expressed disapproval during the time they had lived at home. In contrast, there was a high incidence of homelessness and family breakdown amongst the latter group as a consequence of parental disapproval.

In their analysis of the housing histories of over nine hundred 16–25-year-olds living in five different areas of England in the late 1990s,

Ford *et al.* (2002) distinguish between five ideal-typical housing pathways: chaotic pathways, unplanned pathways, constrained pathways, planned (non-student) pathways and student pathways. They identify three factors which are crucial to the definition of each of these categories, based on the degree of planning and control exercised by a young person, the extent and nature of any constraints, and the degree of family support available to them. Ford *et al.* use the term 'housing pathway' to describe 'the totality of any one young person's housing experiences' (p. 2463), but these distinctions are also very useful for considering the nature of a young person's first departure from the parental home. Importantly, whilst the student pathway is not the only pathway where the initial move out of the parental home is carefully planned, it nonetheless emerges as the route which has the fewest constraints associated with the initial move, by virtue of protected access to various forms of student accommodation. This is another major advantage associated with leaving home in order to study, and is one of the points we consider further in Chapter 5.

5
Student Housing and Households

Introduction

> We never clean the toilet, Neil! That's what being a student is all about. (Rick, *The Young Ones*)

Despite undergraduate students being a captive audience for academic researchers, it is somewhat ironic that the day-to-day experiences of students outside of the lecture room are largely overlooked within the sociology of youth. In a long overdue volume dedicated to the study of student life, Silver and Silver (1997) reflect on 'how little research exists on students as "real people"' (p. 2). This silence, they argue, results from the influence of policy demands, funding pressures and the growing need for institutional accountability. Education and policy researchers, while focusing on student recruitment, learning, attainment and attrition, have thus largely neglected to study student life outside of the learning environment. Indeed, reflecting on the influential Dearing Report (1997), Barnet (1998) notes a continuing 'lack of any serious discussion of... students and what it is to be a student' (p. 17). Most research on housing choices, household formation patterns and transitions to adulthood (within both housing studies and the sociology of youth) has equally failed to consider the experiences of undergraduate students, other than to highlight the growing importance of student accommodation as a first destination on leaving home. The reasons for this specific neglect are somewhat different to those highlighted by Silver and Silver (1997) and will be briefly considered below.

First, it is often assumed that those who move away from the parental home to attend a higher education institution are 'living away' from home, thereby remaining part of the existing parental household. They are commonly viewed as a group who are able to return home during long vacations and on graduating, at which point their 'real' transition into an independent adult home begins. Students are thus often regarded as members of pre-existing familial households during vacations and as members of transitory and temporary non-familial households during term-time. This ambiguous and shifting housing and social status has led to students being perceived as a group whose members are difficult to categorise and locate. This is reflected, for example, in decisions about where students should be enumerated for purposes of the UK's decennial Census of Population.

Secondly, the student housing experience has long been associated with tied institutional accommodation. Many higher education institutions (HEIs) offer rooms or flats in purpose-built accommodation, often priding themselves on being able to house any first year student who wishes to 'live in'. Whilst public funding for special student accommodation has not been readily available in recent decades, since 1995 HEIs have begun to harness money through the Private Finance Initiative (PFI) in order to help them manage and maintain existing accommodation stock and to undertake new developments within the sector. The move of many universities to 'privatise' or 'outsource' their student accommodation has, in part, resulted from the growing pressures placed on universities to become commercially viable businesses. Under such circumstances, student accommodation can be viewed as a resource to attract students and the conference trade to the university, thereby contributing to income generation. In addition, HEIs commonly provide students with an accommodation service that helps them to locate a place to live in their city of study. As a consequence, students are often viewed as existing outside of mainstream housing markets and to be unaffected by broader changes in housing policy. Indeed, it has been noted that there is no clearly defined housing policy for full-time students (Brown, 1992; Rhodes, 1999). Thus, while recent housing research has considered the impact of student housing demand on mainstream housing markets (Rugg *et al.*, 2000), the overall meaning and experience of 'home' for students, alongside changing patterns of student household formation, has received little attention.

Finally, student life has long been associated with middle class transitions to adulthood. As stated in Chapter 2, the pursuit of social justice has led much youth (and indeed housing) research to focus largely on structurally and culturally disadvantaged groups of young people. The belief that students are a privileged subgroup of the youth population who live in a 'special time and space' free from the constraints, demands and structures of real life (Bourdieu and Passeron, 1979: 19) has thus resulted in the student population being largely overlooked by researchers. Nonetheless, it should be noted that students are now receiving greater attention from youth researchers. As Forsyth and Furlong (2000) note, while 'traditional' middle-class students have in the past remained beyond sociology's remit, with increasing access to higher education, students are no longer simply seen as an elite group but are now being seen as a legitimate focus for youth sociology. What is interesting about this statement, however, is that it hints at the continuing unease with which the sub-discipline regards students and/or middle class youth *per se*: it is only the widening of access to higher education to less advantaged groups that has led youth researchers to venture forth into this area of study. Thus, despite calls for a more inclusive youth sociology (for example, Coles, 2000; Miles, 2000) undergraduate students, especially those from the middle classes, still remain an unlikely subject of debate within the sociology of youth and beyond.

In sum, not only is an in-depth consideration of contemporary student housing experiences and household formation patterns absent from the literature but, most importantly, little debate has taken on board the insights of contemporary social theory and the implications of recent social change for the lived experiences of students. This seems somewhat strange when we consider the widely held view that fundamental changes in the labour market are leading to an emphasis on increased training, skills, adaptability and lifelong learning. Participating in education in order to remain 'skilled' is now viewed as a key component in the building of individual biographies in late modernity. Indeed Beck (1992) argues that education has now become the centre of planning for labour suitability in the contemporary period. In the light of these trends it seems timely to consider the contemporary student housing experience alongside, rather than independently of, the housing choices and household formation patterns of other young adults. In the same way that multiple pathways to adulthood are arguably fragmenting household formation patterns and providing a powerful critique of assumptions of linearity and standardisation amongst young people, so too it could be argued that this is the case in the more focused world of student housing.

This chapter, then, focuses on two key aspects of the contemporary student housing experience, reflecting two shifts that have occurred within the student housing market in recent years. First, there has been a relatively recent increase in the proportion of full-time students who remain within the parental home in order to study at their local university or college. Secondly, of those students who continue to move away to university, more are now likely to form households in shared accommodation in the private rented housing sector than in any other type of accommodation. This chapter considers some of the factors underpinning these parallel shifts, considering whether students, in common with other groups of young adults, are becoming increasingly reflexive in their housing choices and whether, in turn, their housing decisions can impact on their 'lifestyle'. The chapter moves on to address some potential implications of these choices for students' subsequent employability, focusing on the importance that many graduate employers place on the idea of a 'rounded' graduate. The discussion draws, in part, on doctoral research conducted in Sunderland during the early 1990s by Kenyon (1998), which considered students' experiences, perceptions and uses of their term-time accommodation and its role in the formation of a student community. Due to the relative lack of sociological research in this area, and the limited space available in this chapter, our discussion of student housing is necessarily speculative and focused in its analysis and conclusions. The issues omitted from our discussion will, without doubt, be as important as those we discuss. Such caveats aside, it is hoped that the chapter will help to pave the way for further debate and future research.

The changing face of student accommodation

Recent commentaries on the two trends in student housing that form the focus of this chapter – more students living in the parental home and more students forming their own households in the private rented sector – have tended to link them to two other recent changes that have taken place within higher education. The first of these is the ongoing emphasis in Britain on widening participation, to facilitate improved access to higher education for hitherto under-represented groups such as mature students and those from more disadvantaged socio-economic backgrounds. The number of individuals undertaking higher education has grown substantially over recent decades. In the academic year 2000/2001 there were 1,176,035 full-time students in higher education (HESA, 2002), and the British Government has pledged to continue this trend by securing some form of higher education for 50 per cent of 18–30-year-olds by the year 2010. The second is the gradual reduction in state financial support for British students over the last two decades (Callender and Kemp, 2000; Christie *et al.*, 2001, provide a comprehensive overview of these changes). Put simply, the drive to widen participation in higher education is believed to have resulted in increased demand for student accommodation. This in combination with the reduction in financial support available for students is seen to have left those without private means with little choice but to remain either in the pre-higher education home or to form student households in the private rented sector (where they can benefit from economies of scale). In the discussion that follows we consider the balance to be struck between these structural explanations on the one hand, and changing student attitudes towards their accommodation, and its link to a distinctive student lifestyle, on the other.

We start, then, with the increasing proportion of undergraduate students who remain full-time residents within the pre-higher education home, studying locally rather than moving away to study. Mori (2001) estimates that 21 per cent of students now live at home, a figure consistent with the Higher Education Statistical Agency's (HESA) figure of 20 per cent of students living at home in 1999. HESA data also suggest that the number of first year undergraduates living with their parents rose by 40 per cent between 1997 and 1999. These national averages should, however, be treated with caution as the number of students living at home can vary enormously between institutions, between regions and over time. The lack of comparable data on this trend is further accounted for by the fact that some estimates of the number of home-based students only list dependent students living with parents or guardians, while others include (usually mature) students who live in their own independent homes. Despite these ambiguities, commentators are clear that in the last few years there has been a gradual rise in the number of students living at home while attending their local HEI, representing a reversal of the post-war trend for students increasingly to move away from home.

In the UK context, the process of moving away to study has often been regarded as an integral part of the post-war student experience. The related assumption that students who live at home are somehow missing out can be traced back to an earlier period of rapid university expansion in the 1960s. The Robbins Report (1963) not only proposed an increase in student numbers by recommending that all young people qualified by ability and attainment should have the opportunity to attend university, but additionally suggested that if this was to materialise,

> ...the gravest of all problems for the universities in the next five years may well be the problem of providing places where students can live...a great expansion of university residence is needed (p. 195).

The foundations of this move to create residential universities were, however, already in place. The Niblett Report (1957) stated that halls of residence were arenas that could be used to 'extend the university day' (p. v); in halls of residence students could experience the civilising and humanising influence of interacting with fellow academics, in a 'living and learning' environment which fostered their academic and personal transition to adulthood. As Brothers and Hatch (1971) state, this idea clearly drew upon the liberal arts theory that a university education should be more than just an academic experience. To underline this viewpoint, the Niblett Report suggested that students living in lodgings, or at home, were likely to be alienated from such social and cultural experiences due to their nine-to-five mentality, as well as their continuing connections with non-academic social worlds: experiences which were both considered to be detrimental to their broader educational career.

While it is widely accepted that mature students clearly have reasons to remain within their established adult homes during their undergraduate years, debt-aversion and/or financial hardship are seen to play an important part in younger students' decisions to remain within the parental home. Research by Mori (2001) has suggested that financial reasons were implicated in the decision to stay at home of just under three-fifths of all students who live with their parents, with this factor having a disproportionate impact on young people from less affluent backgrounds. In support of these findings, Reay *et al.* (2001), for example, have noted how material constraints result in 'limited spaces of choice' (p. 861) with respect to the higher education decisions of many students from working class families, a phenomenon they refer to as 'working class localism'. Research by Callender and Kemp (2000) also found that staying at home was strongly correlated with whether or not a student had taken out a student loan, and that Asian students were particularly likely to be living with their parents: 40 per cent of Asian students were living with their parents at the time of their research, compared with 17 per cent of all students. Home-based students have received particular attention from the media in recent years, as journalists debate the relative merits of 'living at home' versus 'living away' as a student (Swain, 2001). The question which drives both academic and media debates is redolent of a concern central to the Niblett Report (1957): whether home-based students are missing out on key aspects of the student experience which prove central to the student-based transition to adulthood.

As highlighted above, embedded within many of these existing discussions of home-based students is the assumption that financial constraint is the main explanatory factor for students' need to live at home: that given the choice they would prefer to live away from home. In turn, this is seen to impose social constraints on students who are unable to participate fully in student life, and to break away from existing social networks. Thus, in line with the general literature on young people's household formation patterns it is assumed that those who are bucking the main housing trend – in this case moving away from home to live in halls of residence or a student household – do so as a result of constraint. The end result is a common representation of home-based students as unequivocally disadvantaged in monetary, social and cultural terms. What has not been addressed to such an extent is whether home students are indeed reluctant stayers who, given the opportunity, would move away to study. Moreover, little discussion has considered whether, even if they *are* reluctant stayers, they are as disadvantaged by remaining within the parental home as existing literature suggests.

We have noted in earlier chapters that, for some groups of young people, the option of continuing to live within the contemporary parental home may be an attractive alternative to leaving home. Irwin (1995), for example, suggests that continuing dependence may be seen by some young people as an opportunity rather than a constraint. Living with parents, then, may be either a deliberate choice or a reflection of satisfaction and contentedness. Viewed from this perspective, home-based students may not be as disadvantaged as they first appear. Indeed, they may view their parental home as having a number of benefits that far outweigh those gained from forming a household in student accommodation in the private rented sector: a housing sector notorious for the poor quality of its housing stock. As the Mori (2001) figures suggest, factors other than financial resources may then be involved in the decision to stay at home, with commitment to existing friendship groups as well as to cultural norms and expectations also playing their part. Reay *et al.*'s (2001) study of the higher education choices of young people living in London, for example, suggests that many ethnic minority students are reluctant to venture outside of the capital due to the under-representation of non-white students in many old universities. Brooks (2002) has also noted that the option to stay at home and attend a local university may have a particular appeal to young people who are ambivalent about the value of higher education, or who are reluctant to move away from partners who might be remaining in the local area. Further support for the idea that students from lower socio-economic backgrounds are remaining in the parental home through choice rather than constraint is provided by Forsyth and Furlong (2000), who argue

that amongst this particular population, leaving the pre-higher education home for the purposes of going to university is done as a necessity
rather than a choice. For students from groups which have traditionally
been under-represented in higher education, remaining at home may
additionally provide a vital bridge between their own world and the
(middle class) world of academia, with friends, partners and family
members remaining an extremely important source of emotional and
material support.

In failing to consider the actual experiences and the cultural environment of this growing group of students, existing research cannot help us
to understand whether or not they feel disadvantaged by their apparent
inability to leave home and whether the transformative potential of
student life is hindered by this experience. Moreover, a number of questions concerning notions of independence, the attainment of adulthood,
and the renegotiation of familial relations remain unaddressed. In areas
where commuting to a number of institutions is possible, such as
London or Greater Manchester, the restrictions of choice in relation to
programmes of study associated with attending one's local institution
may not occur. We should not, then, be over-hasty in assuming that
home-based student experiences are uniformly limited and of less
value. In reflecting on the variety of housing opportunities available to
them, some students may actively choose to remain at home in order to
maximise the financial and social benefits that such arrangements
bring, and in order to ease the transition between what may be two very
different social worlds.

We now turn to the second shift in student housing trends: the growing number of students renting student houses in the private rented
sector. Despite the recent growth in the number of students living
in the pre-higher education home, it has been estimated that around
75 per cent of students in Britain still choose to leave home to undertake their degree (Christie *et al.*, 2002). While a number of these students
live in institutional accommodation, a growing number are now forming
households in their own right with peers in the private rented sector.
The number of students living in the private rented sector is similarly as
difficult to estimate as the number living in the pre-higher education
home. The National Union of Students (NUS) highlights a particular
reason for this, acknowledging that national estimates are difficult to
access as no one body is responsible for collecting this information
(Kemp, 2001). However, Rugg *et al.* (2000) estimate that on average
49 per cent of full-time students currently live in this sector, a figure
not dissimilar to the more recent estimate of 47 per cent (Mori, 2001).

At first glance it would seem that the proportion of students living in the private rented sector has not risen. Hands (1971) estimated that 49 per cent of students were living in privately rented accommodation in 1965. However, the quantity of students that these figures involve has clearly increased (in the academic year 1965/1966 there were 169,486 full-time students in higher education, a figure which has risen to 1,176,035 in the academic year 2000/2001 [HESA, 2002]). Moreover, significant changes have occurred in the type of households formed by students in the private rented sector: during the 1960s it was far more common for students to live in supervised lodgings or 'digs' with a resident householder. Now students are more likely to rent a house from an absentee landlord and form a household in their own right. As a result of this growth, a niche market has emerged in many cities around the letting of shared student houses in specific neighbourhoods (Ravetz, 1996; Kenyon, 1997; Rugg *et al.*, 2000). Within this market there has also been a rise in student owner-occupation, with increasing numbers of parents investing in property on behalf of their student offspring (Collinson, 2001). This not only helps their children during their student years, but is often viewed as a source of income and/or a longer-term investment.

The history of students coming to rely on the private rented sector for accommodation has been well documented elsewhere and will not be rehearsed at great length here (see Morgan and McDowell, 1979; Kenyon, 1998; Rhodes, 1999). However, in order to set the scene we will briefly highlight some of the historic reasons for this development. The post-war years saw growing numbers of students competing for higher-education places, and growing institutional variations in entry requirements. This resulted in many students applying to universities away from their parental homes. The trend was compounded by the setting up of the Universities Central Council for Admissions (UCCA) in the early 1960s, and the Polytechnics Central Admissions System (PCAS) in 1986, bodies which processed all student applications for higher education. Both systems encouraged students to apply to up to four institutions on the basis of the courses on offer, rather than their proximity to home. As such, more students than ever were offered the opportunity to apply to institutions away from their pre-higher education homes.

By the late 1960s state-funding for specialist student accommodation was first partially, and then completely, withdrawn. The special educational functions which were used as one of the central justifications for promoting and building halls of residence were increasingly questioned, with an acknowledgement that the basis for these ideas had been intuition, impression and ideology rather than objective knowledge (Hatch, 1969). In exploring the basis of these claims, research carried out in the 1960s and early 1970s drew mixed conclusions. Whilst some research concluded that halls could perform a function in promoting wider education, increased and diverse sociability and participation in extra-curricular activities (see, for example, Albrow, 1966; Punch, 1967; Brothers and Hatch, 1971), the debate was certainly not concluded in favour of residence (see, for example, Marris, 1963; Baird, 1969; Nudd and Stier, 1969; McKean, 1975). This very ambiguity helped to sound the death knell for the funding of special halls of residence and as student numbers grew HEIs had to look beyond their campuses into the private rented sector to solve their accommodation crises (Rugg *et al.*, 2000).

However, while such early funding cuts certainly acted to accelerate the trend for students to live in the private rented sector, they cannot wholly explain why shared houses came to be the preferred choice of students living outside their universities. To explain this we need, additionally, to consider student agency. The lowering of the age of majority to 18 in 1969 meant that institutions could no longer require their now adult students to live in supervised halls, lodgings or 'digs'. Many students in the search for increased adult independence thus began to express a preference for accommodation within privately rented 'student houses' with absentee landlords (Morgan and McDowell, 1979; Brown, 1992). Indeed, it has now become a cultural expectation amongst many British students that if they leave home to attend university they will undoubtedly live in a shared student house at some point during their university career.

These various factors, in combination, can therefore be seen to have affected the trend for shared houses and flats to become the main housing option for students studying away from home, with the increased financial costs of studying helping to maintain their popularity due to the opportunities for economies of scale that sharing presents. As student households form on a yearly basis and can be flexible in terms of membership and the use to which rooms are put, they have the ability to adapt to a variety of property types and sizes. This means that they are at an advantage when compared to other households which often have more specific requirements and a fixed membership (Rugg *et al.*, 2000). Moreover, as students tend to regard their shared dwellings as temporary accommodation (occupied for around 30 weeks of the year), they are often more prepared to tolerate certain housing conditions than other groups. For example, downstairs reception rooms are regularly used as extra bedrooms, thus reducing the communal living space in many student houses to one room (usually a kitchen/diner) in order to bring down accommodation costs. Further, the furnishing and upkeep of student properties is often of a notoriously low standard. This has led to concern that landlords, in attempting to maximise their profits, are renting out overcrowded and unhealthy dwellings to students (Humphrey and McCarthy, 1997).

Kenyon (1998) found that the undergraduate students she interviewed in Sunderland were often resigned to their cramped and unkempt living conditions, knowing that they were only a short-term housing solution, and stating the belief that they expected student houses to be like that (findings which correspond with those of Christie *et al.*, 2002). Ultimately, the friendships, the space and the intimacy provided by the term-time home proved to be more important than a nice dwelling. The necessarily flexible student life could take place anywhere, but could not exist without the support and friendship networks that were integral to its formation. Friends from university were believed to take on new importance as for many students they became the first individuals, other than members of the parental family, with whom they had lived and become emotionally close. The new friendships and intimacies that thrived within, and in many ways formed the foundation of, the student community were thus seen to create a homely atmosphere in student flats and houses. Living with friends for the first time 'as a family' created a new level of intimacy with which old pre-university friendships could not compete. For many students the foundation of such friendship networks began in halls where everyone started off on the same footing: all strangers in need of friends and support. As one student from Kenyon's research stated:

> I mean, the student culture here could be anywhere couldn't it? It isn't anything to do with being in Sunderland. We're separate and don't mix with the town or know the town really well, I mean, like I said, I guess if you take away the students, there would be nothing here for us.

This separate culture, in turn, was found to influence, quite dramatically, who students interacted with regularly:

> We have no communication here with adults for the whole of the time we are here. It's another world. It's as if we are cut off from the real world. We don't mix with other people. We're completely encapsulated in a world of students.

Residing in student-only accommodation was therefore not only seen as a by-product of limited finances, but also a positive choice which reflected membership of, and helped to perpetuate, a student-only community.

At first glance it would seem difficult to argue that the social reasons which lead students to share houses in the private rented sector are new, resulting from the particular social climate of late modernity. As stated above, in the post-war period students have been 'encouraged' to move away from home to study for a variety of reasons. The 'living and learning' community is certainly not a new phenomenon. However, some evidence suggests that students may now be more reflexively aware of the benefits to be gained from living in shared student accommodation than in the past. In particular, as the transition to adulthood extends and young adults are no longer expected to leave home as a one-off event (on marriage, for example), young people are increasingly likely to live in a variety of household forms in order to maintain flexibility in their early labour market years. In order to navigate their way in the competitive graduate labour market, students may choose to remain in their city of study or move again to find work. If this is the case then undergraduates may view their first experience of living with peers as not simply 'living away' from their parents, but as their first real step onto the adult housing ladder. Indeed, a number of the young people involved in our own research stated that sharing a house (whether with friends or strangers) seemed the obvious and easiest next step after graduation, as a result of their experiences of sharing as students. The foundations of the importance that many graduates place on living with peers in order to support their independent and necessarily flexible life (a theme we explore in Chapter 6), and the skills needed to find and build a successful shared experience, appear therefore to be built in the undergraduate years.

However, the social importance of this early housing experience may have more than personal value. In particular, it could be argued that the 'cultural capital' gained from living with peers and living a 'traditional' student life, and the practical skills gained through independent living and negotiating the housing market (see Christie *et al.*, 2002) hold more currency with employers than the skills gained through living at home. Indeed, Brown (1995) argues that in the ever more competitive graduate labour market, young people from higher socio-economic groups are finding new ways to consolidate their position and to shelter from competitive pressures. Perhaps, then, a reflexive awareness of the potential gains to be achieved from living away from home is leading the middle classes to continue to follow this traditional route despite the growing economic commitment this entails. Indeed, research shows that lower socio-economic groups are disproportionately represented in the home student category (Callender and Kemp, 2000; Forsyth and Furlong, 2000). It is to a discussion of the different levels of human and cultural capital that can be associated with different student housing choices that the chapter now turns, considering whether there are any longer-term consequences attached to students' housing decisions. In particular, the next section debates whether the experience of living at home can affect the value of the 'graduate' as a marketable product.

Student housing, cultural capital and the graduate labour market

Pitcher and Purcell (1998) note that traditional graduate employers expect applicants to have gained more than 'just' high grades during their time at university. In addition, they look for evidence of participation in creative and sporting activities, and well-spent vacations. A survey of graduate employers in the *Financial Times* provides support for this view, revealing that extra-curricular activities came fourth on a list of experiences which can make a graduate more employable (Kelly, 2001). Above this came structured work experience as part of a degree, other work experience and key skills training. Negotiating and networking skills, the development of self-confidence, entrepreneurial time management skills and the ability to cope with uncertainty are all skills highlighted by employers as desirable in the current climate (La Valle *et al.*, 2000). However, while Lucas and Lamont (1998) argue that most jobs help students to 'acquire social and communication skills, the ability to function in teams and to handle delicate, difficult and occasionally hostile situations with tact, presence of mind and diplomacy' (p. 54), Purcell and Rowley (2000) are less certain. They indicate that it is unclear how far any work experience, as opposed to relevant work experience, can help in securing employment, and argue that this has clear implication for graduates from less advantaged backgrounds. These individuals, through a lack of resources, may have less time and fewer opportunities to look for the 'right' job or to undertake extra-curricular activities or voluntary work. While this literature does not directly refer to graduates' housing choices when analysing the factors that add value to the 'package' they bring with them to their graduate jobs, we argue that there appear to be clear connections between the skills and abilities that employers value and students' housing opportunities and experiences. The notion of the employable, work-ready 'all-rounder' is arguably still based on the notion of the traditional-aged student who lives away from home, has few responsibilities and has the time and resources to pursue extra-mural activities.

Support for this link is provided by Brown and Scase (1994) who argue that it is no longer enough for graduates to gain credentials or to show technical competence. The whole person – the 'personality package' – is now reviewed when selecting managerial and/or professional candidates. Charismatic rather than bureaucratic qualities are increasingly viewed as important for those who are taken on as 'fast-track' graduates. As the number of graduates looking for careers in Britain grows (the percentage of the labour force comprising graduates rose from under 9.6 per cent in 1985 to 14.5 per cent in 1997), a growth in the use of graduates for middle ranking and unrewarding work which potentially underutilises their skills has also grown (Brynin, 2002; see also Rowley and Purcell, 2001). The graduate labour market is therefore becoming increasingly segmented and fragmented. Brown and Scase (1994) thus argue that employers, faced with a wide diversity of graduates, with variable skills bases, are more likely to employ graduates who are 'safe bets'; often identified as those students who have undergone a 'traditional' undergraduate career, which includes living away from – rather than at – the parental home (as indeed the graduate employers may themselves have done), and who have knowledge of certain cultural codes. These cultural codes, they go on, cannot be acquired through formal study but are gained through the lived experience of middle class life; a world where interests and hobbies are cultivated, and specific patterns of interaction serve to 'embellish' educational achievements. For Brown and Scase, those who do not have access to a student-centred social life, where opportunities arise to gain many of the experiences valued by employers, are therefore at a social if not an academic disadvantage when applying for jobs.

In a world where creativity, innovation and habit-breaking are valued more highly than bureaucracy and habit-forming behaviour, those who have remained in the parental home, have continued with a pre-established part-time job and have focused on gaining a qualification and/or financing themselves at university could therefore be at a disadvantage. It could be argued that traditional graduate employers may well believe that students who live in the parental home are somehow restricted in their abilities and outlooks; a viewpoint redolent of that expressed in the Niblett Report (1957) some 45 years ago. If this is so, and given the link between lower social class and a greater likelihood of living at home, the rise of mass higher education seems unlikely to level the playing field and to provide students from poorer backgrounds with access to traditional 'fast-track' graduate jobs. This divide may be further exacerbated by the increasingly flexible world of work where fewer opportunities for promotion through the ranks exist. Those who miss out on fast-track opportunities may quite categorically miss out.

What is interesting when we reflect on these assumptions is that the reality of the two student housing experiences may in fact be very different. Indeed, those who actively buck the trend of studying away from home and for whatever reason instead continue to live with their families may be more adaptive and flexible than those who simply move away to reinvent the wheel of student life, inasmuch as they are having to achieve a continual balance between what may be two very different worlds. Conversely, moving away to university and mixing with young people from a broadly similar background may not necessarily be as life changing and culturally stimulating as is often assumed (Chatterton, 1999). Perhaps, then, what employers are seeking is not so much the ability to adapt and remain flexible *per se* but, as Brown and Scase (1994) suggest, the ability to do so in certain ways and to show understanding of appropriate cultural codes. Students' housing decisions and experiences may therefore be more connected with their employability as graduates than it would seem at first glance.

If, as Brown (1995) argues, members of the higher socio-economic groups are actively striving to consolidate their position in order to shelter from contemporary economic pressures, this may explain the continuing expectations within the middle classes that living away from home is a necessary and valuable part of student life, despite the economic commitment this entails and the trend for more students to live at home. While sending children to university *per se* can no longer be viewed as a middle class activity, sending them *away* to university certainly can. In the light of this discussion we argue that the connection between the 'traditional "graduate labour market" where "traditional" students from established universities continue to have reasonable job opportunities after gaining a degree' (Pitcher and Purcell, 1998: 198) and student housing choices, experiences and opportunities certainly merits further research and debate.

Conclusion

This chapter has considered two parallel developments in relation to the student housing market: the increased proportion of students remaining in the parental home whilst studying at 'local' universities, and the growth in the number of independent shared student households in the private sector. We have suggested that each of these housing options may be perceived very differently by the students living in them, by their peers and, crucially, by potential employers. This last group in particular may regard the decision to remain at home as evidence of a lack of flexibility and adaptability on the part of an individual student, which gives a clear advantage to those students able and willing to live away from home during their university years: increasingly, those from affluent middle class families, whose parents may themselves have first left home in order to move away to attend university. This suggests that the status of 'student' *per se* does not necessarily provide access to a privileged set of transitions; rather, that those who are able to follow the more traditional route of moving away from home to study may be in a position to gain the edge over students who for whatever reason remain in the parental home.

We have also noted that those students who are able to make the move out of the parental home gain access to a niche sector of the housing market, either moving into university accommodation or into a relatively protected sector of the private rented sector. Whilst the quality of accommodation available to students in the private rented sector is notoriously poor, there is nonetheless a ready supply of such accommodation: a supply not so readily available to non-students seeking to leave home. Reasons for this include: restricted access to the niche student market; insufficient funds to rent a whole house or flat; a lack of a ready pool of friends all needing to rent accommodation at the same time, and letting agencies and housing benefit regulations imposing restrictions on the housing that certain groups of young people can rent. Once students have had experience of sharing with their peers at university, many of them then have access to a network of friends and friends-of-friends with whom they may be able to share in the future. In addition, they have developed skills with which to navigate rented and shared housing markets successfully. With these resources in hand, increasing numbers of students are choosing to continue to share, as an alternative to moving back to the parental home or to establishing a household on their own or with a partner, something that few students can afford on first graduating. The growing trend amongst graduates and non-students of living in shared accommodation during their twenties is the subject of the next chapter.

6
Shared Housing, Grown-up Style

Introduction

> House sharing: The best aspects: You're living with your best friends. You're never lonely; there's always someone to talk to. The worst aspects: You're living with your best friends. You're never lonely; there's always someone to talk to (*This Life: The Companion Guide*, p. 81).

Something strange has happened in sitcom land: shared households and bedsits, stock reference points of television comedy and soap, have had a make-over. No longer peopled by lonely individuals (*Rising Damp*), assorted radicals and impoverished students (*The Young Ones*) or slackers (*Men Behaving Badly*), they now house groups of young professionals living affluent urban lifestyles in chic, comfortable surroundings. Today's sitcom sharers have housemates like *Friends* and a *This Life* style to match. And *The Secret Life of Us* is now revealed for all to see, with 24-hour flat-sharing brought to our screens by courtesy of the *Big Brother* cameras. Similarly, the pages of the glossies and Sunday supplements are spreading the message that shared housing is cool; as one such article claimed, 'It's a positive, "I'm all right" statement' (Robson-Scott, 1999: 47). If the media representations are to be believed, then, sharing appears to have become fashionable, a key element of a deliberate life-style choice among single, upwardly mobile post-adolescents.

The media do not, of course, always capture the *zeitgeist* with accuracy, but in the case of shared living there is evidence to suggest that the typical characteristics of sharers are indeed changing. Whilst sharing remains widespread amongst young people on low incomes, particularly amongst students and housing benefit claimants (Jones, 1995a), there is also a growing association between shared housing and relative advantage. In 1991, 48 per cent of twenty-something British sharers were located in Social Classes I and II on the basis of their own occupations, and 39 per cent had at least one degree-level qualification. These characteristics were particularly pronounced amongst women in their mid- to late twenties: 54 per cent of female sharers aged 25–29 were located in Social Classes I and II, and 49 per cent had at least one degree-level qualification (Kenyon and Heath, 2001). These patterns continued through the 1990s: the 1996 sweep of the BCS70, for example, revealed that sharers were, on several counts, the most advantaged group amongst the entire cohort when analysed by living arrangement. Over half of the male sharers in the cohort and nearly two-thirds of their female peers, then aged 26, had a degree or an equivalent qualification, two-thirds of both sexes were employed in professional or managerial positions, and sharers were over twice as likely than any other group to have fathers in professional and managerial occupations (Bynner *et al.*, 1997).

This chapter focuses on the experience of shared household living largely amongst these more affluent sharers. In the absence of much existing literature on shared living arrangements, it draws rather more than earlier chapters in this book on the narratives of the young people involved in our own research, a group which included a number of less affluent members, but which is more generally representative of the changing face of shared housing. We start this chapter by defining the terms of our discussion, then briefly explore our respondents' motivations for sharing, investigating the relative importance of financial savings, housing quality and household sociability. We then focus on the importance of the communal ethic in shared living arrangements, and draw a parallel with Maffesoli's conceptualisation of 'neo-tribalism', a phenomenon which arises under the conditions of proximity, shared space and ritual. We also examine the popular view that shared households are characterised by unusually high levels of conflict and tension, and draw on Natalier's (2002) work on divisions of domestic labour in shared households in exploring the fault lines of shared living. We focus this chapter, then, on the dynamics of shared household living, and by so doing we hope to challenge the assumption that – because they are transitional – shared households and the relationships that exist within them assume little importance in the lives of those who experience them.

What is a shared household?

In comparison with the rest of Europe, shared living arrangements are a largely British phenomenon. Peer sharing in other European countries (with the exception of Ireland) is relatively uncommon, with single person households accounting for the vast majority of non-familial households in Northern Europe (Iacovou, 1998). In Australia, shared households are more common than single person households amongst young adults. In 1996, 22 per cent of 20–24-year-olds lived in shared households, compared with only 5.6 per cent of the age group who lived alone (Australian Bureau of Statistics, 1997b). In Britain, whilst only a minority of young people live in shared households at any given point in time (Heath and Dale, 1994; Heath and Miret, 1996), they are increasingly likely to share *at some point* during their twenties, if not beyond (Berrington and Murphy, 1994; Bell and Jones, 1999). Indeed, according to Datamonitor (2003) house sharing is currently experiencing the most significant rate of growth relative to other living arrangements amongst 18–24-year-olds, whilst across the board the number of shared households is set to rise by three-quarters of a million between 1996 and 2021, many as a result of the breakdown of couple relationships (Office of the Deputy Prime Minister, 1999). Despite this shift, we still know relatively little about shared living arrangements within standard residential housing, not least because shared households are often grouped together for analytical purposes with halls of residence, bed and breakfast establishments, hostels and bedsits under the umbrella category of HMOs. This is an unhelpful aggregation, as we argue here that shared households provide their members with a very different living experience to these other house-hold types.

An HMO is legally defined in the Housing Act 1985 as 'a house which is occupied by persons who do not form a single household', and it is on this basis that HMOs are subject to official regulation, as it is assumed that a lack of connectedness between residents makes them potentially hazardous environments. The 'single household' element of this defin-ition is open to considerable interpretation, but in practice 'if residents are recruited individually by the landlord and allocated a room, do not share facilities, have little communal living, and live in a large property with a rapid turnover of residents, then they are likely to be considered separate households' (DETR, 1999: 30). In other words, HMOs provide an indi-vidualised, non-communal form of accommodation for single people.

It is for this reason that we not only exclude purpose-built institu-tional provision from our own definition of shared housing, but also place bedsit living in a very different category of experience. Bedsits, or 'traditional HMOs', have a reputation for some of the poorest quality housing in the private rented sector, with high levels of unfitness for human habitation as defined in housing legislation (DETR, 1999). It is this type of HMO that provides a common first destination for many young people on leaving home, particularly those not going away to university, as it is typically the only affordable accommodation in the private rented sector. More critically, under-25-year-olds who wish to claim housing benefit will only have their full housing costs covered through living in bedsits, as payments to this group are restricted to the cost of a single room within a non-self-contained dwelling with shared use of a kitchen and toilet, but with no access to a shared or separate living room. Indeed, housing benefit claimants account for approximately half of the 220,000 bedsit tenants in England (DETR, 1999). The higher rents of houses with shared living rooms are rarely met by benefit payments; instead, claimants are expected to meet the shortfall from their own pockets (Kemp and Rugg, 1998). Bedsits are not, then, designed for communal living. Neither are they organised on the basis of mutual trust: most tenants will occupy a single room with a lock on the door, enabling them to keep others out of their private space, and are unlikely to have any control over the selection of new tenants.

In contrast, we use the term 'shared housing' to describe households consisting of unrelated individuals living in self-contained houses and apartments which assume at least a minimal level of sociability between household members and which are organised on the basis of some element of mutual trust. In practical terms, this is usually facilitated by the provision of a shared living room in addition to a shared kitchen and bathroom, and by the absence (or non-use) of locks on bedroom doors. We concede that some overlap may exist between bedsits and shared households in these respects, as we do not rule out the possibility that sociability and mutual trust may come to prevail in a traditional HMO. Nor do we assume that these qualities are necessarily found in households with shared facilities. Nonetheless, given the basic organisation of shared household living, a minimum level of mutual trust and sociability is more likely to develop by default, to the point that it is almost a structural feature of the sector, whereas the emergence of these features in a bedsit would be unintentional and largely unexpected.

Bearing these points in mind, shared households can be placed on a continuum in terms of the strength of existing or developing sociability and trust between household members, ranging from communal households at one end through to stranger households at the other. Communal households are marked by an overt commitment to, and expectation of, operating as a collective, manifest in a variety of shared activities both inside and outside the house, and a broadly similar outlook on life amongst residents. Whilst prior friendship between household members makes the development of a communal environment more likely, it is not a necessary precondition, nor a guarantee that such relationships will develop. In contrast, relationships in stranger households are tenuous, with little sense of commonality beyond sharing the same address. New tenants are most likely to be recruited by a non-resident landlord, with little or no consideration for the views of existing residents (in this respect they are similar to bedsits). Nonetheless, relationships between housemates are not necessarily unfriendly, and housemates will occasionally spend time together in the communal lounge or socialise together outside of the house. These are the extremes; in between are households where individual members may get on extremely well and share a sense of commitment to each other which may not be shared across the entire household. Nonetheless, these are not fixed positions: shared households have the potential to move between the two poles in response to their changing membership, or to changing dynamics between household members.

We also distinguish between three different types of shared household in terms of their tenure: privately rented shared households, households with lodgers, and jointly owned shared households. The first category consists of unrelated individuals holding shared or individual tenancy agreements with non-resident landlords. In 1996, there were approximately 188,000 shared households within this category in England, containing 547,000 residents, 90 per cent of whom were under the age of 30. In the same year, there were approximately 202,000 'households with lodgers', with half of the 253,000 resident lodgers aged under 30 (DETR, 1999). Where owners and lodgers are peers, these households often have more in common with privately rented shared households than they do with traditional images of young lodgers 'rooming' with older (and often partnered) householders. Moreover, these arrangements not infrequently arise out of pre-existing friendships between the owner and the lodger(s). Jointly owned households consist of unrelated young people who have entered into joint mortgage agreements. This group is not easily captured by official statistics, although it is believed to be on the increase (Gordon, 2002; McMinn, 2002). Amongst our own sample of shared households, 17 were privately rented, seven were lodger households, and one was jointly owned by two friends who had taken out a joint mortgage eight years previously.

Why share? material and non-material considerations

Existing research on young people and their housing experiences has tended to assume that shared living arrangements arise largely through lack of choice. From this perspective, the introduction in 1996 of the single room rent (SRR) was widely condemned by housing and welfare rights lobbyists for forcing young people into shared accommodation against their wishes. The Conservative architects of the policy had based its introduction on the assumption that housing benefit was being used to finance the establishment of single person households in self-contained accommodation, thus giving claimants what was deemed to be an inappropriate and unfair advantage over non-claimants. However, as previously noted in Chapter 2, researchers conducting an evaluation of the impact of the SRR on the living arrangements of housing benefit claimants under 25 years of age reached a rather unexpected conclusion:

> Both the policy assumption and the lobbyists' response to that assumption are questioned by research with young adults themselves. As might be expected, a small number of young people in the sample did moderate their search for accommodation on the understanding that Housing Benefit would only fully cover shared properties. In fact, in the majority of cases, even without the prompting of the SRR, young people expected or even wanted to live in shared accommodation (Kemp and Rugg, 1998: 31).

Kemp and Rugg appear to have unearthed a normative expectation of a period of shared living prior to living alone or with a partner, with older respondents no less likely to express a preference for sharing than younger respondents. Nonetheless, they offer two important provisos to their findings. First, they note the importance of distinguishing between preferences and expectations, and point out that the latter tend to operate over and above the former. For many of their respondents, sharing was viewed as an inevitable part of growing up. Secondly, sharing with strangers as opposed to friends was a source of anxiety for virtually all of the sample members: 'control over who they were sharing with was an important qualification to single young people's preferences for shared accommodation' (ibid.: 33). Despite these misgivings, various advantages were associated with sharing: pooled living costs, mutual support and the benefit of company.

In our own research, 'why share?' became a question of crucial importance. In particular, we wanted to explore the balance between choice and constraint in the housing decisions of our sample. Whilst their relative affluence may have afforded them more choices than many young people, certain options may nonetheless have remained beyond their reach given the spiralling of housing costs and the increasing impossibility of buying property on the basis of a single salary. At the start of our research, for example, an averagely priced one bedroom flat in Southampton cost approximately £39,000 requiring a minimum annual income of £13,000, whilst the average price of a two bedroom terraced house cost £55,000, requiring £18,600 per annum. (These prices have increased considerably since 1998.) Whilst housing costs were indeed a key issue for most of our respondents, this was not at the expense of sub-standard accommodation. At the same time, the company of peers was generally regarded as desirable. We have discussed each of these factors in detail elsewhere (Kenyon and Heath, 2001), but summarise them here.

Housing costs

At certain points in time, shared housing had undoubtedly been the only affordable option for our respondents. For some, most notably the non-professionals in the study, this remained so. However, the majority of respondents felt that their options had increased with age and career advancement: they could now exercise greater choice in their living arrangements if they so wished, including the possibility of renting a place on their own. Many had also considered buying a place on their own, but felt that the disadvantages currently outweighed the advantages, not least because the increased financial commitment of a mortgage on a single salary would detract from their ability to use their disposable income for more immediate pleasures, particularly the ability to travel abroad. Buying also carried a heavy weight of responsibility in the minds of many of our respondents, a theme which we discuss in Chapter 10. Sharing in the private rented sector allowed, then, a considerable degree of flexibility and the maintenance of higher disposable incomes, considerations which were of particular importance to those who had clear expectations of geographical mobility in pursuit of their career goals (Heath and Kenyon, 2001).

Of the ten individuals who had already invested in property, five took in lodgers as the only means of maintaining their mortgage payments. The others, however, stated that they had reached the point where they could now afford to pay their mortgages without assistance, yet still chose to share their homes. Damien (household 24), for example, was not only reluctant to forfeit the £300 a month he received in rent, but was also uncertain about the etiquette of asking his tenant – a good friend – to leave. He was also unsure whether he even *wanted* to live alone quite yet. Similarly, Jamie (household 8), a 33-year-old production engineer, had bought a large house on first graduating by entering into a joint mortgage agreement with three friends, subsequently replacing them with a succession of tenants as they had each moved out in order to marry. He had recently bought out his friends' share in the property, and felt he could now manage his mortgage payments on his own without having to take in lodgers. However, his preference was to continue to share for the foreseeable future, largely because he enjoyed the company of his tenants.

The benefits of shared utility bills and economies of scale were also important considerations (as they were for Kemp and Rugg's housing benefit claimants). Whilst few households operated formal 'kitty' systems, most shared the costs of cleaning products and staples such as milk, bread, tea and coffee. Some households operated more elaborate schemes. The chemists (household 7) bought all their food in bulk and shared it in common, additionally clubbing together to employ a regular cleaner. The computer analysts (household 6) each paid an additional £100 a month, on top of their rent, into a joint bank account. All household bills were paid from this account, but any excess was used to finance treats, such as a shared trip to EuroDisney in France.

Housing quality

Our respondents also had very clear expectations of a minimum threshold of housing quality. Those who had experience of living in student households had the strongest views, and generally were not prepared to replicate aspects of their student housing such as bad landlords, noise, damp, run-down localities, neighbourhood disputes, cramped conditions and poor value for money. Exceptionally amongst the ex-students, the six nurses (household 1) had continued to live in their student house, partly in order to channel more money towards paying off their overdrafts, but also in order to save money towards a much-anticipated (and, indeed, subsequently realised) extended overseas trip, travelling together as a group. Nonetheless, decent housing and, in some cases desirable locations, were frequently prioritised over crude cost savings, and were the source of both pleasure and pride for many respondents. Jade and Scott (household 25), for example, neither of whom earned excessive salaries, had chosen to pay £350 each a month in rent – the highest amongst our sample and almost three times as much as the lowest rent, £130 – in order to live in a stylish two bedroom apartment in a prestigious waterfront development. Their close proximity not only to their places of work but to a complex of bars, restaurants, night clubs and cinemas was important both to their chosen lifestyle and to their joint friendship; they had initially met in a local club, and frequently socialised together in the leisure spaces on their doorstep. In this respect, they had much in common with Chatterton and Hollands' 'denizens of the reimagined urban landscape', 'the saviours of the city's new night-time and cultural economy' (2002: 98).

Similarly, the engineers (household 3) had rented a fashionable three bedroom town house, complete with a bathroom apiece, for £895 a month. As well-paid professionals they had enjoyed the pick of the local privately rented sector, and had taken their time to find just the right property:

> Up until that point we'd lived in student accommodation or houses, similar to student accommodation and we just decided we wanted something a little bit nicer. We'd all got reasonable jobs and we could afford something a bit nicer ... [and by sharing rather than living alone] we can live in a house like this, there's no way we could afford to live in a house like this any other way.

This, then, is 'flat sharing grown up style' (Robson-Scott, 1999: 45), facilitating the possibility of living in a relatively luxurious domestic environment. Whilst few others chose to live in quite the splendour of these two households, the theme of progression into better, non-student housing – variously described as 'proper', 'decent', 'professional' or 'sophis-ticated' – was a strong one across our sample, and most of our respond-ents sought with each successive move to trade up in the housing market and to draw a line under previous student sharing. In an echo of these findings, Kemp and Rugg (1998) note that some housing benefit claimants choose to pay extra to live in shared accommodation for similar reasons of progression, preferring to live in large houses rather than 'grotty' bedsits. It would appear, then, that serial sharers and bedsit dwellers alike carry with them a finely tuned awareness of a hier-archy of housing quality. Whilst to many observers all shared housing may appear to be pretty much of a muchness, this is clearly not how sharers themselves experience it.

Household sociability

In addition to considerations of cost savings and housing quality, most respondents also highlighted the draw of sociability in shared housing. Most were well aware that the company of others could be both the major advantage *and* disadvantage of shared living, and readily related a particular variety of atrocity tale: the 'housemate from hell' story, a narrative form perfected by veteran Australian house-sharer John Birmingham (Birmingham, 1997). Nonetheless, ready access to the

company of friends – or potential friends – was an important consideration. Many of the 53 ex-student sharers had developed an expectation
that sharing was what one did on graduating. As Hilary (household 6)
argued, 'having always shared together at university as well, I think it's
just – it was just natural for us to just carry on living together, and it
just made sense as well, 'cos we all got on really well'. In eight households, at least two – and sometimes all – of the residents had previously
lived together as students, and had decided to continue living together
when their work had kept them in, or brought them to, the Southampton area. The three physiotherapists (household 5), for example, had all
lived together whilst training in the West Midlands and – by chance
rather than design – had all ended up working in the Southampton area
on graduating. In a further eight households, the core membership
consisted of individuals with non-university-based friendships, in five
cases stretching back to their childhood years.

Twenty five housemates had moved to Southampton as strangers,
with no prior contacts, usually for work-related reasons. For individuals
such as these, the social aspects of shared housing were seen as particularly important, providing access to a ready-made social life. Heather
(household 4), a market researcher, had recently moved to Southampton, and as she worked mainly from home she felt it was particularly
important to share: 'the only way I'm going to meet people initially is
to house share...I wanted to socialise, I don't want to live alone'.
Similarly, Bobby (household 11), a business analyst, had decided that
sharing would provide a means of making new friends quickly. Within
a week of moving in, she had met the closest friends of the existing
tenants, as well as some of the previous tenants, largely through a
dinner party arranged in her honour. This particular household was
something of a paradox, as in all other respects it corresponded more to
the characteristics of a stranger household rather than a communal
household. Nonetheless, it demonstrated the potential of even relatively
disconnected households to provide some form of social life by default:
having a companion with whom to watch television, for example, or
with whom to share fairly superficial conversation ('beer, birds and
football', as one respondent described it).

Shared households and neo-tribalism

We have explored, then, some of the *reasons* why young adults live in
shared households. But what are some of the *consequences* of these arrangements? In their emphasis on sociability, shared households arguably

have much in common with Maffesoli's conceptualisation of 'neo-tribalism'. We noted in Chapter 3 that Maffesoli uses the term to describe a diversity of groupings, all of which share a commitment to 'the communal ethic', which 'has the simplest of foundations: warmth, companionship – physical contact with one another' (1996: 16). His account stresses the importance of *proximity, shared space* (both real or symbolic) and *ritual* to the nurturing of the communal ethic within neo-tribes. This, he argues, is the stuff of *proxemics*, the socially conditioned spatial factors inherent within ordinary human relations: 'proxemics refers primarily to the foundation of a succession of "we's" which constitute the very essence of all sociality' (p. 139). Interestingly, in applying the term 'neo-tribe' to relatively loose groupings of individuals, he does not use the term to describe *necessarily* close relationships. As such, the term can usefully be employed in relation to shared households, where the communal ethic is similarly underpinned by proximity, shared space and ritual, albeit at times at a rather residual level. We consider each of these points in turn.

Proximity

Maffesoli notes that proximity may arise by force of circumstance as much as by choice – proximity in the workplace or neighbourhood, or indeed through living under the same roof. Proximity can also arise by chance. In ten households, at least one member had moved into the house as a stranger, having responded to a 'room to let' advertisement placed in a local newspaper or in a shop window. From their perspective, it was largely a matter of chance that they and not another applicant had been chosen to be the new household member. For those already resident, it had been a mixture of chance, choice and force of circumstance, depending on the amount of say they were given in the process. In Steve, Miles and Nathan's household (household 14), for example, it was common practice for new tenants to move in without necessarily meeting any of the other residents. The decision was entirely in the hands of the non-resident landlady, whose only interest was assumed to be the financial gain of an extra tenant, rather than the dynamics of the household. In contrast, in Jamie's household (household 8) all housemates were equally involved in the selection process, despite Jamie being the resident owner. Kim, the newest resident, described the process as 'quite formal':

> I suppose formal in the sense that at the other house that I went to you just looked round the room and you sat and had a cup of tea,

whereas [here] you were actually asking questions trying to find out things about me in that sense . . . Like, for example, what my interests were and about my job and obviously try and find out if I would fit into the household. Whereas other households it was just like, 'oh right'.

Jackie, a 34-year-old customer service manager, was the resident owner in just such a household (household 2). Her current household was the second home in which she had rented out rooms, and over the previous six years she had let rooms to a succession of tenants, including one who had moved with her to her second shared house. She appeared remarkably relaxed about the selection process, even though her fingers had been burnt on more than one occasion (including having a tenant who effectively became her stalker). Jackie claimed that she could usually tell whether someone would be appropriate, taking cues from how they sounded over the telephone and their appearance when they came to look round. Nonetheless, she acknowledged that this was by no means an exact science:

So, I don't know, sometimes it's just a chance. I mean I've had people I've had problems with and they've had to go. And then other times, like you think, 'oh, I'm not sure about this one', then it works out well. So it's very easy to jump to the wrong conclusion on the first meeting. So I don't know, often you've just got to give people the chance, and if they take the mickey, then they go.

In the remaining 15 households, none of the residents had been strangers on first moving in. In 12 households they had all moved in together, in most cases with a joint tenancy agreement, whilst in the other three the new members were work-based friends who were already part of the households' respective social circles. In some of these households, the decision to live together had created an extraordinary degree of overlap between the public and private spheres of their lives: not only was there a tendency for residents to have identical jobs – nurses (two households), physiotherapists, engineers, chemical engineers, and computer analysts – but many of these individuals worked for the same company or hospital trust, and on occasions within the same office or ward. Proximity, then, forms the first precondition for the development of a communal ethic, regardless of whether the individual residents come together through chance, choice or force of circumstance.

Shared space

Shared space, both real and symbolic, is the second factor that underpins the development of the communal ethic amongst neo-tribes.
According to Maffesoli, 'space guarantees a necessary security. We know
that limits fence one in, but also give life…the stability of space is a
focal point, an anchor for the group' (1996: 133). In the case of shared
housing, the use of physical space is of critical importance. The shared
living room provided the focal point for domestic life in most of our
households, with residents regularly congregating there to eat and
drink, watch television, or generally 'hang out' at the end of the day
('sit around doing arse all', as one respondent put it). Watching television or videos together was a regular activity in virtually all of the
households, despite most residents having televisions of their own in
their bedrooms. As Jules (household 1) said, 'I never really use it because
I'd rather sit in here'. Considerable time was also spent 'just chatting',
often over a glass of wine or a can of beer, sharing the events of the day
or discussing personal problems. This undoubtedly constituted what
Maffesoli has referred to as the 'emotional glue' of household life (a
metaphor which has much in common with Pahl's (2000) reference to
the 'social glue' of friendship). Certain forms of sociability, then,
develop by default as a consequence of 'spatial affiliation', the sharing
of space and of everyday life under the same roof, and Maffesoli's observation concerning the importance of such moments seems particularly
apposite to life in shared households:

> Having a few drinks; chatting with friends; the anodyne conversa-
> tions punctuating everyday life enable an exteriorisation of the self
> and thus create the specific aura which binds us together within
> tribalism (Maffesoli, 1996: 25).

Perhaps surprisingly, only a handful of respondents ever spent much
time alone in their bedrooms, with the vast majority preferring to spend
their waking hours in the shared spaces of their households when they
were at home. When time was spent in bedrooms, this was usually in
order to secure an element of privacy: to work or study without distraction, to watch a favourite TV programme, spend time with a partner, or
just to get some peace and quiet away from others. The households
were divided on the etiquette of going into each other's bedrooms; in
half, this was a perfectly acceptable practice (particularly if the door was
left open), whilst in the other half bedrooms were either completely off
limits or access to them was based on prior permission. Bedroom doors

had locks on them in only two households, although they were rarely used, except by the resident owners. Jackie (household 2) had used the locks for safety reasons during her 'stalker' period, whilst Robert (household 4) locked his room whenever he stayed away from the house. Robert claimed that he had installed the locks in order to make his rooms more attractive to female tenants, whom he felt might expect a guarantee of privacy. However, in practice it seemed that he had installed the locks as much for his own protection as for that of his tenants, revealing a lack of trust in his housemates which led us to categorise this household as a stranger household. The presence or otherwise of locks in shared households carries, then, an important symbolic value; as Carole (household 8) exclaimed in relation to houses with bedroom locks: 'Ooh, scary houses – don't move in there!'

The sharing of *symbolic* space and territory, in the sense of a shared outlook on life, was also deemed to be of critical importance in many households. This was perhaps most pronounced in the case of the vegan household (household 13), who shared a house which already had a long history as a cooperative housing venture. The original household members had shared a commitment to socialist politics; indeed, for many years there had been a copy of the now defunct Clause 4 of the Labour Party constitution pinned to the kitchen wall. More recently, in response to the household's changing membership, there had been a drift towards a more spiritual and ecological agenda, with meditation having become a regular feature of communal life for some of the residents, alongside an overt commitment to a green lifestyle. All current household members were vegan, and the shared evening meal was an important unifying feature. Holly, a former environmental protester whose previous living arrangements had included 'benders' and the boughs of trees, described how she had found the household:

> I answered this ad because it said 'vegetarian non-smoker'. So I thought, ooh this might be interesting...That was the bit I couldn't ever have dreamed of. I was hoping for a nice house with quite quiet, clean people, but the whole communal cooperative element I just – I didn't think existed in Southampton! There are very few people that I've met here (in the city) that I really connect with anyway. And so you know, I wasn't even hoping for that.

Two other households similarly used carefully worded advertisements as a means of attracting like-minded individuals. In the case of the shared household owned by two yoga teachers (household 15), whose

residents also shared a communal evening meal, vacancies were advertised in the following terms: 'shared environment, vegetarian-inclined,
non-smoking, quiet, friendly house'. Jamie's household (household 8)
advertised for 'broad-minded' tenants, in the hope that this would attract
'people who are sort of relaxed and fairly comfortable with things', and
in particular might filter out applicants who might turn out to be
homophobic. In other households which had advertised for new
tenants, the emphasis had been on the importance of shared interests.
Katie and Viv's social life revolved around relatively heavy drinking
sessions in pubs and nightclubs (household 17). Previous housemates
had often been incapable of keeping up with their lifestyle, so they had
been particularly delighted with their most recent addition, Angie,
whom they regarded as 'our perfect match'. The importance of common interests to the stability of shared households is further underlined
by the case of Steve, Nathan and Miles' household (household 14),
mentioned above. By imposing total strangers on existing tenants and
not allowing them any right of veto, the landlady created a set of conditions that made the emergence of a communal ethic extremely difficult.
In the absence of a shared living room in this household other than the
kitchen, its emergence was rendered even more unlikely, and not
unsurprisingly this household had a very high and rapid turnover of
tenants. Shared space – both literal and symbolic – remains, then,
critical to the fostering of the communal ethic in neo-tribes:

> Whatever the territory in question or the content of the affection –
> cultural pursuits, sexual tastes, clothing habits, religious representa-
> tions, intellectual motivations, political commitments: we can go on
> listing the factors of aggregation – they can also be circumscribed on
> the basis of the two poles of space and symbol (sharing, the specific
> form of solidarity, and so on). This is what best characterises the
> intense communication which in many ways serves as a breeding
> ground for what I am calling neo-tribalism (Maffesoli, 1996: 135).

Ritual

Ritual forms the third element which contributes to the creation of this
'breeding ground' for neo-tribalism. Maffesoli describes ritual as 'repeti-
tive and therefore comforting' and argues that 'its sole function is to
confirm a group's view of itself' (1996: 17). Our households had various
rituals and customs of their own which underlined their functioning *as
a group*, rather than individuals who merely lived under the same roof.
Most households regularly socialised together both inside and outside

of the home, and shared meals on various occasions, particularly in celebration of birthdays and other special events. Other joint events included household outings to local venues such as restaurants, cinemas, nightclubs and bowling alleys, playing sport together, going on holiday or weekends away together, games evenings, and attending events in which household members were involved, such as sporting fixtures and amateur operatic performances. Whilst partners and non-household friends were often involved in these rituals, many were undertaken solely, and quite deliberately so, between household members. Others had developed rituals peculiar to their household. The nurses in household 1, for example, had a shelf in their living room dedicated to a collection of kitsch ornaments bought on group holidays, whilst Jamie's household (household 8) had developed a ritual of sharing a champagne breakfast on Christmas Day before household members went their separate ways. This household also had a reputation for hosting a flamboyant themed party each year.

Through such means, Maffesoli argues, a sense of community comes into existence. Indeed, Maffesoli insists that 'the mechanism of belonging' is fundamental to neo-tribalism:

> Whatever the domain, it is more or less required to participate in the collective spirit. Moreover, the question is simply not asked, and acceptance or rejection depends on the degree of feeling felt both by the members of the group and by the applicant. This feeling will then be either reinforced or weakened by the acceptance or rejection of various initiation rites. Whatever the lifespan of the groups, these rites are necessary. We can moreover observe that they take on an increasing importance in everyday life...At the same time as the aspiration, the future and the ideal serve as a glue to hold society together, the ritual, by reinforcing the feeling of belonging, can play this role and thus allow groups to exist (1996: 140).

It is interesting in this context to note that some of our households had experienced disappointment when new housemates failed to comply with expectations of sociability. Spending too much time in one's own bedroom at the expense of spending time in the shared living room was, for example, regarded as a definite failing in some households, whilst spending too much time with a partner could also attract criticism. Conversely, some individuals entered shared housing expecting to socialise with their new housemates, and felt short-changed on discovering that this was not a shared expectation. It was in households where a mismatch existed between the expectations of the various members that difficulties were most likely to develop, with unequal divisions of labour, different expectations regarding acceptable levels of hygiene and noise, and general thoughtlessness often acting as key flashpoints. These are issues which we consider in the following section.

Neo-tribal warfare?

In her research on gender, domesticity and shared living arrangements in Australia, Natalier (2002) argues that shared households are an example of a 'differently institutionalised' household form. Citing Cherlin (1978), she notes that traditional household forms are based on pre-existing 'ideological templates' which provide scripts for household members to follow. Non-traditional households, on the other hand, are not governed by institutionalised 'guiding principles', resulting in a greater potential for confusion and conflict amongst household members as they try to make sense of the ways in which they relate to each other. According to Natalier,

> Drawing upon this approach it might be argued that share households (*sic*) do not conform to what is sanctioned and supported by society, and as a result their occupants do not have obvious recourse to an off the peg collection of ideological templates. This cultural vacuum potentially undermines the stability of non-traditional household types (Natalier, 2002: 66).

Natalier argues that sharers have to look instead to popular or counter-cultural discourses to understand and manage their relationships with housemates, yet relationships within shared households are nonetheless often judged by both insiders and outsiders in relation to the ideological templates that exist within more traditional household forms. Shared households, then, are popularly regarded as sites of dysfunctional and conflictual relationships in contrast with traditional households, even though in reality they may be no more or less dysfunctional than 'institutionalised' household forms, where conflicts may be masked by the existence of ideological templates governing acceptable behaviour and legitimate grounds for complaint.

This point becomes clearer if we consider tensions over housework, the major source of discord in both Natalier's and our own shared households, as well as in the households included in an earlier Australian study (Baum, 1986). Such tensions and disagreements arose on a regular basis, although in most cases they tended to blow over without materially affecting relationships within the household. Indeed, the majority of housemates in each of these studies went to great lengths to ensure that their frustrations with housemates did not boil over into direct confrontation. Nonetheless, it is disagreements of this kind that are often flagged up when claims are made concerning the dysfunctional nature of shared living arrangements relative to more traditional household forms. This, however, may say more about the transparency of unequal allocations of domestic labour in shared households relative to traditional households, and the lack of an ideological template governing those allocations. Existing studies of divisions of labour in heterosexual couple households, for example, suggest that the allocation and conduct of housework has the potential to be an equally contentious issue (Sullivan, 2000), yet pre-existing scripts in relation to gender and housework – absent in shared households, whether mixed or single-sex – mean that the issue tends to be viewed very differently. Presumably, if roles were not so clearly prescribed in the typical allocation of domestic labour in heterosexual couple households, these tensions would similarly arise. Indeed, the fact that they do arise when one or other partner (usually the woman) is conscious of unequal allocation testifies to this.

In contrast, Natalier argues, shared households do not have such scripts to fall back on, so tensions over housework are more obvious and cannot be sidestepped on ideological grounds. A lazy husband represents a familiar cultural script, and tends not to attract serious admonition; in contrast, a lazy housemate – an equally familiar cultural script – is widely regarded as a legitimate target for bitter complaint, if not eviction. In shared households, then, domestic labour tends to be removed from notions of intimacy and gendered familial obligation. Failings are therefore (legitimately) resented rather than tolerated, and are also more likely to be made public than in a couple household. Thus, a partner who complains openly about household drudgery and an unequal division of domestic labour may be viewed as disloyal, whereas housemates, in contrast, are not expected to be beholden to each other in quite the same way (yet in practice often are). Quite apart from showing how an ethos of care can be used as an ideological cloak for unequal labour in traditional couple households, Natalier's point also illustrates why close friends who move in together may be particularly disappointed when one of them turns out to be less than committed to a fair division of household labour: their 'laziness' may well be regarded as a betrayal of friendship.

Nonetheless, living with others can indeed involve serious tensions and personality clashes. Amongst our own sharers, complaints about housemates failing to do their fair share of housework were particularly common, and occasionally became major irritants, particularly in households consisting of relative strangers. Conflicts of varying degrees of seriousness had also emerged in both past and current households in relation to issues such as personal hygiene, untidiness, neglected washing up, noise, borrowing housemates' belongings without first seeking permission, eating other people's food without replacing it, partners outstaying their welcome, and general thoughtlessness. In discussing the existence or otherwise of 'house rules', for example, most talked of the importance of treating others as they would wish to be treated themselves. However, the majority of households also appeared to have ways of dealing with conflicts of this kind without letting them escalate into major problems. In common with Baum's (1986) study, we found that compromise and an ability to shrug one's shoulders and walk away proved crucial in such circumstances – and this was certainly easier to do amongst households consisting of friends rather than strangers. The more sociability that exists between housemates, then, the better equipped they may be to cope with household tensions.

Conclusion

Shared living arrangements in the United Kingdom are set to increase over the next 20 years. In line with Maffesoli's conceptualisation of neo-tribalism, sociability and the communal ethic are fundamental features of most shared households, even if such sociability operates at a fairly residual level. Whilst many of the sharers in our own research considered some or all of their housemates to be good friends, a theme we explore further in Chapter 8, this is by no means a necessary condition of neo-tribalism. Indeed, Maffesoli uses the term to describe relatively free-floating and often short-lived groupings, features which are characteristic of many shared households. For many sharers, the main point of commonality remains the fact of living under the same roof, yet even here a level of neo-tribalism is likely to emerge by virtue of the proxemics of shared living. Importantly, neo-tribalism does not preclude the emergence of tensions and disagreements, and we have already noted that household sociability can be both the major advantage *and* disadvantage of living in a shared household. In our research sample, although relationships occasionally broke down to the point of collapse, it was more common for respondents to have experienced sporadic periods of heightened tension which tended to blow over with time without materially affecting their long-term relationships with house-mates. This suggests that many sharers become adept at handling the conflicts that can arise when living closely with others.

However, most also acknowledged that, eventually, difficulties such as these would result in a desire for privacy which would override the benefits of constant company, and that this would be a critical moment in deciding either to live alone or to move in with a partner. Whether or not the prospect of living alone was a widespread desire will be considered in the next chapter, when we consider the growth of single person households.

7
Solo Living: Who Wants to Live Alone?

Introduction

> If there were unlimited apartments in Manhattan, we'd all be single forever (Miranda, *Sex and the City*)

> No one said anything about living alone. Or what it does to you. (Zadie Smith, *The Autograph Man*)

Living alone is perhaps the ultimate manifestation of individualisation, marked by access to space and time of one's own. Whilst for some this may be perceived as a blessing and for others a curse, as a domestic arrangement it is undoubtedly in the ascendancy. In the United Kingdom, nearly twice as many individuals now live in single person households than did so in the early 1960s, rising from 4 per cent in 1961 to 12 per cent in 2001 (Office for National Statistics, 2002). An increase in solo living has similarly been noted in the United States and Australia and, as in the United Kingdom, its incidence is predicted to rise throughout the early decades of the twenty-first century, representing the most significant change in household structure during this period. Of course, living alone covers a wide variety of experience: at one extreme associated with bedsit-style accommodation in poor quality housing stock, but at the other associated with a deliberately chosen 'urban chic' designer lifestyle: the world of 'loft living' and purpose-built apartments in expensive locations. Moreover, whilst the former scenario is popularly associated with social isolation, the latter is more associated with the cultivation of an active social life within the urban playground. There is clearly a world of difference between these two extremes, and a range of experience existing in the intermediate spaces, reflecting the unequal distribution of risk and life chances amongst different groups of young people today.

Having first left the parental home, very few individuals live alone *throughout* their lives. However, there is an increasing likelihood of living alone at least once during the life course, with solo living no longer just a prospect in old age following widowhood. Whilst older age groups still account for the biggest proportion of all single person households, the growth of such households in the United Kingdom is fastest amongst younger age groups. The proportions of UK households consisting of 15–29-year-old men living alone, for example, increased threefold between 1971 and 1999, and by just over fivefold amongst the 30–44-year-old age group, compared with a less than twofold increase amongst older groups (Office for National Statistics, 2001b). In Australia, conversely, the growth of solo living has been most pronounced amongst men in the 45-plus age group (Wulff, 2001), but the number of young people in their twenties who live alone has nonetheless almost doubled in the last 30 years (Australian Bureau of Statistics, 2001). Interestingly, whilst higher divorce rates undoubtedly account for some of the increase in the United Kingdom, and are the cause of fastest growth in Australia, it is still the case that never-married individuals form the largest groups amongst both young people in their twenties *and* in their thirties who live alone (Hall *et al.*, 1999; Wulff, 2001), notwithstanding the possibility of prior cohabitation amongst these groups. Living alone during one's early twenties remains relatively unusual in the United Kingdom, United States and Australia, yet becomes increasingly common amongst those in their late twenties and beyond. In the United States, for example, only 4 per cent of 20–24-year-olds were living alone in 2000, compared with 12 per cent of men and 8 per cent of women in their late twenties (Fields and Casper, 2001). Similarly, in the United Kingdom only 7 per cent of single childless 20–24-year-olds were living alone in the mid-1990s, compared with a fifth of single childless men in the 25–29-year-old age bracket and just under three in ten of their female peers, figures which are broadly in line with the proportions amongst this group who were living in shared households (Iacovou, 1998). Within a broader European context, it should be noted that solo living is very much a Northern phenomenon. The incidence of single person households is particularly high in Denmark, accounting for the living arrangements of a staggering 78 and 86 per cent respectively of single 25–29-year-old men and women without children (equivalent to just over a third and a fifth respectively of *all* young people in this age group), compared with only 2 and 3 per cent of their Portuguese peers, nine-tenths of whom remain within the parental home whilst single and childless (ibid.).

Living alone for varying periods of time is, then, an increasingly common living arrangement amongst single young adults in Northern Europe, the United States and Australia, and might be regarded as further evidence of the trend towards individualised lifestyles within these countries. But to what degree is solo living considered desirable by young people? Is it regarded as the ultimate statement of independence? Or is it viewed negatively as a form of social isolation? In this chapter we seek to explore these questions by first drawing together existing literature on single person households. The literature reveals a polarisation of experience, ranging from affluent single urbanites living in prestigious developments in areas such as London's Docklands or Sydney's revived inner city areas, through to disadvantaged young adults living in poor quality bedsits in rundown urban districts. The chapter will then move on to consider the views and experiences of the young people involved in our own research. Strikingly, living alone was viewed as a relatively unattractive option by most of the young people we met, most of whom stated emphatically that they would rather continue to share than live alone, and would only move out of shared accommodation in order to move in with a partner. These responses were related partly to the additional costs of living alone, but mainly revolved around the perceived social isolation of living alone. Of course, if we had interviewed a group of individuals already living alone, we might have met with very different responses, an issue we explore in the conclusion to this chapter.

From rising damp[1] to loft living: diversity in single person households

Hall *et al.* (1999) have noted that the general increase in solo living is attributable to three factors: the changing composition of the population, a changing propensity towards living alone, and the more widespread economic means to do so. With regard to the first of these, the later age of marriage, higher rates of divorce, and the increase in childlessness and later childbirth are most relevant to young people's experiences of solo living. These changes have fed into an increased propensity to live alone at different points in the life course, including in one's

---

[1] 'Rising Damp' was the title of a popular 1970s UK sitcom starring Leonard Rossiter as the live-in landlord of a house divided into bedsits. It is frequently reshown on British television.

younger years, whilst the economic circumstances of some groups of young adults have rendered solo living more affordable, thus creating a market in single person accommodation of a relatively high minimum standard. Importantly, those who live alone through choice are likely to be considerably more affluent than those who live alone involuntarily, the latter group including not only those limited by financial circumstances to live in poor quality bedsit-style accommodation, for example, but also those who find themselves living alone (often without a change of address) as a temporary response to circumstances such as relationship breakdown or the death of a partner.

Single person households occupied by younger people have a very distinctive geography in comparison with those occupied by older age groups. Specifically, they are a largely urban phenomenon, although their incidence within suburban and rural areas within the United Kingdom has nonetheless increased in line with the general rise in solo living amongst younger adults. Hall *et al.* (1999) note the particularly high incidence of lone person households in 'world cities' such as London, Paris or New York, but also point to relatively high rates in other UK cities such as Brighton, Manchester and Newcastle. In their view, the growth of single person households in these locations is not only attributable to demographic change, but also cannot be divorced from changing urban economies, linked to professionalisation and shifts in the housing market. On this last point, many cities are seeking to promote city centre residence as a key element of urban regeneration, and the market has responded with an array of redevelopment schemes aimed largely at childless young professionals (Ley, 1996; Smith, 1996).

Hall *et al.* (1999) expand on this connection by tracing the particularly dramatic growth in solo living in the United Kingdom amongst people from the professional and intermediate classes. In 1971, such individuals accounted for a quarter of all solo dwellers of working age, a figure which had risen to just over a third by 1991, with particularly rapid growth during the 1980s. Amongst younger members of the professional classes, the shift was similarly dramatic: 25–29-year-olds from Social Class I accounted for just 6 per cent of all those living alone in 1971, 13 per cent in 1981 and 19 per cent in 1991. There has also been a particularly pronounced skew towards the 'professionalisation' of single person households consisting of women, with the overall social class profile of women who live alone almost identical to that of men, despite their under-representation within the higher social classes in the workplace. These trends are even more pronounced within capital cities, where solo dwellers tend to be of a higher social status than their peers elsewhere.

This shift contributes to a central component of many studies of urban gentrification. As Smith (1996) has argued, 'popular among gentrification theorists is the notion that young, usually professional, middle class people have changed their lifestyle...(W)ith the trend toward fewer children, postponed marriages and a fast-rising divorce rate, younger home-buyers and renters are trading in the tarnished dreams of their parents for a new dream defined in urban rather than suburban terms' (Smith, 1996: 52). These shifts are captured in a number of recent studies of the growth of city centre living in various cities around the globe. Taylor *et al.* (1996), for example, have highlighted the emergence in Manchester, UK (the host city of the 2002 Commonwealth Games) of a new breed of young 'cultural professionals' living in gentrified areas, often in converted warehouses and disused office blocks in city centre locations. Many of these developments are located within the city's 'Gay Village', and contribute to a distinctive lifestyle amongst more affluent members of the city's large gay and lesbian community (Skeggs, 1999). Whilst the number of young professionals living in the city centre is relatively small, their presence is nonetheless affecting Manchester's physical landscape, with new facilities such as health clubs, cafe bars, restaurants and grocery stores springing up in response to growing demand. For those able to afford such housing options, these gentrified areas offer the opportunity to be close to the action. Decisions to live in the city centre, then, 'imply some very contemporary choices', including 'the attempt to identify oneself – to 'distinguish oneself'... as a member of the fast-moving vanguard of Manchester's cultural professional class', and constitute 'an attempt to construct a flexible individual life project, surrounded by a range of alternative diversions, pleasures and challenges' (Taylor *et al.*, 1996: 295).

A number of studies have also explored the growing demand for inner-city living amongst young adults in Australia and New Zealand (Vipond *et al.*, 1998; Morrison and McMurray, 1999; Watling, 1999). Each points to the transformation of established 'downtown' areas and the growing appeal of living, working and socialising in the same location. Commenting on the apartment boom in inner-city Melbourne, Watling (1999) notes for instance that 'the flat and the bedsit of the past, with their associations with cheap temporary rental accommodation and high-rise public housing, have been rehabilitated to become the apartment and the studio, apparently now the choice for many of the fashionable and wealthy' (p. 100). Vipond *et al.* (1998) similarly note the demand for inner-city accommodation amongst under-35-year-olds in Sydney (who in 1996 accounted for just under a third of all residents in inner Sydney, compared with just over a fifth in outer Sydney). Morrison and McMurray (1999) point to a similar trend in New Zealand's capital city, Wellington, highlighting a desire amongst those opting into the city centre for an alternative to high-maintenance housing in the outer suburbs. They note that young people in their early twenties are over-represented amongst Wellington's apartment-dwellers, and that apartment-dwellers amongst younger age groups tend to be unattached, either living alone or with friends. Interestingly, Morrison and McMurray argue that these new apartments are not targeted exclusively at the rich, but are meeting the demands of middle-income households for 'downtown living'. They also note the particular importance to apartment-dwellers in their twenties and early thirties of close proximity not only to shops and recreational spaces, but also to friends and relatives.

Hall *et al.*'s (1999) study of solo dwellers living and working in London's Docklands offers insights into the attitudes towards their living arrangements of a group made up largely of professionals. A third of the sample were under 35 years of age. Most had moved frequently within London before moving to their current homes, and most had experienced shared housing. All but one stated that their current decision to live alone represented a deliberate and positive choice, although in several cases the precipitating factor had been a relationship break-down. Nonetheless, a strong desire for independence emerged as an important reason for living alone, alongside the need for time and space of one's own. None considered him or herself to be lonely; many spent weekends with otherwise non-resident partners, and all nurtured a range of close relationships outside of their homes, although this was more of an effort for some than for others. In contrast to city centre living in Manchester, however, many felt that the supporting infra-structure in Docklands was inadequate for their needs. As one woman noted, 'I couldn't live here if I wasn't always out'.

Despite the focus so far on the growth of solo living in fashionable downtown locations, it should be noted that such housing is still very much a minority option. Situated at the other end of the spectrum of solo living arrangements is a group of rather less privileged individuals, consisting of young people living alone in poor quality housing, often in bedsit-style accommodation. Indeed, bedsits are a living arrangement which – at least until recently – have perhaps best represented the popular image of solo living amongst younger people. In contrast to the purpose-built developments inhabited by young professionals, bedsit accommodation tends to be located within large pre-1919 houses. These houses are usually sub-divided into single rooms which are rented out on an individual basis, and tenants rarely have exclusive use of cooking or washing facilities. Bedsits also have a relatively poor record of safety, particularly in relation to fire regulations, and are highly likely to be in some state of disrepair. There were approximately 220,000 bed-sitting rooms in England in 1996, distributed across 56,000 dwellings (DETR, 1999). Just under half of these bedsits housed a single adult living alone, with approximately 40 per cent of all bedsit dwellers aged under 30, and 75 per cent male. Seven out of ten residents were in employment, but many only part-time, and six out of ten earned less than £10,000 per annum. Unsurprisingly, half of all tenants were in receipt of housing benefit. Indeed, under-25-year-olds claiming housing benefit not uncommonly end up living in bedsit-style accommodation, rather than the type of shared accommodation described in the previous chapter, as the regulations governing the single room rent define a single room in shared accommodation in terms of the exclusive use of a bedroom, the shared use of kitchen and bathroom facilities, and *no* access to a separate or shared living room (Kemp and Rugg, 1998).

The provision of social housing targeted specifically at single young adults is relatively unusual. Some local authorities have experimented with the exclusive allocation to younger tenants of flats and apartments in housing estates where it is difficult to let accommodation to other groups, particularly to families and the elderly. Stewart and Stewart (1988) note that these schemes are often centred on high rise developments in inner-city locations, with high levels of disrepair. Moreover, Anderson (1999) has noted that younger tenants (particularly those still in their teens) are often perceived to be a problematic group, with many local authorities insisting on provision of support by some other agency in order for a young person to qualify for council housing. Some housing associations and the voluntary sector have also stepped in to provide purpose-built transitional accommodation for single young adults deemed to be in housing need (Quilgars and Pleace, 1999). Such provision often consists of hostel-type accommodation, or developments of self-contained one bedroom flats, with access to a common room if so desired, and with tenants having access to a support worker to assist them in their transition. Many schemes are also part of the growing foyer movement across Europe, a scheme whereby accommodation is tied to provision of support for employment and/or training.

Supported schemes of this nature tend to be targeted at vulnerable young people in their late teens or early twenties, particularly at the point at which they first leave the parental home. They are by no means a mainstream form of provision, although one could argue that in certain important respects there is little difference between a supported housing scheme and certain types of university-provided student accommodation – both, after all, provide affordable accommodation during a critical time of transition. This of course reinforces the degree to which student status provides a relatively cushioned transitional pathway into the housing market. For non-students seeking to leave home at a similar age to their student peers, there are few guaranteed routes into independent housing, whereas students expect to be able to reap the benefits of access to a niche housing market, whether in the form of halls of residence or in the privately rented student housing sector. It is also striking to observe that bedsit living remains relatively unusual amongst young graduates, a group who are more likely to move into privately rented self-contained shared housing than into bedsits, often secured through networks of friends or acquaintances with whom they may have shared as students. Amongst the graduates involved in our research, for example, only three had the experience of living alone in a bedsit. It is to the experiences of our respondents, and their perceptions of solo living more generally, to which we now turn.

Who wants to live alone?

Beck and Beck-Gernsheim (2002) have coined the term 'self-culture' to describe 'the compulsion and the pleasure of leading an insecure life of one's own and co-ordinating it with the distinctive lives of other people' (p. 42). They argue that the emergence of this 'self-culture' is, then, both simultaneously a key manifestation *and* a consequence of the individualisation processes prevalent within late modernity. They emphasise their argument by highlighting specific demographic changes within western societies, including the rise of single person households and 'the correspondingly high value placed on separateness in every lifestyle', expressed in 'the basic need – developed and established historically – for "space" and "time of one's own"' (p. 43). Access to personal space and time have, then, they contend, become increasingly valuable commodities within a world of increased risk and uncertainty, and the degree of access that a young person has to these commodities is arguably an important consideration in young people's housing choices. Nonetheless, the spatial and temporal aspects of household formation amongst young adults have tended not to receive explicit recognition, despite, for example, the centrality to many young people's leaving home narratives of the need to escape from a living arrangement where space and time are rarely their own, and the importance of addressing related issues within the organisation of shared households. Living alone can then provide the ultimate sense of freedom and self-determination: 'it's *my* space and I can spend my time within it how *I* choose!'

This rather assumes that living alone is conducted within a space where someone would be happy to spend a considerable amount of time on their own. For young people with limited resources or at the start of their housing career, however, this is often not the case. This is apparent in the accounts of the eight young people involved in the biographical interviewing phase of our research who had previous experience of living alone, four in bedsits and four in self-contained flats and houses (an additional four sharers had experience of living alone, but did not participate in the one-to-one interviews). Bedsit conditions had been universally poor for the four young men who had experienced them. Nathan (household 14), for example, had lived for a year as an undergraduate in a six foot by ten foot attic room containing a sink, fireplace, bed, table, an armchair and a chest of drawers with a Baby Belling cooker on top:

> I had about two square feet of space in there, to actually move around in. Half the room was covered with a sloping ceiling there, anyway, and it was stinking hot. I had a lovely view of the gasworks out the window ... It was always a let down coming home again to that place, I never enjoyed it. Again, space, *I didn't have any space at all*. Definitely not a home. It was just somewhere to eat and sleep and to do my assignments if I couldn't be bothered to go into the library (our emphasis).

Even though Nathan had exclusive control of his own space, he clearly did not perceive it to be a desirable space, nor did he feel that he had sufficient space. However, in some cases the mere possession of any space to call one's own can represent progression, as illustrated by Jimmy's rather more complex relationship to his year of living in a bedsit (household 18). He described his bedsit as 'dirty', 'dingy', 'noisy' and generally 'disgusting', yet having previously been forced to return to his mother's house for six weeks, and before that having lived for ten months in a rather disreputable hostel, he considered this stage in his housing career to be a step upwards, not least because his move coincided with getting a job after a long spell of unemployment. Indeed, he said that his bedsit eventually came to feel like home to him, helped by having acquired some drinking buddies from amongst the other residents. Nonetheless, throughout this period he had aspired to live somewhere rather nicer, and was very relieved when the opportunity arose to share a house with his brother and a friend.

Matt and Ivan's accounts of bedsit living centred less on the physical conditions of their accommodation, which had nonetheless been typ- ically poor, and focused instead on the social aspects of living alone. Matt (household 13) described his 'dismal' bedsit in Liverpool whilst a postgraduate student as 'about the most isolating place I've ever lived in'. Ivan too hated his spell of bedsit living (household 22), describing it as 'bleeding awful', made worse by having a room next door to some- one who played music at high volume at all hours, and living across the landing from someone he described as a thug. He too hated the sense of isolation that came with living alone, and talked of there being 'no one there to notice' when things happened in his life. In Ivan's view:

> Living alone is bloody crap, to be honest...it's dull...I mean like normally when I was living in a bedsit I'd be storing up things, and at work the next day for the next hour no one would shut me up.

Ivan also noted that living in a bedsit had impacted negatively on his sexual freedom. He gave the example of 'pulling a bird' at a nightclub, yet not feeling able to take her back to his place. As the woman in ques- tion still lived with her parents, neither had they been able to return to her home: 'I had to blow her out simply because of my room, the state it was in, and that's a bad situation to be in.'

The other four who had lived alone had done so in self-contained apartments and houses rather than bedsits. Kath (household 22) had rented an entire house whilst studying for a masters degree for the sum of only £25 a week. The house had belonged to a friend's late father, and she lived there as a favour to the friend. Initially she lived alone, with most of the rooms in the house full of packing cases containing the belongings of the deceased owner, although eventually her sister had moved in to keep her company. Kath had not enjoyed living there alone, and had consequently spent a lot of her time at her boyfriend's house. Randall (household 13) had also lived alone for a while follow- ing the break-up of a long-term relationship in his early thirties. He acknowledged the sexual freedom that living alone had given him, but had eventually moved into a commune for what he described as 'a long retreat'. He is now the joint owner of a communal household, and cannot foresee a time when he would ever live alone again: 'I am a communal beast. I have lived on my own, but it doesn't actually suit me very well.'

The experiences of Ellie and Miles raise other important issues concerning the conditions of solo living. Ellie's story points to the importance of perceptions of personal security in relation to one's living arrangements. Ellie (household 6) had briefly lived alone in her early twenties after having lived in a variety of shared households, including two spells of cohabitation with boyfriends in shared households. On the break-up of the second of these relationships, she had moved into the spare room of a friend of her ex-boyfriend, but this arrangement had not worked out: 'I thought: time for independence, not relying on other people'. Consequently she had found a one bedroom flat that was self-contained except for a shared bathroom, accessible through her kitchen. Her landlord had promised to rent the second flat to a woman, but had instead let it to a young man, and to her dismay she had entered her flat one day to find one of his friends helping himself to a drink of water in her kitchen. She had felt unsafe in the flat after this incident, and for the remaining eight weeks of her lease had preferred to sleep on friends' floors than in her flat. Ellie's experiences had led her to reappraise her self-identity as an independent person:

> I had this really romantic idea of living on my own, it would be suddenly great and I'd have all my own space and I'd be able to decorate – well, not decorate it, but put all my own things up and it would be fantastic and I would spend all these evenings in watching telly because I could. And have my own space because I could and I'd cook for myself every night and the fridge would be empty because nobody else would be cramming it full of stuff and it wasn't like that at all. And it broke every expectation and it was horrible. It's funny, because at the time I was thinking about buying and I had all these romantic expectations of buying a house as well, and it would be great and I'd just spend all my nights decorating it. And I think that made me realise that I'm just not that sort of person and that I'm just hopeless at occupying myself . . . *And so I think it changed my view of me a lot* (our emphasis).

Lastly, Miles's story highlights the difficulty of finding decent quality accommodation whilst living alone, one of the factors that led many of our respondents to continue to share in order to maintain the standards of their housing. Miles (household 14) had lived alone in three consecutive flats on first relocating to Southampton, and would happily have continued to live in the third of these if his work had not taken him away from the city for a while. He had initially decided to live alone because he no longer wanted to share with others: 'I thought I'd come to the stage when I wanted a flat of my own, or somewhere of my own.' His early experiences of living alone, however, had been marred by his lack of resources and far from being able to move into his desired 'yuppie flat in a converted warehouse', his first flat was an unfurnished and unheated maisonette some distance from his workplace. After the six-month tenancy had expired, he had decided to move nearer to his workplace, but had inadvertently moved to a fairly rough area of the city whilst nonetheless paying over the odds for his rent. Finally, he had moved to an affordable but rather small studio flat near his workplace, and had felt quite settled there until his move away from the city and his subsequent decision to share on his return.

Of the eight young people who had prior experience of living alone, only Nathan now felt that he would like to live alone again at some future point, although for the time being he preferred to continue to share. As he noted, 'in my most depressed moments, I do still see myself living in a shared house when I'm 50 years old . . . It's fine for a young person, but I really want somewhere where I can walk around in my pants and just sit watching the telly – and not have to consider other people'. In contrast, Miles was set to move in with his girlfriend, whilst all the others were committed to sharing until such time as they felt ready to move in with a partner. The main drawback to future solo living was seen very much in terms of the lack of company, rarely a problem in shared housing. Jimmy (household 18), for example, noted that 'I couldn't go back to a house and know that no one is going to come in eventually. It would just feel cold'.

Whilst one might think that the reluctance to live alone amongst those who had already done so was attributable to their largely negative experiences, it transpired that living alone was viewed with ambivalence by the majority of those we interviewed, not just those whose first-hand experiences had served to deter them. Only seven respondents willingly embraced the possibility of living alone in the immediate future, in most cases – they hoped – in the form of an owner-occupied house or flat. However, one young woman in this group acknowledged that this was probably an unrealistic aspiration, whilst four others were aware that even if they were able to buy a place of their own they would probably have to take in housemates to cover their costs, at least initially. Nell (household 21) was particularly insistent that she would *not* share with a partner if she was able to secure a place of her own. However, our last contact with Nell revealed that she had indeed achieved her ambition of buying a flat, but had invited her boyfriend to live with her. They are now engaged to be married. Similarly, Sean (household 8), one of only two aspirant solo dwellers who believed that they could afford to live alone, recently bought a house with his girlfriend, again after having earlier vowed not to do so. Jules (household 1) was the most enthusiastic about the potential of living alone, feeling that this was the logical next step after four years of sharing with nursing friends:

> I've done the shared house thing, and I really enjoyed it, but now I'm more content with myself and my own company. And I could quite happily live on my own and have like my own mess and my own ways of doing things. Because I just feel happier with myself now ... I feel more equipped to live on my own inside.

Eight others did not rule out the possibility of living alone if the circumstances arose, but only as a default option rather than a positive choice. Some amongst this group argued, for example, that they would choose to live alone if the only alternative was to share with strangers, but continuing to live with friends or moving in with a partner were both considered to be preferable. Similarly, both Kim (household 8) and Viv's (household 17) prime motivation was to move into a place of their own, alone if necessary, but their clear preference was to do this with a partner. It should of course be noted that several of our respondents had already achieved the status of a place of their own, in the sense that they were the resident owners of their shared houses. Nonetheless, as we saw in the last chapter, most were happy to share their houses, although Warren (household 10) felt that he could quite easily live alone if necessary, his response hinting at both the positive and the negative aspects of living alone:

> I'm sure I could live on my own because when I first moved into the house I was here for about three weeks on my own before anybody else moved in. The first week I hated coming in and nobody about ... I'd just come in and eat my meal and the telephone wouldn't ring and I'd just get bored with the telly and have a bath and go to bed. And I thought 'God!' But then after a week or so I actually revelled in the solitude. I really liked it. I started going out and going into pubs and started to go out more meeting new people and this sort of thing, and I knew that I had the solitude to come back to, or that I could bring people back home and have a coffee or a drink. And then everybody would wend their merry way and I'd be left here and I'd go off to bed and back on my own again ... So I think I'd be

happy either way. Easier to be happy on your own, because if you're sharing with the wrong people then it's a nightmare. But luckily I'm sharing with the right people and so I'm perfectly happy sharing my home with other people.

In contrast, almost twice as many young people were emphatic that living alone had little or no attraction to them, and could not imagine choosing to live by themselves in the foreseeable future. A number of reasons emerged across the group, including the loss of financial savings accrued from sharing and, for a young woman who suffered from epilepsy, the importance of having someone around in case she had a fit. However, by far the most common reason for rejecting solo living was the assumption of loneliness, boredom and isolation, and the overwhelming desire for company. Liz (household 1), for example, described her compulsion to make telephone calls to friends and families even when alone in the house for only a few hours, whilst Paul (household 7) talked of his appreciation of always having someone around in the house to keep him company: 'it's great and I do like that, and yeah I'd much rather have that than the added privacy of having a flat to myself.' Another young man felt that returning home to an empty house would effectively mark the end of his day, regardless of the time at which he returned, as there would be no one at home with whom to share his evening.

Overall, then, the majority of respondents actually enjoyed living with others, and felt that they would miss the daily interaction with their housemates if they chose to live alone. This overwhelming desire for company rather than solitude might appear surprising, given that so many of our respondents also highlighted various tensions and difficulties arising from a lack of privacy in shared households. Indeed, Morgan (1996) has argued that issues of time and space are not only crucial to the study of households, but are often difficult to disentangle from issues of 'bodily density' within living spaces, a term he uses to refer to spatial proximity between household members, and to the monitoring and knowledge of each others' bodies which comes with such proximity. Housemates (whether friends, family members or even partners) may presume to know more about each other's lives than might sometimes be considered appropriate, for example, and on occasions may be concerned to monitor aspects of household and personal cleanliness, or each others' sexual behaviour and eating habits. However, for many of our respondents the monitoring of each other's bodies in space and time was, perhaps surprisingly, a valued and comforting feature of sharing (albeit within limits), and an aspect of domestic life that they claimed they would miss if living alone.

Conclusion

In this chapter we have explored the growth of solo living amongst younger adults. Demographers have tracked the changing profile of single person households, yet little research has focused specifically on the day-to-day experiences of single young adults who live alone. The literature on gentrification has provided us with some limited insights into the experiences of the archetypal 'yuppie' choosing to live alone within the urban playground, but in a reversal of the usual trend within the sociology of youth, we know even less about the everyday experiences of less advantaged solo dwellers. The young professionals who have gradually colonised city centre space over the last few decades appear to be a very distinct – and relatively small – group: on the whole, affluent white middle class professionals, exercising a high degree of choice and reflexivity in their living arrangements. Not surprisingly, the limited evidence available would seem to suggest that those who live alone through choice enjoy the experience and value the opportunity to exercise control over their own time and space. In contrast, the archetypal bedsit dweller is unlikely to be living in such an arrangement from choice, and will probably be all too well aware of the limitations of spending too much time alone in too little space. Nonetheless, some bedsit dwellers may still consider their situation an improvement on former shared living arrangements, where they may have had too little time alone, albeit in a potentially larger space.

Amongst the young people involved in our own research, there was a marked lack of enthusiasm for the prospect of living alone, although in only a small number of cases was this based on prior experience. Only a minority could see the appeal of having access to time and space of one's own, with the majority claiming that they valued the company of others above the benefits that might accrue from having greater privacy. The majority, then, said that they would only consider moving out of shared accommodation in order to live with a partner, or if they faced the prospect of otherwise sharing with strangers. We are of course aware that the experiences of the young people involved in our research represent a very partial account of the appeal or otherwise of living alone amongst twenty-somethings. This is a group which generally – but by no means universally – shared a strong commitment to living with others, so it is not surprising that as a group they tended to express a preference for sharing over solo living. We certainly do not argue that their views are typical, but they nonetheless represent the views of a particular sub-group of young people. More generally, of course, it is likely that those who actually live alone are by definition more sympathetic to solo living, although those who did have some prior experience had been less than enamoured with this part of their housing career.

Significantly, however, where solo living did have an appeal it tended to be amongst those for whom the disadvantages of constant company were beginning to outweigh the advantages. This suggests that shared living is regarded by many single young people as a rite of passage that one enjoys whilst the going is good (and the going *was* still good at the point at which we interviewed most of our respondents), but that once the balance shifts, the allure of living alone or with a partner becomes greater. It is also the case, of course, that solo living in at least half-decent accommodation tends to become more affordable with increased earnings and advancing age, hence its growth amongst those in their late twenties in particular. This is important: just as shared housing on a graduate income appears to be qualitatively different to shared housing as a student, so living alone later in one's housing career is likely to be more attractive than living alone earlier in that career.

In closing this chapter, we end our consideration of the specific living arrangements of single young adults: living with parents, living in student accommodation, living in shared housing and living alone. The next three chapters shift the focus away from the specific context of young people's living arrangements to focus more on their relationships with a range of intimate others: with parents, with friends, with partners, and to consider how contemporary young adults are redefining 'home' and 'settling down'. As in previous chapters, we begin each of these chapters with an overview of some of the key trends and themes in research in these areas, and we then illuminate some of these themes in the specific context of the experiences of the house sharers involved in our own research.

8
Friends and Family

Introduction

> I know I've got it great, really. I've got good friends, good job, loving family, total freedom, and long bubble baths. What more could there be? (Ally McBeal, *Ally McBeal*)

> We're right behind you, only further back. (Xander, *Buffy the Vampire Slayer*)

Since its launch in 2000, Friends Reunited – a website devoted to catching up with former school friends – has become one of the most popular websites in the United Kingdom. With over eight million members and about five to ten thousand new members joining every day, it has spawned rival websites and at least one spoof site, Bullies Reunited, and now sells a series of Friends Reunited 'nostalgic music' CDs and related merchandise. As a measure of its success, and of the simplicity of the idea underpinning it, it has now extended its coverage to other countries, including Australia and South Africa. Its popularity arguably reflects a sense of nostalgia for the straightforwardness of childhood friendship, but also reinforces what seems to be a widely held ideal concerning the increased significance of friendship within contemporary society. Such a view is similarly reinforced by the popularity of any number of friendship-based sitcoms, with the hugely popular *Friends* leading the way in a paean of praise to contemporary friendship. Partners and family members may, after all, let you down, but at the end of the day old friends are, as the theme tune of *Friends* suggests, always 'there for you' – and, should you have mislaid them, Friends Reunited can now help you find them.

In Chapter 3, we introduced the arguments of a number of writers who lend varying degrees of support to the view that friendship has become more important within contemporary society. Giddens (1992), for example, contends that the sphere of intimacy is undergoing considerable transformation, with the pure relationship between friends forming the prototype for *all* intimate relationships in late modernity. Pahl (2000) has further argued that one of the reasons why friendship has taken on greater significance is the increasing inability of family members to provide day-to-day practical support to each other, so that friends are now stepping in to fill the gap. In the case of young adults, this needs to be understood within the context of the later age of couple formation. As the age of first marriage creeps ever higher amongst heterosexual young adults, it might be reasonable to assume that friends will inevitably take on greater significance within young people's lives, particularly during periods between partners. As a consequence, we now expect far more of our friendships than ever used to be the case. Indeed, Beck (1992) has even argued that friendship is 'the pleasure offered by the single life' (p. 122). Jamieson (1999), however, poses an important question when she asks '*are* good friends all you need?' Or is it the case that we actually continue to remain largely reliant on family members and sexual partners?

Where single young adults actually *live* with their friends, however, we might expect those friendships to take on increased importance, with the potential for housemates to adopt some of the supportive roles otherwise adopted by family members or partners. This chapter, and the one that follows, explore this contention amongst the sharers involved in our research. We start with an overview of some of the key themes within the rather scant existing literature on friendship and family relationships amongst single twenty-somethings. We then consider the conduct and relative importance of sharers' relationships with housemates on the one hand and family members on the other, whilst the following chapter pursues these themes in relation to sharers' sexual relationships. In our view, platonic friendship with housemates has the potential to provide an important source of pleasure and support within the lives of single young adults. Nonetheless, family members, particularly parents, continue to be important and influential figures within their lives, albeit often within a framework of obligation and duty.

Exploring networks of intimacy amongst twenty-somethings: friends and family

The ability to form friendships in childhood and as a teenager is regarded by developmental psychologists as an extremely important developmental task, with failure in this sphere having serious negative consequences for adult development. 'Adolescence' is widely constructed as a period when young people are strongly peer-orientated, to the point that 'the sense of adolescents and peer pressure being synonymous has entered the realm of the common sense' (Lesko, 2001: 4). Functionalist sociologists have also pointed to the crucial role played by young people's friendships in easing the transition between the traditional values and culture of the family of origin, and the values and cultural norms of the wider adult world. Within both of these frameworks, friendships developed in one's childhood and late teens are viewed as essentially transitory: to achieve full adult status, young people are expected to transfer their primary affections away from childhood friends towards potential sexual partners and, ultimately, towards their 'life partner' and, possibly, their own children. From this perspective, if platonic friendships are indeed taking on greater significance in young people's lives, and at the expense of establishing couple relationships, this might be regarded as evidence of the delayed attainment of maturity amongst contemporary youth rather than evidence of a progressive transformation of intimacy. We noted in Chapter 3, for example, that Côté (2000) has linked this trend to the increased 'other directedness' of contemporary youth, a trait which he associates with a disregard for generational continuity.

It is also widely assumed that the older a person becomes, the less attached they become to their family of origin. Gillies (2000) has noted, for example, that the overriding focus of much youth research on transitions in the spheres of employment, housing and partnership formation as an essentially individualised experience tends to reinforce a view that these transitions exist largely independently of family life, with no apparent repercussions for other family members. As such, young people's relationships with their parents are often portrayed as being characterised by a straightforward transition from dependence to independence. This is despite evidence of the often reciprocal transfer of emotional and financial resources between parents and their children, and the increased likelihood of returns to the parental home on first leaving (Jones, 1995a,b). Moreover, studies of the negotiation of responsibility and obligation amongst parents and their adult children suggest that parent–child relationships in many respects become increasingly *inter*dependent, rather than less so, with advancing age (Finch and Mason, 1993). A recent survey found, for example, that nearly one in four young people in their twenties who had already left home had given financial help to their parents at some point (Social Market Foundation, 2002). Gillies argues, then, that,

> The essentially normative framework for understanding the family life of young people works to obscure the emotional, material and economic dependence many people continue to share with their families throughout their lives. Rather than allowing the researcher to explore the ways in which family relationships change and develop over the course of individual lifetimes, the concept of 'transition' pre-interprets the direction of those changes by constructing a theoretical template to interpret the experiences of young people and their families (Gillies, 2000: 222).

For as long as youth researchers continue to focus on *individuals* in transition, this framework will be difficult to resist. Consequently, the degree to which the transitional pathways of individual young adults are in fact closely entwined with those of their friends, partners and family tends to remain obscured (Heath, 2002).

Despite the widely held nature of these assumptions about changing loyalties and levels of dependency, surprisingly little empirical research has been conducted specifically on the networks of intimacy of single twenty-somethings, in contrast to the relatively established literatures on friendship and family commitments amongst teenagers and the middle aged. Studies of teenage friendships have pinpointed a number of key themes. They have, for example, tended to emphasise the particular intensity of female friendships, and often distinguish between girls' close dyadic relationships and boys' more loosely affiliated 'gang-based' friendships (Coleman and Hendry, 1999). In contrast, Schneider and Stevenson (1999) suggest that friendship groups amongst American teenagers of both sexes are increasingly fluid: 'students often move from one group to another, and friendships change over a period of a few weeks or months. Best friends are few, and students frequently refer to peers as "acquaintances" or "associates"' (p. 190). They also note that outside of school hours American teenagers spend twice as much time alone or with family members than they do with their friends, suggesting that the contemporary American teenager is not a particularly social animal beyond the realms of the nuclear family.

Existing literature also suggests that same-sex friendships are the norm during the early to mid-teen years, followed by the development of mixed-sex friendship groups in one's late teens (Banks *et al.*, 1992). Some writers have argued that heterosexual young women tend to prioritise their relationships with boyfriends over those with their girlfriends during their teen years, often effectively dropping their female friends on acquiring a boyfriend, whilst heterosexual young men experience few, if any, restrictions on the continuation of their male friendships on acquiring a girlfriend (Griffin, 1985). This view has been challenged by Morris and Fuller (1999), who argue that heterosexual young women develop strategies to allow for the simultaneous maintenance of relationships with boyfriends and same-sex friends. Nonetheless, some of the literature on friendship amongst older heterosexual women suggests that the marginalisation of female friends may continue past marriage. O' Connor's (1992) study of working-class married women, for example, found that only a minority claimed to have a close female confidante. Other studies, however, suggest that female friendships remain important to married women; as Jamieson (1999) notes, many married women may use their female friendships 'to compensate for the lack of emotional intimacy in their marriage and to encourage each other to stick with it despite the failings' (p. 102).

But what about the friendships of twenty-something singletons? Do they have more in common with teenage friendships or with those of older individuals? Mackay (1997), writing in an Australian context, has argued that members of what he calls 'the options generation' place a strong emphasis on cultivating friendships with both men and women, and that they tend to 'stick with the group' rather than pairing off. He notes too that these close platonic friendships can be misinterpreted by older generations, who find it hard to believe that there is not a sexual element to these relationships. This assertion of a tendency amongst single young adults to form larger cross-gender friendship groupings is congruent with Maffesoli's contention, explored in earlier chapters, that we are living in a 'time of the tribes', with young people forming fluid allegiances across a number of different social contexts. Bennett (1999), for example, has highlighted the existence of neo-tribal friendship groupings within dance subculture, characterised not just by the inclusion of both men and women, but of men and women from a variety of different social backgrounds. Single sex friendship groups nonetheless remain important to many young adults, particularly in the context of 'the big night out' with 'the lads' or 'the girls'.

Pahl (2000) has argued that the recent expansion of higher education is a particularly significant factor in the recasting of friendship amongst young adults in their twenties, as it has provided increased opportunities for the expansion of existing friendship networks. He claims that friendships forged whilst at university have the potential to develop a particular potency, framed as they are by a time of often unparalleled transition, change and uncertainty, and that they are thus likely to continue well into adulthood:

> Learning to live on their own, away from family, forces young people to come to terms with who they are and how they want to live. Leaving college and seeking employment can be a very unsettling period and friends who supported them through their twenties are bonded with ties of gratitude and mutual experience (Pahl, 2000: 117).

Of course, not all university-based friendships survive beyond graduation, and there is no reason to assume that the formative relationships of non-graduates – those formed, for example, amongst workmates in a young person's first place of employment – may not take on similar significance. Pahl's broader point, however, is that university provides young people not only with the opportunity to expand their friendship networks, but also to *diversify* those networks quite dramatically. Given the social homogeneity of many university campuses, this may be an overly optimistic view of student friendships. Nonetheless, what may be of greater significance for the recasting of friendship amongst young adults is the exposure of increasing numbers of students to independent living arrangements, whether in halls of residence or in student households. Such arrangements provide an opportunity for young people to form intimate relationships at an accelerated pace, and in a group context. As one of the students in Kenyon's (1998) research on student households noted:

> You can have best mates back at home who you have known for sixteen years, but you have never lived with them so it has taken you, say, all that time to get to know them well. But you come to university and live with people and because you live with them you get to know them so much faster, you fit in sixteen years of getting to know them in three years. And it is at the time we really are becoming adults, so we are getting to know the developing adult in a way no one else does.

Of course, as we discussed in detail in Chapter 5, there has been a recent increase in the proportion of students who now remain within the parental home for the duration of their studies, a trend which has been associated with students from social backgrounds traditionally under-represented in higher education. The relatively privileged housing transition associated with a niche market of student accommodation remains, then, largely the preserve of more affluent students.

Alongside a relative lack of knowledge regarding the platonic friend-ships of single young adults in their twenties, we know even less about their family relationships during this period. In Chapter 4 we referred to some of the literature on young people's relationships with their parents whilst they remain within or are in the process of first leaving the parental home. But what about their relationships in the years following their departure? Many young people experience an improvement in their relationships with family members once they have moved away from the parental home, regardless of the circumstances of their leaving, and subsequently either continue to experience or manage to regain a strong sense of connection to the family home. Scott (1997) has argued, for example, that in general terms the family remains the primary concern in most people's lives. Younger people tend to make fewer references to family events than older people, but often because they are more likely to be geographically distant from members of their immediate family. Increased geographical distance rather than family breakdown has also been invoked by McGlone *et al.* (1999), alongside the pressures of work, as an explanation for their finding that visits between parents and children became less frequent in the mid-1990s in comparison with the mid-1980s. It is interesting to note in this context that a survey conducted in 2002 suggested that around a third of British twenty-somethings currently live over a hundred miles away from their parents, with a further third continuing to live within ten miles. The same survey nonetheless found that a quarter saw their parents at least once a week (with young women twice as likely to do so as their male peers), whilst half saw them at least once a month (Social Market Foundation, 2002).

More generally, however, the mechanisms by which parent–child relationships are nurtured and renegotiated once having left the parental home are under-researched, a neglect that contributes to the broader assumption, noted above, that family life becomes of marginal import-ance to young people once they have first left home. Despite this lack of empirical evidence, Giddens (1991) has nonetheless argued that parent–child relationships have the potential to develop facets of the pure rela-tionship. Whilst he feels that they 'stay partly distinct from the purview of the pure relationship' (p. 98) because of the unequal power relations that exist between parents and their children in childhood, he feels that as children get older there is at least the potential for an equalisation of their relationships: 'A person who has left home may keep in constant touch with his (*sic*) parents, as a matter of obligation; but reflexively ordered trust must be developed, involving mutually accepted commitment, if the relationship is to be deepened' (ibid.). This is arguably a tall order given that parent–child relationships invariably come 'with baggage'.

In the sections that follow, we draw upon data from the *Single Young Adults and Shared Household Living* project to explore two pivotal sets of relationships in the lives of sharers: their relationships with housemates and their relationships with their parents. The specific domestic setting of these relationships is crucial. In particular, we explore what can happen when friends become more than 'just friends' and become living companions. Do such friendships blur the traditional boundaries of friendship and family? And if so, what are the implications of setting up home with friends for how a young person relates to their parental home and how, in turn, their parents relate to their offspring's new home? We consider each of these points below.

Housemates: the new family?

Choosing to live with friends, or with people whom one anticipates will become good friends, subverts normative expectations of the place of platonic, non-kin relationships within most people's lives. Such relationships are more typically played out at a level above the territorial and social domain of the home and, on the occasions when friends enter the home to socialise, they tend to do so in ways that underline their continuing 'outsider' status and which also serve to maintain varying degrees of privacy and territoriality. Friends tend not to come and go as they please, for example, whilst certain household spaces usually remain out of bounds to visitors (Allan, 1986). In contrast, shared households blur the usual boundaries of public and private space that exist between friends. Nonetheless, friendships that are made and consolidated in the context of shared household living have the potential to be of long-standing significance in an individual's life, based on shared participation in important transitional experiences such as leaving home and standing on one's own feet for the first time, negotiating relationships with sexual partners away from the parental gaze, and learning how to cope with the idiosyncrasies of non-family members.

In Chapter 6 we argued that the coming together of individuals within shared households can be seen as an example of 'neo-tribalism'. However, in many cases the friendships that develop between housemates are far from fleeting and are of lasting significance. The biographies of two-thirds of the young people involved in our own research were, for example, already closely intertwined with those of their housemates. As noted in Chapter 6, 16 of the 25 households included at least two (and often all) residents whose friendships predated their current living arrangements, with housemates either having been students together, having worked together or having known each other since childhood. In the nine other households, close friendships had often developed between individuals who had initially moved in as strangers. It was commonplace for friendships with past housemates to have continued well beyond the life of the household in which they had originated, with many respondents stating that their current best friend(s) had at one time lived with them – or still did. Many housemates had developed strongly interdependent housing histories, brought together through the sharing of formative transitional experiences and in turn resulting in new levels of intimacy.

Particularly close relationships had developed, for example, amongst the four computer programmers (household 6). Three of them had first met at university six years previously, with two of them having subsequently lived together across six different households. All four women viewed their current household as a discrete social unit with a natural lifespan of its own, and they had no intention of finding a replacement tenant following the imminent departure of Hilary to move in with her boyfriend. Rather, they planned to keep the fourth bedroom free for return visits by Hilary, even though, with a shared tenancy agreement, this would increase the monthly rent of the remaining three by an additional £72 each – a third of their existing rent. Moreover, all four friends described Hilary's departure in terms reminiscent of a parent talking about the impending departure of a child from the parental home. The household members were also well aware that the closeness and degree of overlap that existed between their lives was regarded by outsiders as rather odd:

Ella: It's sort of a standing joke. There's a lot of talk [at work] about how close we are.

Hilary: People can't believe that we can live together and work together and socialise together and not hate each other's guts. But yeah, we've all just sort of slipped into doing stuff together.

Justine: People at work tend to see us as the four of us sticking together and they don't see anything else, they always say we're a night-mare, sort of really cliquey…I'm beginning to worry now about how people see us at work…'cos we went on holiday together as well, three of us, I think they thought that was really sad.

These comments underline the common-sense assumption that shared households are not sites where one would usually expect to find intimacy of this kind. Such closeness is evidently unsettling to outsiders and demands some sort of explanation, not least because it appears to breach the usual limits of platonic friendship. Scott and Jade's shared living arrangements (household 25), for example, were frequently questioned by friends and acquaintances who found it hard to believe that their relationship was purely platonic. The implications of domestic intimacy that can sometimes follow from living with friends may also prove to be unsettling to *sharers*, as we found when we interviewed Sam and Damien (household 24). Damien in particular was anxious to impress upon us that he and Sam shared solely for reasons of mutual convenience, as if we might otherwise have considered two single men choosing to live together to be sexually dubious. When asked whether or not they felt their living arrangements provided a source of mutual support, Damien responded defensively: 'I wouldn't say there's any sort of emotional feeling there – sounds a bit dodgy.' Similarly, when later in the interview we alluded to the practice of sharing clothes that we had discovered in several other households involved in our research, including some of the all-male households, Damien's response was one of incredulity: 'were they gay?'

Damien's reaction was the exception that proved the rule; in most other households, sharers were clearly proud of the friendships they had nurtured within the context of their living arrangements. Many households demonstrated a strong sense of mutual commitment between their respective members not just through acknowledging the importance of the emotional support they provided to each other on a regular basis, but also through a variety of very practical measures: reducing noise levels if someone had gone to bed early, for example, telephoning a sick housemate from work to check they were alright, cooking for each other, or giving each other lifts at night to avoid walking home in the dark. Housemates in these households actively sought to make their shared living space – however temporary they perceived it to be – as supportive an environment as possible: a stark contrast to some of the abiding stereotypes of life in shared households. Indeed, Carole, who had lived with Jamie in household 8 for the previous six years, favourably compared the emotional support she received from housemates with that which she received from partners:

> I think it's just the idea that someone's there for you. I mean I think, you know, obviously some people get that through being in a

relationship or boyfriends or whatever...whereas it's like, I like doing my own thing. It's fine when I'm in a relationship, but when I'm not in a relationship I'm very happy. Because I think I've still got a close relationship and a lot of support [within the household]. And you know that if things are bad, whatever, I don't have to drive to somewhere, I don't have to pick up the phone, I can just chat to the people around. And it's the same for them.

For these reasons, Carole spoke of her ambivalence concerning the possibility of moving in with her current boyfriend, given that partners tended to come and go, whereas her friendships had the potential to be more enduring.

The possibility of creating a warm and supportive environment with friends is an aspect of shared living which may hold a particular appeal for individuals – like Carole – who, whether straight or gay, do not readily aspire to traditional patterns of family formation. Outlet, a London-based lesbian and gay shared accommodation service (one of whose directors is *Big Brother 2001*'s Josh), emphasised these aspects within early publicity material, stressing the way in which sharing with like-minded individuals can facilitate friendship and mutual support in a big city. Noting the cost of living in London, Outlet's website used to include the claim that,

> Shared accommodation is now the most popular way lesbian and gay people choose to live...(it) not only cuts living costs – it distributes the day to day domestic responsibilities, provides support and often develops into a surrogate 'family'...for many it is a way of life, but for everyone it is an opportunity to share our varied lesbian and gay lives, learn from our differences and make new friendships that often last for a lifetime.

Writing in the lesbian magazine *Diva*, Carolin (1999) makes a similar point:

> While straights might process from rancid, rowdy student houseshare to suburban married quarters via an urban apartment with a couple of yuppie pals, or from family home to cramped council flat with a baby on the way, my experience is that dykes often leave home younger and stay in shared housing longer – out of social idealism or financial necessity, or a combination of both (p. 36).

Indeed, sharing with friends emerged as a common living arrangement in Weeks *et al.*'s (2001) research into friendship and kinship networks amongst gay men, lesbians and bisexuals. One in eight respondents, mainly drawn from those in their mid-twenties to mid-thirties, were living in shared households, with part of the appeal of sharing derived from a perception that its benefits were similar to those associated with living with a partner: 'love, stability, emotional support, and an equal and reciprocal relationship' (p. 97). Returning to the example of Carole and Jamie in household 8, this was a theme that emerged in Jamie's account of the importance he attached to his platonic friendships with housemates, amidst a strong sense that his living arrangements had evolved around his identity as a gay man. Sharing was Jamie's preferred option, even though he expressed uncertainty about how this might work out in the longer term, particularly when he reached an age when most of his straight contemporaries were likely to be married with families of their own. Nonetheless, his housemates – Carole in particular – had become an important part of his world:

> Although I am single, I am in a relationship but it's one with another man and so that makes a sort of difference to my perceptions. He lives with an ex- of his and I live with this group of people. And [he and I] sort of get along, but I don't think we'd ever, I can't, I don't imagine we'd ever live together. So I like to have almost like a family around me. And also he feels very much part of that, and I think that's perhaps how I like to see life really.

Choosing to live with certain friends and not with others also had the effect in some households of creating a distinction between an inner circle of housemates and an outer circle of non-household friends, with friendships formed within the domestic setting often conducted on very different terms to those formed outside of that setting. Friends in the outer circle, for instance, often continued to enter the shared household under mediated conditions, and were unlikely to be invited into private spaces, such as bedrooms, even if housemates often wandered in and out of each other's bedrooms with impunity. Bodily intimacy was also permissible within the inner circle of some households, in as much as it was often acceptable to share clothes, wander round the house wearing very little clothing, or even to share bathroom space. Housemates were extremely unlikely to extend these practices beyond the inner circle.

Relationships with housemates can, then, be marked by a high degree of intimacy and interdependence. These are not insignificant relationships in young people's lives, as a focus on shared households solely as 'zones of transition' might suggest, and the temptation to deny their importance strikes us as an example of the tendency highlighted by Roseneil (2000) 'to trivialise, infantilise and subordinate relationships which are not clear parallels of the conventional heterosexual couple' (p. 8). However, platonic friendships also tend to be subordinated to *kin* relationships within popular culture, reflected in Rubin's (1985) observation that 'the idea of kin is so deeply and powerfully rooted within us that it is the most common metaphor for describing closeness' (pp. 16–17). Within our own research, this was a metaphor that was often used to capture the closeness of friendships with housemates, with particular individuals referred to in terms of being 'like a brother', 'like a sister' or 'like family'. This also reflects the way in which traditional family networks, based on blood or sexual ties, are still regarded as the primary framework within which domestic intimacy is expected to develop, in contrast to which the language of 'families of choice' has emerged. But what are the implications for young adults' traditional family networks of the formation of 'families of choice' within the domestic setting of the shared household? We now turn to a consideration of this theme.

Renegotiating parent–child relationships

As noted in Chapter 4, the vast majority of our respondents recalled childhoods spent in relatively secure, supportive and happy environments, marked by shared activities with other family members and the general enjoyment of their parents' company. Those who had been able to leave home via the socially sanctioned route of going away to university noted that their relationships with parents had remained largely intact, whilst those who had been unable to leave for this reason were more likely to have reported a deterioration in their relationships in the run-up to, and immediately following, their departure. Whilst most in this latter group had been able to renegotiate their relationships with parents over time, for others their relationships remained somewhat precarious – or, in a few cases, non-existent.

In considering the nature of their current relationships with parents, most sharers maintained some degree of regular and ongoing contact with their parents. Most spoke to them on the telephone on a regular basis, and the majority also visited their parents at least once every two to three months. A handful visited their parents on a weekly basis – notably, but not exclusively, those whose parents lived locally. This group consisted of younger and/or female respondents, and their return visits often revolved around a regular shared meal, for example Sunday lunch. In contrast, the parents of three respondents lived overseas, rendering home visits infrequent, whilst five respondents – all men – appeared to have no contact whatsoever with either one or both of their parents following the irretrievable breakdown of these relationships. A further six stated that their contact with parents was extremely infrequent, often confined to a duty visit at Christmas.

In almost all cases the frequency of return visits had declined with increasing age, whilst the reasons for returning had also shifted over time. In particular, catching up with old friends – a widely cited reason for return visits in the first few years after leaving the parental home – had gradually become less important, not least because many of these friends had themselves moved away. Instead, rather than using their parents' houses merely as convenient bases for socialising with childhood friends, the older respondents spoke of their increasing desire to spend time within the parental home itself on their return visits. Paul (household 7), for example, argued that:

> When I was living there full time, if you like, there were quite a few times when I didn't particularly want to be there at all. I mean I suppose you could look at it when I was younger I would much rather be out with my mates and having a good time and going down the pub or whatever. But I would say more and more now I would prefer to some extent going home and just sitting with my parents and chatting away.

Although in Paul's case he increasingly enjoyed spending time with his parents, this was not always the primary reason why respondents preferred to spend more time within the parental home. Instead, many highlighted the importance of the parental home in providing an occasional haven from the stresses of their busy working lives. A desire to spend time in the parental home, then, was often less about catching up with one's parents but more about 'recharging batteries', being spoiled by parents and indulging in the home comforts of childhood memory: a warm house, home cooking, one's old bed, the background presence of family members.

Of the respondents who were still in regular contact with their parents, most seemed to enjoy return visits, yet they were acutely aware that their own status had, with time, shifted from being a member of the household in their own right to that of *visitor*. One young man said that his visits home were now 'more like a member of the family coming to stay', and he noted, for example, that he was no longer expected to get involved in household tasks when he returned home. Another young man noted that whereas he used to spend a lot of time alone in his bedroom on return visits, he now spent far more time in the lounge: 'even though the bedroom hasn't changed that much, it doesn't feel as if I can do as much as I used to be able to do there. It's just a bedroom now. Used to be a lot of things'. In a small number of cases, parents had separated since their child had first left home and were now living with new partners. This was particularly disorientating for those concerned; Katie (household 17), for example, spoke of feeling the need to ask permission to do things in her father's new house that she would never previously have checked out first. (The implications of these shifting relationships with the parental home for young people's broader conceptualisations of 'home' are considered in Chapter 10.)

Sharers' accounts of their relationships with their parents were invariably permeated by a deep awareness of change. This was expressed in a variety of ways: for example, some spoke of their parents becoming 'more like friends' (at the same time, as we noted above, that many argued that their friends were becoming 'more like family'), others felt that their parents now treated them as equals or regarded them as adults, whilst others noted that previously tumultuous and argumentative relationships (particularly with fathers) had now become much calmer and more 'adult':

> At first when I moved away I'd be on the phone to them all the time in tears and things. And they'd be supporting me. But now I'm sort of happy here and they'll ring up and say 'you're never going to come home now?' and things like that, 'we really miss you'. And they get upset and I feel like I'm supporting them. Because at first I was so reliant on them and I told them all the time how much I missed them and stuff and then I'd go home like a lot of weekends and then as I got more and more settled, I sort of haven't rung them up as much, things like that, and they've noticed (Jules, household 1).

> My relationship with my father as well, that's changed as well because he's not really my father any more, he's like my mate. Do you know what I mean? He doesn't tell me what to do any more. I ask him for advice instead of him telling me things, you know what I mean? (Martin, household 23).

Despite the changing nature of their relationships, in the main for the better, most stressed that return visits nonetheless reinforced the undesirability of a more permanent return to the parental home. A visit of two or three days was usually sufficient, and beyond that most found their patience with their parents wore thin (and often vice versa). The comfort of family-style routine and expectations soon became a constraint for a group of young adults used to independence within their own household spaces. This is a feeling captured well in the novel *Generation X*; commenting on a return visit to the parental home, the book's central character notes that 'already, after ten minutes, any spiritual or psychic progress I may have made in the absence of my family has vanished or been invalidated' (Coupland, 1991: 159).

Nonetheless, it is significant that most of the sample continued to visit their parents, despite the experience sometimes being a disappointment for all parties. This was most marked amongst those who felt that they now had little in common with their families. Holly (household 13), for example, who had first left home to live at an environmental protest camp, argued that 'I make myself [go home] occasionally, because my parents get upset if I don't', yet the experience was invariably a painful reminder of how far she had moved away from her parents' expectations for her. Similarly, Warren, a gay man who shared his house with Rick, a transvestite, both spoke of their unease on return visits to the parental home (household 10). Both men felt unable to 'be themselves' on such visits, in contrast to their feelings of ease and acceptance within their own home (see Kenyon, 2003). Paula (household 19), a 28-year-old British-Asian, felt similarly out of place on her rare return visits, and had created a new life for herself outside of the parental gaze. Unbeknown to her parents, she had had a white boyfriend for the past eight years, and return visits merely served as a reminder of her 'double life':

> But now I have to mentally take time out to go and see them ... You know, when I go there it's fine, everybody gets on and it's almost as if – I almost get the feeling from them as if we've lost her, you know, and it's just like everyone has decided to go with the flow now. You know, I'm just like sort of, sort of, gone out to sea and it's like, you know, I'm waving at them. I'm here, still. But not so close to them now.

The importance of sharers maintaining contact with parents through visits to the parental home becomes even more significant if we consider that most parents rarely visited their children in return. Indeed, unless our respondents were prepared to make these trips, face-to-face contact with parents would have been extremely limited, if not non-existent. On the occasions when parents did come to Southampton, these visits were often regarded by parents as conferred 'treats', and usually involved taking their child out for a meal rather than being entertained in their son or daughter's home. Such arrangements, welcome though they usually were and undoubtedly underpinned by practical considerations such as limited space or privacy within shared households, had the effect of reinforcing an assumption of ongoing dependency upon parents whilst remaining single. This is underlined by the experience of Ella (household 6), who noted that the first time she had ever entertained her parents in her own home, rather than being picked up and immediately taken out for the day, was when she had briefly moved out of shared accommodation in order to live with a boyfriend (whom her parents did not even like). This had also been the only occasion when she had ever cooked for them.

It was also not uncommon for parents to combine visits to their children with another purpose, not just in order to visit their child, or whilst 'passing through' en route to another destination. Huw's parents, for example, were keen sailors, and tended to visit him during sailing events in the city, such as the annual boat show (household 3). Moreover, parents from out of town very rarely stayed overnight in their child's shared household, preferring to stay in local hotels and guesthouses, if at all. Even parents who lived locally seemed to need a specific reason to visit. Nell's parents, for example, lived only a few miles away, but would only visit after attending football matches at the nearby stadium (household 21).

There were, however, perceived advantages to this apparent reluctance on the part of parents to visit their children in their own homes, as it reduced the opportunity for parents to intervene inappropriately in the lives of their single offspring. In the previous chapter we noted Morgan's (1996) use of the term 'bodily density' to refer to spatial proximity between family and household members and the consequent monitoring and knowledge of each others' bodies within household space. Whilst bodily density is most acute whilst living with family members, and the opportunity to escape bodily density a reason why many young people choose to leave home in the first place, Morgan argues that the monitoring of bodies can also occur *across* household spaces. As such, the behaviours and lifestyles of single young adults may still be subject to the scrutiny of parents, albeit from a distance. Parental reluctance to visit their single offspring in their own homes clearly reduced the opportunities for this to occur.

Many parents, then, had little knowledge of the practicalities of their children's living arrangements, and their children believed them to be largely unaware of the degree of independence they enjoyed. Consequently, sharers felt that their true level of independence was rarely acknowledged by their parents, who continued to regard them as semi-dependent at best. A reluctance to visit their children in their own homes was one manifestation of this unwillingness, but so was the disappointment of some parents that their children no longer regarded the parental home as 'their' home, a theme we discuss in detail in Chapter 10. Such parents appeared to associate 'home' with 'family' and, according to their children, appeared unwilling to accept that a shared household could realistically constitute an alternative home for their single offspring, or that close friends could take on the role of confidante that a parent might otherwise assume. Nonetheless, the family of origin remained important to the vast majority of our respondents. They were prepared to maintain regular contact with parents, often negotiated over considerable geographical and emotional distance, and, despite a widespread ambivalence in relation to the parental home as a site that embodied both the best and the worst aspects of family life.

Conclusion

This chapter has sought to explore the conduct of relationships with housemates and parents in the lives of the sharers in our research. It has done so against the backdrop of debates concerning the transformation of intimacy and the assertion that friendships have assumed increased importance in the late modern era, particularly in the lives of younger generations. We have demonstrated that friendships conducted within the domestic sphere have the potential to take on considerable significance in young people's lives, with housemates providing the sort of day-to-day practical and emotional support more usually associated with blood relatives or sexual partners rather than with friends. This is not to suggest that sharers choose to share *in order* to nurture these relationships, but that supportive relationships can occur as a consequence of sharing. Whether or not they share the characteristics of Giddens' 'pure relationships' is, however, debatable. In some instances, pure relationships based on equality, reciprocity and mutual self-disclosure may be easier to sustain between friends who live apart, given Giddens' contention that 'a balance between autonomy and the sharing of feelings has to be obtained if personal closeness is not to be replaced by dependence' (1991: 95). Living in a shared household can, after all, place an extraordinary strain on even the closest of friendships, and there is no doubt that, in an echo of the conditions of the pure relationship, friendships with housemates only work well for as long as both parties benefit equally from the arrangement.

We have also considered relationships with parents amongst our respondents. Parents remained important to and well-loved by most of our respondents, but they nonetheless became increasingly marginal to their lives the older they became and the further they moved away geographically. Return visits served to bring parents and children together, but often reinforced their differences and reminded each party of their former ways of relating to each other. Many young people felt that, despite their best efforts, they automatically reverted to a position of dependency even on the briefest of visits to their parents, despite feeling independent and very much in control within their own domestic settings. These sorts of considerations have implications for the degree to which parent–child relationships can feasibly move towards Giddens' (1991) ideal of the pure relationship based on 'reflexively ordered trust' and 'mutually accepted commitment' (p. 98). Until young people feel that their living arrangements receive the parental seal of approval, such equality is hard to achieve; and our research suggests that most parents do not regard shared households – or even single person households (except, sometimes, if owner occupied) – as 'proper' adult households.

Housemates are, then, important and ever-present in the lives of sharers, whilst parents are also important, but tend not to be physically present to anywhere near the same extent. But what about housemates' girlfriends and boyfriends? Whilst our respondents were single in the sense of not actually living with a partner, most were involved in sexual relationships, or had had partners in the past even if they were currently not part of a couple. How were these relationships conducted against the backdrop of shared living? And how did these relationships fit into a longer-term view of household formation? These issues form the focus of the next chapter.

9
Negotiating Current and Future Partnerships

Introduction

> 'Why aren't you married yet, Bridget', sneered Woney (babytalk for
> Fiona, married to Jeremy's friend Cosmo) with a thin veneer of
> concern whilst stroking her pregnant stomach. (Helen Fielding,
> *Bridget Jones Diary*)

Contemporary young adults may well be spending longer periods of
time living alone or with friends rather than partners, but there is little
evidence to suggest that they are rejecting the pursuit of sexual relationships *per se*. A casual stroll down any urban high street on a Saturday
night would confirm this, not to mention the proliferation of dating
agencies and singles clubs all dedicated to finding the perfect partner – or
at least the *next* partner. In 1998, nine out of ten 25–34-year-old Britons
reported having had at least one sexual partner in the previous year,
with most having had more than one (Office for National Statistics,
2000), whilst a third of never-married men aged under 35 and four in
ten of their female peers claim to be in a steady relationship with someone they consider to be a partner (Ermisch, 2000). Early marriage may
be going out of fashion, but sex, love and romance appear to remain high
on the agenda for most twenty-somethings.

In this chapter we focus on young people's experiences of negotiating
sexual relationships with partners whilst living independently from
them, and then go on to consider their longer-term domestic aspirations.
Whilst there were perceived advantages to living apart from sexual
partners for most of our respondents, the majority aspired to quite
traditional domestic arrangements in the longer term, notwithstanding
their awareness of the high costs associated with committing oneself to

one partner. These perspectives need to be set against the evidence of broader demographic shifts in relation to family formation, so we begin this chapter with an overview of key trends in relation to marriage, cohabitation and partnership formation, before revisiting some of the themes introduced in Chapter 3 about the increasing difficulties associated with the attainment of co-resident sexual relationships. In this light, we then explore some of the tensions around these issues as experienced by the young adults involved in our research.

We are conscious in writing certain sections of this chapter that our primary focus is on the experiences of heterosexual young adults. At the present time, marriage or even formal registration of a partnership is not an option available to lesbians and gay men in most parts of the world, whilst the desirability of such options is also the subject of considerable debate within the gay and lesbian community. Weeks *et al.* (2001) capture this debate in the following terms: 'is the general goal one of wanting to be included in a society still dominated by a strong heterosexual assumption; or is it to seek a recognition of different ways of life?' (p. 191). In other words, should gay men and lesbians be seeking to emulate the straight world, or should they be seeking to challenge its underpinning assumptions? Contemporary academic debate about the transformation of intimacy holds out the possibility that some of these assumptions are being turned on their head by younger generations, resulting in a challenge to the assumptions of linearity which often underpin the study of personal relationships. This is a challenge we have tried to reflect throughout this book, yet the evidence of this chapter, as well as the next, suggests that in many respects the old assumptions underpinning the desirability of marriage – at least in the longer term – remain firmly in place, even though the routes by which heterosexual young adults achieve this status are no longer as straightforward as they once were.

Trends in partnership formation, cohabitation and marriage

During the 1960s, the age of first marriage was often used as a fairly reliable proxy for the age of first leaving home (Kiernan, 1985). Over the last 40 years, this relationship has declined rapidly in line with the dwindling appeal of marriage and a significant rise in the median age of those who do choose to marry. The number of first marriages registered in the United Kingdom in 1997, for example, was less than half the number registered in 1970 (Office for National Statistics, 2000), whilst the median age of first marriage rose from 23 for men and 21 for women in 1971, to 30.6 and 28.4 respectively in 2001 (Bynner *et al.*, 1997; Office for National Statistics, 2003). Similar trends in relation to a drop in marriage rates have emerged across Europe, albeit with significant variations in the north and the south, as well as in the United States and Australia (European Commission, 2000; Fields and Casper, 2001; Australian Bureau of Statistics, 2003). The median age of first marriage has also risen significantly in both the United States and Australia, although it is still lower in both countries than in the United Kingdom: in 2000, the median age of first marriage in the United States stood at 25.1 for women and 26.8 for men (Fields and Casper, 2001), whilst the equivalent figures for Australian women and men in 2001 were 26.9 and 28.7 respectively (Australian Bureau of Statistics, 2003).

Before concluding that young people are rejecting couple relationships during their twenties, it is important to note that much of the shift towards later marriage is attributable to the growth of cohabitation, and the majority of young people will have cohabited at least once during their twenties. In the United Kingdom, rates of cohabitation have more than doubled over the last 20 years (Office for National Statistics, 2000), and cohabitation as a precursor to marriage has now become the norm in many westernised societies. In Australia, for example, one study found that nine out of ten young people who were married had previously cohabited with their spouse (Kilmartin, 2000), whilst more than half of all Americans who married in the mid-1990s had cohabited with their spouse prior to marriage (Bianchi and Casper, 2000). Many young people cohabit for the first time quite early on in their twenties (Ermisch and Francesconi, 2000), which might suggest that cohabitation has replaced the sig-nificance of marriage as a reason for first leaving home. However, the proportion of young people who leave home in order to create *any* form of couple household, whether married to or cohabiting with a partner, has declined. Amongst Britons born in 1958 and leaving the parental home in the late 1970s and the 1980s, for example, couple households formed the first destination of 60 per cent of women and 55 per cent of men, compared with only 46 per cent of women and 38 per cent of men from later cohorts who first left the parental home during the 1990s (ibid.).

Recent evidence suggests that cohabiting relationships are not as stable as marriages. In the UK, only a fifth of relationships based on cohabitation continue beyond five years, although of those that come to an end, three-fifths discontinue as a result of the partners marrying each other rather than as a consequence of the partners splitting up (Ermisch and Francesconi, 2000). The breakdown of a cohabiting partnership has a delaying effect on subsequent partnership formation, with a median period of three years before the next live-in partnership. Consequently, this is a period during which there is an increased likelihood of a young person living alone, sharing with others or, in some cases, returning to the parental home, although such arrangements do not, of course, preclude having a non-resident sexual partner. The rise of cohabitation as the norm for first partnerships is, then, widely regarded as a crucial factor influencing changing marriage patterns amongst younger generations.

Significantly, this is no longer a trend confined to the 'experimenting' middle classes, with young people from all social class backgrounds now similarly likely to cohabit in their first residential partnership. Nonetheless, it is still the case that young people whose fathers are in higher status occupations are more likely than those whose fathers are in lower status occupations to be neither married *nor* in a cohabiting union, a difference which is in part linked to the greater likelihood amongst the former group of continuing into higher education (Ermisch and Francesconi, 2000). Amongst the 1970 cohort, for example, those who were married at age 26 were less qualified than cohabitees, and both married and cohabiting 26-year-olds were in turn less qualified than those in the cohort who were either living alone or with friends: just over one in ten spouses and two in ten cohabitees had a degree-level qualification compared with four in ten who were living independently (ibid.). Blackwell and Bynner (2002) argue further that the relationship between higher education and household formation is strongest amongst women: the higher the educational level achieved, the less likely a woman is to marry, whereas amongst men, less educated men are the least likely to marry or cohabit.

Willmot (2001) has explored the influence of educational experience on patterns of relationship formation amongst heterosexual young women through comparing the 'discursive constructions of love and intimacy' amongst those who leave full-time education by the age of 18 and those who continue into higher education. She suggests the existence of two dominant but oppositional discourses: a discourse of romance associated largely with early leavers, based on notions of love at first sight, exclusivity and 'foreverness', and a discourse of contingency associated largely with those who stay on, based on the necessity of balancing intimate relationships with other life choices. Willmot argues that it is not the higher level of education *per se* that explains these differences, but the influence of the distinct 'socio-cultural milieux' linked to each route. Those who leave school by the age of 18, for example, are more likely to have remained in their home towns and to have continued to live in the parental home into their early twenties, in contrast to their peers who continue into higher education, who tend to be geographically mobile and to experience living arrangements outside of the parental home, usually in the form of living with friends:

> My analysis is thus not based on the idea that higher qualifications engender a certain kind of intimate consciousness amongst young women. Instead, I am suggesting that it is the socio-cultural experiences and relations which surround the following of different educational routes which establish different conditions for and practices of intimacy (Willmot, 2001: 232).

Willmot's argument reinforces our own view that exposure to the student lifestyle opens up young people's options in ways which go far beyond those linked purely to the more usual assumptions of financial and occupational advantage. Being a student also provides young people with access to alternative living arrangements which have a significant impact on their subsequent domestic choices. Her argument also supports du Bois-Reymond's (1998) distinction between the choice biographies of well educated young people and the rather more standardised biographies of young people who leave full-time education at a relatively early age. The practices that follow from Willmot's 'romantic discourse' can be clearly linked to a traditional, gendered biography associated with early marriage and parenthood, in contrast to the practices that follow from the contingent discourse: frequent yet often short-lived periods of cohabitation, geographical mobility as a single person, deferred marriage and parenthood.

Current trends in cohabitation and marriage have, then, led to a situation where certain groups of young people – notably, but not exclusively, graduates – are single for longer periods of time than their parents' generation, and as a consequence are living in a variety of independent living arrangements between periods of time spent in couple households with a partner. We have noted in earlier chapters that a perceived need to be geographically mobile in order to prioritise one's career often places considerable obstacles in the way of partnership formation amongst young people, particularly those in professional occupations. However, many form non-resident couple relationships despite these obstacles. In 1998, for example, a quarter of never married, childless men aged under 35, and a third of their female peers, were involved in a non-resident partnership of at least six months duration, with around two-fifths of these partnerships having lasted for at least two years (Ermisch, 2000).

In many instances, particularly amongst younger single people, partners may be living apart because they have not yet even considered the possibility of cohabitation or marriage, or do not feel themselves ready for such a step. However, it has also been suggested that there is also a growing trend towards 'living apart together' (LAT), whereby couples who in earlier periods might well have moved in together deliberately choose to live apart from each other (Lovatt, 2003). A French study of such couples suggests that two-thirds attribute their living arrangements to external pressures, such as family or work-related commitments, with the remaining one-third living apart quite deliberately in order to retain their independence (Villeneuve-Gokalp, 1997, cited in Bawin-Legros and Gauthier, 2001). In the United Kingdom, analysis of the British Household Panel Survey paints a slightly different picture of this phenomenon, with more than 60 per cent of LAT couples in long-term relationships stating that the arrangement suits them on a permanent basis (Ermisch, 2000).

Whether or not an LAT relationship is regarded as a permanent arrangement, many young people nonetheless conduct their relationships with partners across at least two household spaces (their own, their partner's, and possibly across their parents' living spaces too). Those whose work commitments preclude them from living in the same locality as their partner may only see each other at weekends, such that time spent alone with a partner is at a premium. Such arrangements present particular dilemmas for young people who live with their parents, as noted in Chapter 4, but young people who live in shared accommodation nonetheless can face equally difficult negotiations in relation to issues of household space and time. In the sections that follow we first consider some of the practicalities of conducting relationships across households in this manner. We then put the spotlight on young people's aspirations in relation to future couple households.

Negotiating couple relationships in shared households

Throughout this book, we have suggested that shared households increasingly form the focus of many young adults' aspirations at certain moments in their housing careers. Importantly, few of the young people involved in our own research appeared to feel that their status as independent adults was compromised by sharing with other single adults. Instead, it allowed them to experiment with economic independence within a space that also supported the maintenance of two parallel statuses: living a single lifestyle with unrelated peers, *and* initiating and maintaining intimate sexual relationships with partners, yet partners who were semi-resident at most. Sharing thus provided a site for developing independence away from the constant gaze of both parents *and* partners. Moreover, their strong sense of independence suggests that one of the more traditional indicators of adulthood – a place of one's own with a resident partner – was not of primary significance to them in defining the attainment of adulthood, even though it remained an important longer-term goal in most cases.

Thirty six of the young people involved in our research had a girlfriend or boyfriend living outside of the shared household at the time we interviewed them, whilst most of those who were 'unattached' at the time referred to earlier relationships in which they had been involved. With the exception of two gay men, all of these past and current relationships were or had been heterosexual. Most current partners lived within a 30 mile radius of Southampton, with contact often frequent and potentially at any time during the week. Ten partners lived at some geographical distance (including one based in Germany), with contact largely confined to weekends. Twenty-seven young people had previously cohabited at least once, with two individuals having been married, and relationship breakdowns were specifically cited as the primary reason for a housing move in 18 cases.

Many spoke of their previous experiences of maintaining long-distance relationships, particularly when they had moved away from home for the first time, or had moved away from a partner on graduating from university, with partners not infrequently ending up in different parts of the country. Piers (household 7), for example, had had a steady girlfriend throughout his university years, but he had split up with her within six months of graduating:

> The reason we split up was distance. I decided I wanted to move down here, I had a choice of a job in London originally when I was deciding, or near London, but I'd be in Edinburgh within the year. So I wasn't really going to be in London. And she had a job, she was training to be a solicitor so she had at least four years of training. We didn't see each other for the summer because she went on holiday with some of her friends. I went on holiday with some of mine. She had exams, which meant we didn't see each other, she was studying hard for those. And we just drifted apart through that and felt that neither of us were prepared to give up all the weekends to go and visit...

Several others talked of relationships that had faltered because of the distance factor, whilst those currently in long-distance relationships pointed to the unsatisfactory nature of their arrangements. Liz (household 1), for example, said that she and her boyfriend were 'fed up of having separate lives', and wished that they could find jobs rather closer to each other, whilst the difficulty of maintaining a long-distance relationship had led Hilary (household 6) to decide to move in with her boyfriend to a town equidistant to their places of work. Nonetheless, she had mixed feelings about leaving her housemates of the past six years:

> It was a really hard decision to make because I don't want to move out, I love everything about living here and I wouldn't change a thing about it. But, on the other hand, I really want to live with Sam as well...and so it is just the sensible thing because Sam and I really want to live together and we're going to do it and it's the right thing to do.

Similarly, Paula (household 19) had been involved with the same partner, Richard, for the past eight years. However, they had never lived together, and were currently living several hundred miles apart, meeting only at weekends. She identified earlier points in time when they could have lived closer together, but at the cost of a good job for her, and noted how they had decided that her career must come first. Reflecting on the possibility of living together in the short term, she regarded it as 'just bloody impossible, it's just not realistic at all':

> We just want to get our careers sorted out, and if that means being apart from each other to do it, we'll do it. Because we know we're going to end up together no matter what.

For those with partners living locally, tensions of a different nature often arose, concerning the appropriate amount of time to spend in each other's houses. Where the other partner lived alone, this was less of a problem, with a greater amount of time tending to be spent in the partner's home. If a partner lived in the parental home, however, the shared household became the main domestic space within which their relationship was conducted. However, where both partners lived in shared households, judgements tended to be made about which household was more welcoming, or more appropriate as a regular base. Privacy was a big issue, too, as David's comment suggests:

> It's difficult to have a blazing row or doing something very noisy without other people noticing...I think it's just difficult in that,

sometimes if my girlfriend comes round and you want to spend some time with her, and I know I'm guilty of it, she comes in and you go straight upstairs...the big downside to it is, you know, if you had a house to yourself, if you just wanted to get a video in and sort of snuggle up on the sofa that's pretty much an impossibility, in our house anyway (David, household 7).

In David's case, he would go to his partner's house if they wanted a quiet night in, as she shared with only one other person in contrast to David's household of four young men. In some cases, though, it was quite clear that partners were not readily tolerated in each other's household spaces. As a consequence, the most easy-going households tended to be the most crowded, with partners coming and going at regular intervals. Indeed, five of the household interviews included partners who were visiting at the time. In one all-female household new boyfriends were always subject to the scrutiny of the other housemates, and referred to as 'one of the girls' once accepted ('I think we make life for the men much more difficult. It must be a nightmare, mustn't it, to walk into a house with girls who don't have any privacy from each other at all, so none of your relationship is actually sacred! But we don't tell them that'). In contrast, in two all-male households the impression was given that other people's partners were at best a necessary evil, at worst a downright nuisance and a distraction from 'laddish' lifestyles. In one of these households (household 3), a girlfriend was actually in the house during the group interview, yet remained in the kitchen throughout and eventually left without saying goodbye to her boyfriend, despite our repeated suggestion to her boyfriend that she might like to join in.

Not surprisingly, then, negotiations of the boundaries of privacy and intimacy in shared households emerged as a key flashpoint in sharers' narratives, no more so than with respect to the appropriate conduct of couple relationships in shared households. Indeed, stories concerning nightmare housemates often revolved around breaches of these boundaries. The introduction of new partners into shared households tended, therefore, to be carefully policed by fellow housemates, and the collective approval or disapproval of household members made clear. A particular difficulty related to the problems arising from perceptions that partners were spending too much time within the shared household. This was problematic for a number of reasons, including the diversion of the resident partner's energies from their commitments to fellow household members (spending too much time in their own room, for example, instead of socialising with others in communal spaces) and the perception of non-resident partners as freeloaders. In Huw's household (household 3), such behaviour had been the subject of past tensions:

> We were quite looking forward to living with this guy (a new house-mate), cos we'd known him from uni, but we'd never lived with him. But from the very first day his girlfriend was sort of – I think the first two weeks that we were here she spent more time here than we did. And then she started cooking his dinner before he got in from work and things like that.

Mindful of this experience, Huw's housemate Jack subsequently expressed some misgivings concerning the impact of his relationship with his current girlfriend (the woman, in fact, who remained in the kitchen):

> There's more space in my house and I've got a double bed and she's just got a single bed. It's very tempting to stay at my house a lot of the time. That's not really fair for the others. But it's difficult to keep it 50:50. Because on the one hand if I'm around her house, her house is smaller so I'm more likely to be noticed by her friends, whereas here I can disappear into my room.

Unfortunately, in some households the decision to spend time away from the shared household was viewed as similarly problematic, albeit for different reasons. Rick and Warren (household 10), for example, both felt let down by their new housemate precisely because she was spending all of her free time with her new boyfriend in pref-erence to spending time getting to know the people she now lived with.

In some of the households in which our respondents had lived, tensions had also arisen as a result of the breaching of the boundaries of acceptable behaviour with regard to sexual intimacy. Most household members respected each other's right to privacy in this regard, for example not barging into someone's bedroom if their partner was known to be around, as well as each other's right not to be embarrassed by displays of intimate behaviour in the shared spaces of the household (or to at least ensure that other housemates were out of the household before having sex in these spaces!). Other households had clear limits about what was permissible in shared spaces. The household of six nurses (household 1) spoke about this with some humour:

Daisy: If you're in the lounge, as long as they're not sort of slobbering on each other it's alright. Or they'll go to their room if they want to slobber.

Jane: I don't mind someone putting their arm around their boyfriend.

Daisy: Yeah, sitting and having a cuddle and that.

Ray: Holding hands. On top of each other might be going a bit far.

Jane: Removing each other's clothes.

Daisy: Kissing.

Jane: Nibbling at the ears, yeah.

Daisy: Fondling breasts and things is out.

Jane: Whispering sweet nothings whilst you're trying to watch ER.

Ray: Being a bit pukey is a bit of a no no, isn't it?

Nonetheless, excessively noisy sex was a frequent cause for complaint even when – as was usually the case – having sex was confined to a housemate's own room, although one respondent noted that the noise of sex was less of a problem than the post-sex chatter into the small hours of the morning which had kept her awake in the early stages of her housemate's latest relationship (see also Gurney, 2000). Cathy and Jackie (household 2) similarly complained of two previous housemates who had started going out together and had become 'too much of a couple'. They had eventually moved into the same bedroom, and could frequently be heard having sex. In most households, whilst generally regarded as mildly irritating, noisy sex was also the subject of a lot of humour. However, one respondent had once lived in a household where, in order to minimise some of these difficulties, boyfriends had been restricted to a maximum of two visits per week.

Whilst this last instance was an extreme case (and one of the reasons behind the respondent's early exit from this particular household), there was nonetheless a general view expressed across all of the households that it would be most undesirable for a partner to move into the household on anything approaching a permanent basis. This view was equally shared by those *with* partners, who might stand to gain from this, suggesting that the space to be *apart* from a partner provided by a shared household was equally as important as the space to be *together*. The shared household is very much a halfway house in this regard: it provides a space where partners can come and go with relative ease (importantly, free from the parental gaze), yet also provides a space which is a step removed from the commitment and responsibility of actually living together. For many young people, this appeared to represent the best of both worlds, and this independence was highly valued by the majority of those who had partners. However, few regarded this as a desirable set-up in the longer term, and we turn now to a consideration of our respondents' attitudes towards the prospect of eventually living with a partner on a permanent basis.

'Settling down' with a partner

The later formation of couple households amongst contemporary young adults is often described as a *delayed* transition, implying that, were it not for constraining factors, most young people would prefer to be living with a partner than alone or with friends. Whilst this may be the case for some young people, it is by no means universally so and implies further that most young adults lack agency in controlling the timing of a major life decision. There is, of course, an important distinction to be drawn here between subjective views regarding the 'right time' to 'settle down' with a partner, and the objective conditions which might make cohabitation and marriage more or less difficult at any given point in time. Nonetheless, there is also plenty of evidence to suggest that many young people are more than happy to prioritise other aspects of their lives before choosing to live with a partner – or even to have a partner at all. Jamieson *et al*. (2003), for example, found amongst a sample of 246 twenty-somethings in Fife, Scotland, that 'just over half were not oriented to a long-term commitment, either not being in a relationship and not looking for either a partner or a romance or else being in a relationship which they viewed as short term' (pp. 138–39). Moreover, BHPS data suggest that around a third of never married childless women aged under 35 who are in non-resident relationships of at least six months duration have no plans to cohabit with or marry their current partner (Ermisch, 2000).

Amongst our own sample, cohabitation was seen as desirable *at some point* by around eight out of ten respondents of both sexes. A similar proportion of women regarded marriage as desirable, yet only just over half of the heterosexual men regarded marriage in a similar light. One in ten of the young men were adamant that they did not want to marry whilst a third were at best ambivalent, compared with comparable figures amongst women of one in twenty and one in eight. Some were on the verge of moving into a couple household when we first met them: one young woman was about to get married, another about to cohabit, and one of the mature students was planning to share his girlfriend's house in the next academic year (although not without severe misgivings concerning the wisdom of this move). We learnt that at least five others had moved in with partners within a year of our research, and that a fifth was planning to do so following her boyfriend's relocation to the area. However, most respondents, including those with partners, were in no obvious hurry to cohabit, even where opportunities had arisen.

Many were acutely aware that decisions to cohabit involved complex trade-offs between varying degrees of dependence and independence. Some believed, for example, that their current flexibility of lifestyle would be hard to sustain if they were to cohabit. Others, particularly those with partners at some geographical distance, expressed concern about the potential impact on their career aspirations, reflecting their awareness of the advantages of being flexible in relation to their employment. As stated earlier, Paula (household 19), who had moved to the area with a new job, was emphatic that her career should currently be prioritised over her eight-year relationship with her boyfriend:

> We talked about it, we know where we're heading, but it's just getting there. Because there's no point in getting all hitched and everything when you're struggling (in your career) . . . I think that in itself, being together, and then trying to get where you are, I don't know, maybe it could affect our relationship, I don't know.

Those without partners were equally ambivalent about the appeal of cohabitation and/or marriage at this stage in their lives. A number of women in their early twenties spoke of their desire to travel prior to settling down. Several others considered themselves too young or too immature to settle down with a partner, others spoke of not yet having met the 'right' person, whilst others were enjoying their independence too much to settle down:

> I'm fairly independent and I take life as it comes. I'm not, you know, banking on [marriage]. There are more girls than guys in the world and I've got fairly high standards, which makes things difficult! Finding Mr Right might be quite difficult! (Susan, household 19).

> At the moment I can't see myself having a better time with my wife than I would with my mates (Ivan, household 22).

There was, however, a clear distinction drawn between the revokable semi-commitment of cohabitation and the legally binding, 'serious' nature of marriage. Indeed, many regarded the commitment implied by marriage with not inconsiderable awe, if not fear, and were conscious that marriage would involve a huge commitment and change of lifestyle for which they were not yet ready:

> I've got nothing against marriage. Complete lack of ability at finding a partner, but not through want of trying! So yeah, I think it's a possibility one day. Yeah, it scares the hell out of me, the thought of it, but I have no moral objections to marriage. I think I probably will. (Nathan, household 14).

> At some point, yes … [but] I'm not 'me' enough to share that much of my life with another person yet, I'd become half of them. Well, I don't become half of them, but we'd become as one and I find it difficult to have my own life and not just wanting to be with them all the time … *I don't want to be essentially changed by being with somebody else* (Holly, emphasis added, household 13).

> I think I've always said that my attitude to marriage is once you're married that's for life. I've got the opinion that if I want to play around and be naughty, now's my chance to do it … if people are ever disapproving, I say yeah, but you know I'm not married, I don't owe anyone anything. But when I am married I can say well, I know what it's like to fool around, I know what it's like to have different relationships, and this is the one that I want (Jill, household 12).

For the most part, then, our respondents recognised the degree of commitment required to make cohabitation and particularly marriage 'work', and whilst marriage was something that most of the women and just over half of the men wanted for themselves at some point, the general consensus was that the 'right time' to do this was not quite yet. A small number of respondents, mainly non-graduates, expressed surprise that they were not yet 'settled down', as they had always imagined that they would be married by a certain age that had now passed, but were not particularly regretful about this. Others, in speaking about a 'right time', spoke of the way in which this right time remained at a fixed distance from their current age, and never really appeared to get any closer, despite their advancing age (as one 28 year old put it, 'my parents seem to have the same idea of what's too young to marry as I do, which stretches out as you get older. It's currently hovering around the 40 mark!'). Whilst acknowledging that 'the right time' was not now, some young people nonetheless hinted at the fear of missing out on a partner. Simon (household 18), for example, stated that he would be 'worried' if he was still single in his mid-30s, and expressed the hope that at some point in the future he will be able to share his life 'with just one other'.

For the most part, a strong sense of caution pervaded these accounts of future cohabitation and marriage. Whilst some accounts, most notably those of young women rather than young men, were couched in glowingly romantic terms ('I want to be a princess for a day'), most were intensely practical and underlined the importance of finding the 'right' person and of exercising caution before rushing into living together. Some of these concerns were pragmatic financial concerns, such as making sure that couple households were based on joint ownership or tenancy rather than only one partner having legal rights over the property, but in the main these concerns were about the need to get to know someone before making a commitment to them. Cohabitation before marriage formed an important safeguard in this respect, with only a tiny minority having strong views against living together outside of marriage. Some of these views arose from religious belief, whereas others were more pragmatic. Luke (household 11), for example, acknowledged that his position might seem strange, but 'if you're going to make that kind of commitment, then why not just get married?'

The examples set by their own parents' relationships had also influenced the views of many young people. A number of those from stable family backgrounds wished to emulate their parents' happy marriages, whilst a number whose parents had divorced expressed more negative views concerning the attractiveness of marriage. More frequently, though, ambivalence towards marriage was expressed in terms of whether it was strictly necessary to achieve a sense of commitment with a partner. Richard (household 16), for example, referred to marriage as 'just a slip of paper' or 'a tax benefit', whilst Rick (household 10) felt that commitment could be legitimately expressed outside of the institution of marriage, and took comfort from the increasingly acceptable nature of this practice. Marriage was also regarded as more 'difficult to get out of' by some respondents, whereas others had doubts about the religious underpinnings of marriage.

Overall, then, the majority of our respondents were not at all averse to the idea of 'settling down' with a partner at some point, either in the form of cohabitation prior to marriage or cohabitation as an end in itself. Importantly, however, these were regarded very much as mid- to long-term plans, either through current lack of opportunity or, more commonly, through a desire to retain their independence for the immediate future. Nonetheless, it is also important to consider the impact of the vagaries of romantic love and desire on processes of household formation, and their potential for undermining even the best laid plans. Love and romance, unlike sexuality and to a lesser extent desire, have generally been neglected by sociologists (Jackson and Scott, 1997), yet they are arguably integral to a serious consideration of the factors that influence young adults' domestic and housing transitions. 'Being in love' and/or 'in lust' can often act as the spur to a radical and far-reaching change of direction in a young person's housing and domestic career. Some such moves appear to be quite rational and well thought out, but others can appear to be quite the opposite: irrational, unplanned and spur-of-the-moment. Earlier in his housing career, for example, Nick (household 18) had returned to a doomed sexual relationship despite having finally sorted out his housing situation, whilst Nell's boyfriend moved in with her when she finally completed a long-planned flat purchase (household 21), despite her protestations six months earlier that this was a move for *her*, and that there was no way that she would countenance him moving in. They are now engaged to each other. A more extreme example is provided by Angie (household 17), who first left her London home and her job at 20 in order to move to the south coast to live with her new boyfriend, an arrangement that had lasted for three months before breaking down irretrievably. When interviewed, she vowed never to repeat such a mistake (as she now saw it), yet six months later had moved to Durham with a new boyfriend. As Stewart (household 23) noted, 'there's always a danger when the love hearts are stuck on your eyelids that you do things like that'.

Conclusion

This chapter has examined recent trends in relation to partnership formation, noting the growing evidence of a strong link between the level of educational attainment and the likelihood of a young person living with a partner during their twenties and early thirties. We have also considered evidence from our own research concerning the desirability of cohabitation and marriage as a future option, and have explored some of the practicalities that single young adults must wrestle with as a consequence of negotiating their sexual relationships across at least two distinct household spaces. For most of the young people involved in our own research, there were some distinct advantages to living arrangements which simultaneously allowed for sexual freedoms in one's own domestic space but which also provided space away from a partner when desired. In the longer term, however, most anticipated moving in with a partner at some point although, in the case of those who had partners, not necessarily the partner they were currently involved with. Significantly, living with a partner was regarded as a serious commitment, particularly in the context of marriage, and therefore not to be undertaken lightly. In the following chapter, we consider the link between intimacy and 'home', noting that traditional constructions of home tend to have placed a heavy emphasis on the presence of family members: whether of one's family of origin or of destination. Some of the points raised in this chapter take on added relevance in this debate. As we shall demonstrate, whilst young people may be redefining the parameters of 'home' during their single years, they nonetheless attach considerable significance to the role of a partner in future constructions of the concept.

10
Redefining Home?

Introduction

> This was not a good idea coming home for Christmas. I'm too old ...
> the days of revelation about my parents, at least, are over. I'm left with
> two nice people, mind you, more than most people get, but it's time
> to move on. I think we'd all appreciate that. (Douglas Coupland,
> *Generation X*)

Despite the growing destandardisation of young people's living arrangements, and the implications this has had for relationships with friends,
partners and family members, the belief that young people only fully
'leave home' when they form a family of their own still maintains
widespread cultural currency. 'Home' is invariably conflated with 'family',
a popular view underpinned by the association of the parental home
with childhood memories. As a corollary, it is often assumed that living
arrangements which stop short of this domestic ideal, such as living
alone or with friends, cannot provide young people with the ontological security associated with the parental household or a future couple/
family household of their own, and are therefore unlikely to replace
a primary attachment to the parental home. Independent living
arrangements tend to be viewed, then, merely as stepping stones en
route to more permanent family-based housing and households, rather
than as sites which may at the time nonetheless constitute 'home' for
those involved.

Such assumptions are of great importance, given that leaving the
parental home and setting up an independent home of one's own has

been recognised as a key indicator of emergent adult status (Coles, 1995; Jones, 1995a). As Cooper-Marcus (1995) states:

> Moving into young adulthood, relationships and career may be at the forefront of our consciousness, but in the establishment of our first home-away-from home, we begin to express who we are as distinct individuals, apart from our family of birth (p. 12).

Over three decades of discussion across diverse fields of inquiry have indicated the varying and intricate roles that home can play in reflecting and building personal identities, social and cultural status, citizenship, a sense of belonging and ontological security; all of which are commonly regarded as aspects of the adult individuality and independence to which Cooper-Marcus refers. Nonetheless, an individual's ability to secure adulthood through housing can depend very much on the place that they inherit in the existing social structure, as well as the wider cultural environment in which they live. For example, the common sense conflation of home and family works to reinforce a 'modern domestic ideal' (Allan and Crow 1989: 1) towards which young people are expected to aim, even though for many young adults this may be little more than a distant and unattainable dream.

The conceptualisation of the family home (whether of one's family of origin or of destination) as the only 'real' adult home nonetheless continues to endure. It is this conflation of home and family-life that underpins the oft-cited aphorism of Leonard (1980) that a home based on living alone or with unrelated peers is a 'contradiction in folk terms'. Jones (2000) has questioned this assertion, noting that such a view impacts upon the potential of those who live independently to develop and reflect their adulthood through their homes, often to the point of denying that potential. If meanings and expectations of 'home' remain static in this way, then the wide variety of non-familial living arrangements that are increasingly adopted by young adults may be regarded as temporally, socially and materially unsatisfactory, in contrast to settled, traditional 'family' homes.

This association is reinforced in countries such as Britain and Australia through the strong emphasis placed upon the desirability of owner occupation. In these countries, home ownership is relatively widespread, yet independent households continue to be formed largely within the private rented housing sector. This is a sector which in everyday understanding is viewed as a flexible and short-term source of accommodation for young and/or geographically mobile households, and therefore is assumed to be 'unhomely' by definition. This link is further consolidated by housing legislation such as the 1996 Housing Act (England and Wales) which identifies 'assured shorthold' tenancy agreements as the default arrangement within the sector. Such tenancies are fixed term for a minimum of six months and, although it is often possible to move on to a rolling contract after an initial six month contract, landlords nonetheless retain the right to terminate the contract within a specified period of notice. Legislative discourse thus creates an image of dwellings in the private rented sector as temporary precursors to more permanent accommodation, in what Kemp and Keoghan (2001) call the 'waiting room' perspective:

> This 'waiting room' perspective on private renting is implicitly based on the notion of a housing ladder in which there is a hierarchy of tenures, up which households move over time. Owner occupation is seen as forming the top rung, social housing the middle and private renting the bottom rung (p. 22).

Young adults who live in non-familial housing, particularly as private tenants, are often viewed then in one of two ways: either as a group in transition, unable to set up a 'real' home of their own (due to social or economic constraints), or as part of an increasingly mobile and individualistic generation for whom the establishment of a home linked to traditional family life is becoming less important. This latter viewpoint is reflected in the work of Kumar (1995) who states that 'the home is becoming less of a haven in a heartless world for the family, and more like a hotel for paying (and non-paying) guests' (p. 159, cited in Perkins and Thorns, 1999: 132). Overlooked by both viewpoints, however, is the possibility that experiences and ideals of home may in fact be adapting alongside the changing household formation patterns of this group. With the formation of settled couple households now occurring at a considerable distance in time from first leaving the parental home, the possibility that growing numbers of young people are redefining the meaning of home should come as no great surprise. Our own research has suggested that this may indeed be the case, with 'home' no longer defined solely in terms of the presence of immediate family members or partners within a permanent 'home of one's own'.

A key argument within academic debates on the meaning and experience of home has been the suggestion that notions of 'home' can coexist as both an ideal *and* a reality, as can the experiences of inhabiting, and the meaning given to, particular dwellings (Somerville, 1992; Kenyon, 1999). Moreover, an individual might believe their current home to be ideal for the present, but may view other home ideals as aspirations to be realised in the future (Kenyon, 2003). Whilst the complexity and fluidity of home is now widely recognised, discussions have nonetheless remained largely individualised in their focus, considering for example the impact of climactic events and individual status passages, such as the death of a partner, or the impact of employment, on the meaning and experience of home (Sixsmith and Sixsmith, 1990). In contrast, there has been little consideration of the ways in which broader social shifts are affecting individuals' navigation of home, or the day-to-day experiences of and meanings attached to *transitional* housing in the contemporary period. As Perkins and Thorns (1999) state, the focus in existing work on the home is,

> very much on individuals and their shifts and changes as they alter through life. It pays less attention to the wider social, economic and political context in which individuals and their homes are set... While place meanings result from individual human activity, individual interpretations of place always operate in a social context' (pp. 125, 130).

If individuals are indeed becoming increasingly detached from the traditional social structures upon which identities were founded during the modern period, then 'home' may become an increasingly import-ant signifier of adult identity in the late modern age. And if home is becoming a key locus of identity, expectations of and the meanings attributed to 'home' may also be shifting. Viewed in this light, young people could arguably be making sense of their housing, households and homes in new ways, necessitating a reassessment of the meaning and experiences of living in so-called 'transitional' housing and house-holds in the contemporary period (Jones, 2000; Kemp and Keoghan, 2001). This chapter seeks to explore these arguments through consider-ing the construction of 'home' amongst the young people involved in our research. A distinction is nonetheless drawn between their renegoti-ations of meanings of home whilst in their twenties and early thirties, and the rather more traditional constructions of home that the vast majority of the sample aspired to in the longer term. This latter discussion is played out within the context of debates concerning the desirability of owner occupation as a preferred housing tenure within which to locate future 'homes'.

The meaning of home

MacGregor-Wise (2000) clearly captures the intricacy of the role that home can play in our lives, and the various elements that constitute a home:

> The markers of home...are not simply inanimate objects (a place with stuff) but the presence, habits, and effects of spouses, children, parents and companions. One can be at home simply in the presence of a significant other. What makes home-territories different from other territories is on the one hand the living of the territory (a temporalisation of the space), and on the other their connection with identity, or rather a process of identification, of articulation of affect. Homes, we feel, are ours...the process of home-making is a cultural one (p. 299).

Landmark research in this field found home to exist at a number of levels: as territory, as a locus in space, as a reflector and mediator of self-identity, and as a social and cultural unit (Hayward, 1975). Three decades of research within housing studies, architecture, sociology, psychology and geography have built on this breakdown of the meaning and experience of home in order to construct an ever more comprehensive understanding of the concept. Home is now recognised to exist at a number of levels and in a number of forms, as part of lived experience, memories and imaginations, and is so wide a subject that to dwell on it in detail would be to defer the main purpose of this chapter. Nevertheless, it is important to recognise that the home has been located as a space in which to reflect and build personal identities (Cooper, 1976; Appleyard, 1979), adult citizenship (Jones and Wallace, 1992), social and cultural status, tastes and values (Csikszentmihalyi and Rochberg-Halton, 1981) and ontological security (Saunders, 1990). Moreover, home is often viewed as a place of privacy and relaxation in which one can escape from the outside world, and a place of love and security (Abbott-Chapman and Robertson, 1999). And while it should be noted that home can have a darker side and can be seen as a place of fear, of subservience, of loneliness, and of exclusion (Moore, 2000), idealistic and comfortable images and experiences of home still continue to maintain importance in most people's lives either as lived experience, as memories, or as desired futures.

As noted above, the elements that constitute home can exist both as ideals and/or as realities. As such, whether they are experienced in the present, are reflected in our real or imagined memories of past homes, or are imagined in future homes, they should never be assumed to be singular, permanent or static. An individual may hold more than one ideal of home, such ideals can adapt over time, and a home whose social and material composition is ideal for the present may not be viewed as ideal in the longer term (Kenyon, 2003). Those living in shared houses, for example, may expect their current social unit of home to comprise of friends, yet when reflecting on their future homes may speak of partners and/or children. It is in breaking down the home into various experiential levels (the personal, the social, the temporal, and the physical) and in understanding that such categories can contain a variety of elements which are neither necessary for a home to exist, nor static, nor permanent, that common-sense assumptions that *non-familial* housing cannot become a home can be challenged. This is what we seek to do in the following discussion, which focuses on constructions of 'home' amongst the sharers involved in our own research.

Resituating home in the here and now: 'home home' and 'here home'

In Chapter 8, we gave some consideration to our respondents' relationships with their parents, focusing in particular on the nature of their face-to-face contact. Most regarded their parents as important people in their lives, had happy memories of their childhood homes and valued their return visits. Nonetheless, in focusing on the meanings they currently attached to 'home', we found that the most common position was a rejection of the conflation of home with conventional/idealised notions of family life. Indeed, only five young people continued to associate home *solely* with their parental home, and argued that this association would only be broken at the point at which they acquired a house of their own – usually, but not necessarily, linked to the parallel acquisition of a resident partner. Paul (household 7), for example, noted that 'the only home that would overturn my parents' home is if and when I got married'. Similarly, Lucy (household 12) not only retained a strong link to her parents' home, but also continued to associate herself with the town in which she had grown up, despite having lived and worked in Southampton for four years. In common with Paul, having her *own* home was linked to the future prospect of having a house and family of her own: until then, her parents' house constituted her 'home'.

However, in direct challenge to this assumed link between home and past or future family life, the majority of the sample – just under two-thirds – considered their current shared household to be their *only* home at the present time. Amongst this group, the concept of home was linked not to the presence of family but to the quality of their relationships in any given setting, and to the presence of features such as security, emotional warmth, privacy, and physical comfort. If a living arrangement met these criteria it was regarded as home; if not, it was *not* a home. Ella (household 6), for example, shared a comfortable house with three friends whom she had met through work, and with whom she had developed a close friendship. She had lived in five previous shared households, none of which she had experienced as homely, due to the absence of the features mentioned above. However, she described her current house as 'the best place I've lived in, so far. This is the first time in ages I've called it home.' Indeed, as a measure of her sense of attachment and security, Ella no longer gave her parents' address as her postal address for official purposes, a practice she had hitherto maintained despite having left home six years previously.

In most cases, the parental home nonetheless remained an important reference point. Indeed, even those sharers who no longer considered their parents' house to be their 'real' home noted that they would inadvertently talk of 'going home' when they visited their parents. Thus an important distinction emerged between 'here home' – where one lives, and where one is surrounded by one's personal belongings – and 'home home' – where one's parents' live, or where one's childhood memories are located (Kenyon, 1998). This often produced an element of confusion in young people's discussions of what constituted 'home', although the majority nonetheless insisted that their 'real home' was the one where they currently lived, not least because most felt that, in practice, they could never return to living with their parents on a long-term (or even a relatively short-term) basis.

Eight young people nonetheless considered 'home home' and 'here home' to be of equal importance in their lives, and consequently felt that they had *two* homes. The reasons for this were varied. Richard (household 16) and Ellie (household 6), for example, both had very close relationships with the lone parents who had raised them, and felt a strong pull to the parental home out of a sense of loyalty and responsibility to their mother and father respectively. Considerable importance was also attached by this group to the continuing presence of their own possessions in the parental home, including in some cases the maintenance of their old bedrooms, untouched and ready for their exclusive use on return visits. As such, strong ties continued to exist not only at the emotional level but in terms of a material connection to the parental home.

A further seven young people stated that they felt 'homeless', with neither their shared household nor their parents' house feeling like a home to them. Again, this was the case for various reasons, including an equation of home with personal space and with living with trusted friends rather than strangers, an equation of home with owner-occupation and/or with feeling settled in one's living arrangements, and an equation of home with future coupledom. In these cases, then, some of the classic indicators of 'home' were considered to be absent. Finally, Paula (household 19) felt equally at home in her shared household and in the parental home of her long-term boyfriend, and felt no attachment whatsoever to her own parental home, whilst Angie (household 17) stated that she did not really know where her home was, given her weekly visits to the parental home: 'If *I* haven't got a clue what my home is, my parents probably haven't got a clue either!'

The responses of the majority of sharers nonetheless suggest that shared housing can indeed provide a meaningful 'home space' for single young adults and, in line with earlier research involving students living in shared accommodation (Kenyon, 1998), home was found to exist on four experiential levels: the personal, the social, the physical and the temporal. This list in many ways corresponds with those of earlier analyses (Sixsmith 1986; Desprès 1993), while clearly reflecting the housing experiences of the specific group under study: young adults living in peer group households. Home, then, was evaluated and made sense of from within the particular personal, social, physical and temporal contexts inhabited by sharers. The social context of home for sharers has already been considered in detail in earlier chapters, and we now briefly consider each of the other three contexts.

The personal home

Shared households undoubtedly met an important need amongst our respondents to establish their own personal space and to thereby gain independence from their immediate family. Indeed, the majority of respondents expressed the view that it was impossible to gain independence whilst living in the parental home. Interestingly, however, many graduates felt that their earlier *student* shared households, despite providing them with a private space away from the parental home, had similarly denied them full independence, as they had invariably continued to receive both financial and practical support from their parents during this period. As such, student accommodation was often referred to as an extension of the parental home, albeit with rather more freedom. Moving away to university was seen as a crucial first step towards independence, but it was largely characterised as a time of living away from, rather than actually having left, the parental home. In contrast, current *non*-student shared housing was seen as free from parental influence, as a place in which our respondents could begin to build lives of their own. Talking about his student accommodation and then comparing it with his current living arrangements, Piers (household 7) for example told us that

> ... I still felt my parents' home really was my base and these were just term-time places to live. I felt at home in one respect there because it was my stuff, it was my retreat. But I still didn't feel I was separated from my parents' home. So it was very much like having my bedroom distanced from my parents' house in a lot of ways ... It's only in moving down here that I felt real difference in a house. It wasn't as nice a house as my parents', you know, it wasn't as convenient for as many things, but suddenly it was my place ... I just felt I moved up from halls and from the other places I lived because suddenly I wasn't relying on somebody else to provide – it wasn't a cheap alternative. It wasn't cheap accommodation because of the job I was in or because I was a student or because of friends, it was something that I'd gone out and got independently. So that felt like a bit of a step up.

In some cases, the physical space of the home in which young people had grown up no longer existed, either because parents had moved or had made substantial changes to the house through redecoration or through a reallocation of bedroom spaces. For some respondents, such experiences had served to make their shared households more homely to them. Moreover, the process of parents moving house was clearly a dislocating experience for many young people. Jules (household 1), for example, referring here to an entry in the housing history form that each respondent completed for us, told us that,

> When I moved here my parents moved to Torquay so I've never actually lived there ... That's why I haven't put it on the list because I've never actually had a bedroom, I've never actually lived there with them. I go and stay there but I haven't got my own room. I mean I've never lived there, I never will live there. So that was a bit odd as well, coming away with my parents moving at the same time as I did. Sort of felt I had no identity in a way because, you know, where you come from is one of those things you discuss a lot.

Similarly, Tammy (household 16) spoke of 'being devastated' when her parents had moved from their idyllic country cottage to a nearby city in order to establish a guesthouse. Whilst she visited most Sundays, she rarely stayed overnight, despite a room being kept free for her should she wish to stay. When once asked by her mother why she never stayed, she had replied 'I'm not being funny mum, you know, but I get a better night's sleep at Southampton than sleeping in some bed that loads of people have slept in and I haven't slept in that much'. Others talked of the strangeness of visiting parents' new homes and, whilst many still had rooms put aside for them, these were not associated with childhood memories even when old furnishings and artefacts were sometimes transferred to these new spaces. Interestingly, these reactions appear to suggest that the comfort associated with childhood memories of a particular house or room was often more significant than the comfort to be derived from spending time with parents, which highlights the importance of the *physical* home.

The physical home

The process by which any given shared house came to be constructed as 'home' was also closely linked to the conditions of the physical space occupied by housemates. We noted in Chapter 6 that the graduates in our research were generally keen to distance themselves from their student identity and the poor conditions of their student accommodation. Part of this distancing included a greater willingness to assume responsibility for their physical surroundings than at earlier points in their housing careers. This is a shift which can be explained in part by their wish to use their current homes as indicators of their emergent adult status, even though this status was often overlooked by others (including parents). The computer analysts, for example, related how they had found it difficult to shake off their student past whilst looking for their current house:

> When we were looking for a house we'd go into the agencies. Lunch times we were all in our suits because we have to dress quite smart for work, and they just assumed we were students because it was four girls living together (Hilary, household 6).

This desire to distance themselves from their past status as students and the problems associated with being a student tenant, such as noise, mess and generally unkempt housing (Kenyon, 1998), appear to parallel the findings of Rowlands and Gurney (2001), who argue that untidy housing can often impact negatively on the status of an individual, as an untidy house is often conflated with personal fecklessness. Our respondents were thus using their management of the home and general upkeep of the dwelling to construct an image of adult responsibility linked to a lifestyle based on full-time paid employment.

Many households had accordingly made cosmetic changes to their living spaces in an attempt to project a more 'grown-up' image, whilst at the same time rendering them more homely. In some cases, tenants had redecorated bedrooms or shared living spaces, or had carried out do-it-yourself repairs and home improvements as a further means of creating a sense of home, although less permanent changes to the physical space of a house, using items such as photos, posters, furniture and soft furnishings, were more common. Sometimes these items were jointly chosen and purchased, and reflected the households' sense of group identity. This was most marked in the case of the six nurses (household 1). The decor of the shared living room reflected their collective commitment to creating a homely physical environment: they had tie-dyed a pair of curtains and spray-painted the light-shade, whilst a boyfriend had painted the walls. Various items of second-hand furniture had been jointly purchased, and the room was packed with personalised effects. One wall was covered by a collage of photographs from a recent joint foreign holiday, with a framed group photograph on the window ledge. A selection of posters and holiday postcards graced the adjacent walls and fairy lights were strung around the window. Shelving on either side of a fireplace contained an assortment of cookery books, bottles of alcohol, glasses, and video tapes. The pièce de résistance was, however, 'the tacky present shelf', consisting of the 'tackiest, most disgusting souvenirs' from their joint holidays: Russian dolls, seashells adapted to perform various functions, a fan-shaped letter holder, dolls in national dress.

Significantly, the shared spaces in the minority of households which we referred to in Chapter 6 as 'stranger households' were largely devoid of personal effects. Luke and Bobby's shared living room, for example, was virtually empty, except for two settees, a TV on a wooden chest, and a glass coffee table – with nothing on it – in the middle of the room (household 11). Shelving on one wall contained a handful of abandoned books and magazines. On the other walls a number of framed prints were hung: mostly rather bland landscapes of the type often found in impersonal corporate hotels. Luke informed us that 'everything in here belongs to the house. Well, to the landlord, obviously. Nothing in the room at all is mine. Nothing'. Sharers in households such as this, unsurprisingly, had little sense of mutual commitment and were less likely than other sharers to regard their living arrangements as 'home'. We found, then, a strong relationship between the layout and use of shared space, the degree of sociability and mutual support that existed between residents, and the construction of 'home'. In other words, emotional closeness or distance tended to have a physical and spatial manifestation, with implications for the extent to which any given household might be regarded as 'home'.

Household sociability and the nurturing of 'homeliness' could also be helped or hindered by the allocation of rooms and their specific uses within shared households. Occasionally, for example, downstairs reception rooms were expected to be used as bedrooms. Our respondents described such arrangements as 'studenty', cramped, less than ideal and often unhomely, serving to remind them of their status as renters rather than home owners. Ellie (household 6), recalling an earlier shared house, described how these circumstances could affect the balance of social interaction within the house:

> So they'd be getting ready [to go out] upstairs...And I used to feel 'but I'm all left out down here'. 'Cos I was downstairs and I used to keep bringing my stuff upstairs just to get changed and get ready 'cos I felt like I'd be missing out on everything upstairs, didn't I?

In such households, the existence of a shared space where housemates could interact with each other, or into which they could invite guests instead of having to take them to their bedrooms, took on even greater importance. Indeed, the absence of such spaces in past and present shared households was often pinpointed as a factor which could render a shared household *un*homely. The importance of shared space was frequently stressed by those who considered themselves to be living in 'grown-up' shared houses, and who contrasted their relatively spacious current living conditions with the cramped conditions of earlier student houses where often every room in the house bar the kitchen and bathroom had been let by landlords in order to maximise rental income. Likewise, Nathan (household 14), who was disappointed to find himself currently living in a household whose only communal space was the kitchen, reflected on how the presence or otherwise of a shared living room,

> has a big effect on how much you socialise with people in the house. Because, you know, just dossing in front of the telly of an evening, you know, it sparks off conversations and you end up getting to

know people a bit better. And there's less incentive to hide in your room and not come out and see anybody.

The temporal home

'Home' is often linked with permanence and security, yet the extent to which this is a necessary requirement is brought into question by the finding that over two-thirds of our sharers regarded their current shared household as either their sole home or one of two homes. Nonetheless, as noted in Chapter 8 and despite the transitional and short-term nature of most shared houses, several of the groups of housemates in our sample had been together for a number of years, and had moved together from house to house. As such, while the physical environment in which they lived had fluctuated, other elements of their home, including the household members, had often remained stable. Nonetheless, most respondents were clear that whilst household stability might be desirable, it was often difficult to attain. Indeed, since the age of 18, each had, on average, experienced three moves involving a geographical relocation, with a change or loss of job the primary reason for moving on one-third of these occasions. There was, then, a strong awareness of a need to remain socially and geographically flexible, either because of a strong personal desire to be mobile, or because they believed that it was expected of them by employers:

> I would like a foreign assignment at some point. I would like to work at their central office in marketing. And these things I know I'm going to have to move for... I'm sure when I get older and when I have family and things I may completely change my mind, but at the moment I can't see myself more than three or four, five years in any one place (Paul, household 7).

> I won't stay here forever because it's not good for your professional development to stay in one hospital (Julia, household 5).

> If one's doing a PhD then, say, probably, I don't know, I'll have to accept that a job will take me somewhere else. Especially if I want to stay in academia. You know, you have to go where the work is, or where the positions are, so it's a bit open (Rick, household 10).

Shared households, then, were rarely regarded as having a life beyond the short to medium term, given the need to be mobile. However, there was also a general awareness that sharing with others, regardless of how close housemates were, could potentially become quite wearing, particularly in larger households where it was often difficult to secure and protect privacy and time alone. Jules (household 1), for example, one of the six nurses who shared, argued that dealing with such a large number of people and the associated interactions could often become overwhelming:

> If you're getting ready to go out everybody wants to know where you're going, what you're doing, who you're going with, what time you're going home. That sort of thing. And that's not always a problem, but sometimes you just want to say no, I'm just going out, all right? Leave me alone. And just sometimes everyone likes to have an opinion about what you're doing or who you're seeing at the time and that sort of thing. And that can be a bit much.

This lack of time to oneself has the potential to detract from the sense of independence that is often sought in a shared household. However, most sharers felt that they were usually able to get away from the attentions of housemates if necessary, and the support and sociability that arose from living with others for the most part overrode any genuine desire to live alone. Indeed, as noted in Chapter 7, few respondents relished the idea of living alone in the near future, even in order to gain privacy. Those who did reflect on the benefits of such a living arrangement stressed that it would only be feasible if they had a partner or a strong social network outside of the home. The message was certainly not privacy at any cost:

> I don't know what will happen, but I'd like to have a little cosy flat of my own. Lots of people coming to visit, not actually being on my own all that much, but yeah, having my own place (Holly, household 13).

> I am quite happy to stay in shared housing. As I say, buying – living down here, I wouldn't want to go and live or buy on my own, at the moment, anyway, 'cos I just don't know enough people. If I got to the stage where I did, I don't know, to be honest with you. I think if it was anywhere other than this particular house, if I got to know – I had a big social circle – I would probably go and do the rented flat thing, just so you could, like, have your own place and you'd still have that whole social circle (Steve, household 14).

The analysis so far has identified the meaning of home for young adults and the ways in which living in shared housing can be understood as homely or otherwise in the here and now. While few viewed sharing as a feasible longer-term option, this did not detract from the construction of their current living arrangements as home. The young adults in our sample were simply aware that home was a fluctuating and developing phenomenon. Thus while their current home was often more than adequate for their current needs, they were equally clear that future housing, and ideals of home, would necessarily adapt to fit in with their own changing life circumstances.

Future expectations, settling down and owner occupation

We have so far demonstrated that although shared households rarely form an end point in an individual's housing career, they can nonetheless provide young people with a legitimate and stable base from which their adult lives can operate. As such, sharing is often chosen not simply because it is the cheapest or indeed the only housing option, but because this particular living arrangement resonates with, and provides support for, the chosen 'lifestyle package' of many young adults. The young adults in our sample therefore appear to be actively engaged in redefining the meaning of 'home' and re-evaluating transitional home experiences in the light of their own changing housing and household needs. This suggests that for some individuals the process of individualisation is affecting their experiences of, and the meanings they attribute to, 'home'. Our analysis supports the conclusion of Birdwell-Pheasant and Lawrence-Zuniga (1999) that, despite 'home' being a powerful and all invasive agent of western hegemony, which has the potential to affect our everyday and most intimate lives, residents may resist hegemonic intrusions in surprising and creative ways. Many of the young adults in our sample were certainly presenting a challenge to the common-sense conflation of home and family by defining their shared households as meaningful adult homes.

Nonetheless, some caution should be exercised before concluding that this will inevitably result in a proliferation of alternative constructions of home as the post-1970 generation moves into its mid- to late thirties and beyond. Despite evidence of resistance to more traditional modes of home life during their twenties, the young adults in our sample appeared unable to imagine 'alternative' homes as either future ideals or realities. As we saw in the previous chapter, most had a much more conservative view of the future, largely describing their ideal future home in terms of living with a partner in an owner occupied dwelling, albeit not necessarily in the context of marriage. Their apparent conformity is reflected in the findings of Rowlands and Gurney (2001) who, reporting on research into the housing perceptions of 15–17-year-olds, state 'paradoxically, for a label conscious, risk-taking, fashion-articulate group, the young people here held remarkably conservative ideas about housing choices they might make in the future' (p. 127).

Why might this be the case? As highlighted at the beginning of this chapter, wider common-sense understandings of home appear to lag behind the lived experience of many young adults who are 'doing home' on their own terms. This results from the fact that our everyday understanding of home is 'derived socially and arises from the historical development of local and global interaction, deeply embedded cultural values and economic activity' (Perkins and Thorns, 1999: 130). The effect of such ideologies of home and family life should be taken into account when attempting to understand the future orientations and expectations of young adults, and the continuing conflation of 'family' and 'home' is one such example of the deeply embedded cultural values to which Perkins and Thorns refer. Indeed, recognition of this overlap is necessary for an understanding of the ideological nature of 'home', certainly within British culture. Despite the growth of shared household living, homes created by friendship groups continue to lack cultural authenticity, compounded by the non-sexual nature of the intimacy associated with friendship, which stands in stark contrast to idealised images of permanent sexual partnerships. As Jamieson (1999) states, 'given that friendship is culturally defined as a non-sexual relationship, and a pervasive public story is that adults need a sex life, then friendship is not all you need' (p. 105).

In speaking of their future housing expectations, respondents indicated that they did not wish to end up 'lonely and sad' ('sad', in this context, referring both to unhappiness and being seen as pitiable and pathetic). Indeed, loneliness was one of the most feared outcomes of housing choices. Thus despite the rising number of separations, divorces and lone-adult households (all of which may make such fixed future ideals uncertain and unpredictable) our respondents continued to view couple households as their ultimate goal. While striving towards this, they were happy to choose shared accommodation and the single lifestyle that such households support. However this was only seen as practicable and desirable insofar as their peers entertained similar lifestyles and were available to provide the friendship groups necessary to support a single life. Nathan (household 14), for example, revealed that 'in my most depressed moments, I do see myself still living in a shared house when I'm fifty years old. I could live with that, but I wouldn't want to be'.

In a world which continues to place a great emphasis on 'pairing up', and which still views sharing with friends as an unusual phenomenon, these twenty and thirty-something young adults clearly felt that sharing as the basis for a sustainable sense of home had a limited shelf life.

A further example of deeply embedded cultural values in relation to housing and the construction of 'home' is the widespread acceptance in the United Kingdom, as well as in Australia, that owner occupation is the most desirable form of housing tenure, despite the increasingly high financial costs associated with taking out a mortgage. Stone (1998), for example, has noted the continuing power of 'the great Australian dream' of home ownership, even though its attainment is increasingly beyond the means of many young Australians. In the United Kingdom, Hunter and Nixon (1999) argue that the negative image of the rented sector is now deeply embedded in policy construction, whilst Gurney (1999) has noted that commonsense metaphors and language have helped to create the pervasive ideology that renting is 'dead money' and that getting onto the property ladder is an important economic and social investment. This trend has been intensified in the United Kingdom by 20 years of the promotion of housing as a private commodity rather than a social right of citizenship (compounded in recent years by the fear that pension funds will no longer provide for a comfortable retirement), thereby resulting in the widely held view that owner occupation is the 'preferred tenure'. This preference was clearly reflected in the narratives of our respondents. Luke (household 11), for example, who was 28 at the time of interview, made the following observation:

> Can't be Peter Pan forever . . . I'm growing up really and you can't live in rented accommodation forever, can you? That's the British and that's what we do and that's what I'm gonna do.

Rowlands and Gurney (2001) have also argued that owner occupation is regarded by many young adults as an integral part of an upwardly mobile 'lifestyle package', 'a bundle of positional goods and social attributes which together define social status' (p. 125). Indeed, some of the strongest support for owner occupation in the United Kingdom during the 1980s came from under-35-year-olds (Ford, 1999), who regarded home ownership as an indicator of independence, responsibility and adult status. However, this level of support tailed off dramatically through the 1990s and, whilst there was some evidence of an increase in the late 1990s in line with broader economic growth, support for home ownership amongst younger people has yet to return to the high levels associated with earlier periods of economic growth. In identifying broadly similar trends in Australia, Reed and Greenhalgh (2002) have questioned the ongoing attractiveness of owner occupation to younger generations. They argue that the flexibility afforded by the private rented sector may be increasingly perceived as its chief advantage over owner occupation amongst young people in their twenties and thirties. Other Australian research confirms this view, with Vipond *et al.* (1998) noting that a high proportion of inner-city dwellers in Sydney could well afford to buy property, yet choose to rent out of choice rather than necessity. Nonetheless, owner occupation remained a popular option amongst the young people involved in our own research, at least at the level of aspiration.

For some of our respondents, owner occupation was a tenure they had already secured, with eight households based in properties which were being purchased by one or more of the residents. In five cases, this had been the only sustainable way of gaining a foothold on the housing ladder and, indeed, the only way they managed to meet their mortgage payments. Renting rooms to other young people may then become an increasingly common strategy for single young adults who are struggling to cover their mortgage costs, whilst for those who are financially better off it can be an effective way of supplementing their disposable income. Damian, for example, noted that he was no longer reliant on the contribution of his housemate to meet his mortgage payments, but would be reluctant to live alone because he would miss the additional spending power. Moreover, given the difficulties that first time buyers increasingly experience in trying to gain a foothold on the property ladder on a single income, entering into joint mortgage agreements with friends is likely to become an increasingly common arrangement (Browne, 2003).

Conclusion

'Home' remains an evocative concept within most people's lives, whether an imagined home, an actual home or a future aspiration. The conflation of home and family is an enduring tendency, reinforced by public and political discourses which continue to promote an ideology of family and owner occupation as the basis for 'home'. Nonetheless, increasing numbers of young people are experiencing a variety of non-familial living arrangements between leaving their family of origin and settling down (if at all) in a family of destination, and there is evidence to suggest that they may be engaged in a reconceptualisation of the meaning of home in their lives. Some of the classic signifiers of home are still drawn upon – the importance of personal space, the comfort of others, physical markers, stability – yet these are no longer necessarily, or only, linked to family life in the minds of many young adults, at least in the short term. Popular conceptualisations of home, then, appear to lag behind the everyday lived experiences of many young people. However, given the entrenched nature of these conceptualisations, and young people's wish to avoid loneliness and uncertainty, it seems improbable that non-familial living will be embraced widely by young adults as the basis of home in the longer term. Instead, alternative futures such as these are equated with loneliness, failure and unhappiness, even though young people's experiences of these living arrangements during their twenties and early thirties often suggests otherwise. Of course, future homes based on the traditional association with family may not necessarily unfold in their planned or imagined form, yet are nonetheless regarded by most young adults as less problematic than choosing consciously to remain single.

Owner occupation also remained a widespread long-term goal in young people's conceptualisations of their future homes, despite the increasing difficulties of gaining a foothold on the property ladder. Nonetheless, the spiralling of house prices may mean that taking out a joint mortgage with friends may become the only means of gaining this foothold for many single young adults, in turn contributing to the projected growth of shared households over the next 20 years (Browne, 2003). Such arrangements create legally binding relationships between friends, at a level well above the legal relationship implied by being joint tenants in the private rented sector. Arguably, this will have a major impact on the nature of platonic friendships between housemates, and not necessarily for the better. Decisions on the timing of moving out and/or selling up will inevitably take on far greater significance once a house is jointly owned rather than rented, and may indeed become critical tests of the limits of friendship.

11
Conclusion: Twenty-somethings and Household Change

Introduction

And what of his long-term plans? He turns 35 this year, so in theory the pram in the hall beckons, but he still feels he wants a refund on his adolescence. 'I've always been a bit immature, you know, in that I never saw much attraction in becoming an adult. 'He thinks he *might* buy a house (at present he shares a rented flat with friends) but 'I don't want to get too settled . . . I probably couldn't hack it, if I tried to live a domestic life . . . I think it's much more difficult nowadays because there's so many distractions and so many options. I don't *like* choice . . . You watch the telly, and there's so many lifestyle choices, so many things that will make you feel dissatisfied with what you've got in your life. And so, for two people to stay together and be happy and not resent each other, it's very difficult' – Jarvis Cocker, lead singer of Pulp, now a married father (Barber, 1998: 46)

This book has explored the ongoing destandardisation of patterns of household formation amongst young people in Northern Europe, Australia and the United States, with a particular focus on the United Kingdom. As such, the transitional experiences of contemporary twenty-somethings tend to be markedly different to those of their parents. We have noted that contemporary young adults are now more likely to leave home in order to continue into higher education, to return to the parental home for extended periods once having left, to experience periods of shared household and solo living arrangements alongside periods of cohabitation with opposite sex and same sex partners, and to marry and have children, if at all, at a later age and after first cohabiting with their eventual spouse. As a consequence of these developments, there is little consciousness amongst many young adults of an automatic and linear route from parental dependency to (co)dependency on a partner, even though available evidence suggests that most heterosexual young people continue to aspire to such a trajectory in the longer term.

In Chapter 3, we argued that these changing patterns of household formation cannot be understood solely in terms of economic constraint, but that equal consideration needs to be given to broader shifts within contemporary society. These include the demands of the labour market and the particular tensions these create for young women; the emergence of post-adolescence as a new and distinct phase of the life course; and the possibility that younger generations are at the forefront of a re-evaluation of the significance attached to intimate relationships and household forms in young adulthood. In our view, such a focus – alongside an emphasis on risk, individualisation and the distinction between choice biographies and standardised biographies – forms the basis for a more rounded analysis of changing patterns of household formation than models which focus purely on constraining factors, one which is capable of embracing the experiences of groups of young people who have been largely neglected in earlier youth research. In this final chapter we reconsider the usefulness of this framework, focusing in particular on the growing distinctions which are emerging between graduates and non-graduates. We briefly consider the implications of changing patterns of household formation for the design of new housing, include some pointers to areas ripe for further research, and finish with a reflection on current representations of young adulthood as a life phase.

Risk, individualisation and the destandardisation of young people's biographies

Throughout this book, we have stressed the significance of the destandardisation of young people's pathways to adulthood. The weight of recent research in the sociology of youth continues to point to the fracturing of traditional standardised biographies in a variety of spheres, including work, housing and family life (see, for example, Bynner *et al.*, 2002; Jones, 2002). Some interpretations of the processes underpinning the destandardisation of hitherto key transitional experiences suggest that social class differences are no longer important in considering broader processes of change. We do not share this view. Whilst all young people are increasingly subject to greater risk and uncertainty in relation to processes of household formation, it is nonetheless the case that certain groups of young people remain more likely than others to follow a rather more traditional or standardised pathway to adulthood, marked by the relatively early formation of a family of their own. A key marker in this respect is whether or not a young person continues into further and higher education (Bynner and Pan, 2002), a route which opens up new possibilities for economic advantage and also provides exposure to independent living arrangements. Those who do not continue into higher education, a group which continues to consist overwhelmingly but not exclusively of young adults with access to limited financial resources, remain more likely to follow 'accelerated transitions' (ibid.: 25) into early partnership formation and early parenthood, often first leaving home in order to move in with a partner rather than in order to achieve independence through living alone or with peers. Young women with few educational qualifications are particularly likely to follow this route (Blackwell and Bynner, 2002).

There is, then, a strong association between social class status and the degree to which a young person's biography is more or less standardised or 'traditional' in nature. It is also the case that young people from working class families tend to face greater levels of risk in their housing careers than their middle class peers as a consequence of their relative economic disadvantage and their restricted access to certain sectors of the housing market (Ford *et al.*, 2002). This is not to argue that more affluent young people do not also face risks related to their housing careers. However, the risks faced by young people from working class backgrounds tend to be those that compound their vulnerability with respect to housing, whereas those faced by their middle class peers are more likely to arise as a direct consequence of the compelling need to maintain their financial advantage. An example of the former would be the risks associated with an inability to afford decent, safe housing, whilst an example of the latter would be the risks associated with the need to be geographically mobile and the consequent strain this places on relationships with partners or on the ability to form a partnership in the first place.

For graduates, there are also very specific risks associated with the rising costs of higher education which may, in themselves, deter certain groups of young people from applying to university in the first place. We noted in Chapter 2 that increasing numbers of young people are leaving university with unprecedented levels of debt, which will only be exacerbated by the planned introduction of additional top-up fees in both England and Australia. These developments create particular risks for young people when they first graduate, and are already linked to the propensity for increasing numbers of students to return to the parental home on first graduating. They are also likely to have a significant impact on the ability of young people to move into the property market on an individual basis early on in their graduate careers, which in turn may result in the creation of more shared households in both the private rented and the owner-occupied sectors.

Financial constraints such as these, as well as others which we have highlighted in earlier chapters, are of course extremely important in understanding changing patterns of household formation, particularly in the early stages of a young person's independent housing career, yet as we have argued in this book, we also appear to be witnessing a parallel transformation in young people's attitudes towards the desirability of certain forms of living arrangements at particular moments in the life-course. Broader structural changes, including those that have had a particular impact on graduates, have undoubtedly acted as powerful catalysts for recent demographic trends, but we have sought to give equal consideration to the possibility that many young adults are also questioning the relative attractiveness of different domestic arrangements during their twenties. As we have seen, this does not preclude a parallel adherence to relatively traditional longer-term domestic aspirations. It does suggest, however, that many young people may, for a variety of reasons, be choosing to defer the process of 'settling down' with a long-term partner and are quite content to live independently at various points in time during their twenties.

In the current climate of economic uncertainty and risk, many young people feel under pressure to remain responsive to labour market demands, which in turn appears to frame their housing choices. However, some of the more sensationalist predictions concerning the assumed end result of these processes, such as the creation of a society of career-oriented and inward-looking loners, appear to be a far cry from the reality of the lives of most contemporary young adults. Whilst the writing of complex and uniquely individualised choice biographies translated for some of the young people involved in our own research into strongly individualistic lifestyles, for the most part we would by no means equate processes of *individualisation* with *individualism*, not least because of the high degree of interdependency with friends and housemates that marked the housing careers of many of the young people we met. This was partly tied to an awareness of the potential risk of loneliness which could arise as a consequence of their single lifestyles, with the decision to share representing for some a deliberate defensive strategy against this possibility. As Weeks *et al.* (2001) have argued in a slightly different context, 'the new narratives of intimate life that we have pinpointed do not represent a thinning of family commitment and responsibilities, but a reorganisation of them in new circumstances' (p. 23).

In the context of our own research, then, instead of finding individuals who were prioritising their careers above all else, we found a group of extremely sociable young people who were consciously engaged in the building and maintenance of close platonic friendship networks and who were at the same time nurturing their relationships with parents and partners across a variety of household settings. Nonetheless, although most were content to be sharing for the foreseeable future, very few regarded it as a serious long-term option, with most talking of 'settling down' at some unspecified future date. Interestingly, 'settling down' was not constructed solely in terms of living with a partner, but often in terms of a baseline of 'having a place of one's own', although the most desirable form of this arrangement ultimately included the presence of a partner, more often than not within an owner-occupied house. Once again, it is important to note that whilst most of our own respondents aspired to these possibilities in the longer term, most were also quite content with their current living arrangements *for the time being*.

These findings, along with other evidence presented in this book, lend strong support to the view that we are witnessing the emergence of a new and distinct phase in the life course, marked by economic and residential independence alongside a freedom from the domestic responsibilities associated with traditional conceptualisations of adulthood, most notably marriage and parenthood. As we have noted, this new phase is by no means universal, but is particularly associated with well educated graduates and young professionals, who are increasingly choosing to sideline some of the more traditional markers of adulthood, in some cases indefinitely. Significantly, this new life phase is linked to both young men and young women, suggesting that amongst the well educated gender is no longer as significant a factor in determining a young person's biography as it once was. Côté (2000) for example, refers to a trend in recent decades towards 'gender reconvergence', particularly amongst the middle classes: 'using a person's sex to predict a life course, and especially a lifestyle, is becoming less accurate, as more men and women face increasingly equal odds of various fortunes and misfortunes' (p. 24). Thus the United States has its 'genderquakers' (Wolf, 1993), Australia its 'girl heroes' (Hopkins, 2002) and the United Kingdom its 'can-do girls' (Katz, 1997): terms used to capture the powerful sense of optimism and ambition prevalent amongst contemporary young women. Across the rest of Northern Europe and North America, as well as in

Australasia, there are also constant reminders of young women's unprecedented levels of success within the education system (Epstein *et al.*, 1998). The possibility that we are witnessing a fundamental shift in the aspirations and expectations of contemporary young women, linked to the ongoing equalisation of access to higher education appears, then, to be central to constructions of post-adolescence as a distinct life phase, despite broader evidence which suggests that important inequalities continue to exist (Franks, 1999; Dench *et al.*, 2002).

However, it is often suggested that the emergence of post-adolescence has come at a high cost for individual young women, as well as for broader society, given the strong association which is often highlighted between educational success, single status and childlessness. Blackwell and Bynner (2002), for example, note that 'there are very few single, childless women amongst those with few or no qualifications' (p. 7); in contrast, the higher the level of qualification attained by a woman, the less likely she is to marry or to have children. These trends towards later marriage and parenthood are often construed in terms of 'delay' or 'postponement'. Aside from ignoring the possibility that the single and/ or childfree status of many women may be the consequence of a positive choice, rather than something which 'hasn't yet happened', discussions of family formation in terms of delay can all too readily slide into value-laden discussions about the dangers for young women – but rarely young men – of 'leaving it too late'. In summer 2002, for example, the British media made much of the publication of the book *Baby Hunger* (Hewlett, 2002). Originally published in the United States under the title *Creating A Life: Professional Women and the Quest for Children*, the book was a cautionary tale for professional young women about the dangers of trying to 'have it all'. In a similar vein, 'delayed' marriage is commonly implicated in debates concerning the so-called 'crisis of masculinity' in many western societies, with women implicitly, if not explicitly, held responsible for the rise of 'new laddism' by virtue of depriving young men of the 'civilising influence' of early marriage and fatherhood (Whelehan, 2000).

Popular culture also promotes a rather contradictory set of messages regarding the desirability of women's labour market success. Whelehan (2000) notes, for instance, that magazines aimed specifically at heterosexual women consistently promote the message that 'having a career is all well and good, but not if it is at the expense of finding Mr Right. They all warn implicitly that the heady days of youth, glamour and social freedom are all too soon replaced by the lengthy twilight of terminal single status' (p. 136). Shows such as *Ally McBeal* and *Sex and the City* likewise depict glamorous and professionally powerful single women whose private lives are invariably beset by angst and emotional turmoil. These images, alongside the portrayal in most singleton novels of 'a *Cosmopolitan* view of single womanhood, sexuality and sacrifice' (ibid., p. 137), represent powerful moral tales concerning the perils of putting career before relationships, with tensions between work and relationships remaining firmly in place for many young people (Franks, 1999).

Much of the public disquiet that underpins popular discussion of contemporary patterns of family formation arguably derives from the growing link between post-adolescence and the movement away from some of the traditional – and highly gendered – markers of adulthood. In this context, and amidst constant reminders of the necessity not to 'leave it too late', many young people may feel themselves to be in limbo with regard to their claim to 'adult' status. For as long as considerable emphasis is placed on marriage and parenthood as the ultimate markers of maturity, it is likely that young people who have not 'settled down' in these terms will continue to be regarded by older generations as 'not yet adult' or, at best, not *quite* adult – regardless of their own sense of adulthood, their level of financial independence, or their employment and educational success. Our own research suggests, however, that in these and other important respects, post-adolescents are not necessarily lacking in the mysterious 'adult' factor, nor are they a group who will necessarily remain 'forever young', even if some young people are currently rejecting 'adulthood' as it is understood by older generations. Rather, they are a group who are – often unconsciously – developing a range of alternative responses to 'doing adulthood', often from necessity as much as from choice. After all, 'adulthood' is as much a social and cultural construction as 'youth': it is by no means a static concept, but one that has evolved and adapted across time and across different socio-economic and cultural contexts. These developments have practical implications in a number of areas. In the next section we focus on one particular area, in relation to the supply of housing to meet young people's specific needs.

The infrastructure of individualisation

The redefinition of youth and adulthood has created both opportunities and challenges for those who would seek to capitalise on the growth of the single 'lifestyle'. The market has been quick to spot the opportunities presented by contemporary patterns of independent household formation, particularly in relation to the rise of the single person household. We noted in Chapter 3, for example, responses ranging from the development of singles nights and the growth in the ready meals market, through to housing developments which include in-house gymnasia, bars and restaurants. In a brochure promoting its 2003 report *Young Adults' Living Arrangements: Changing Needs of 18 to 24 Year Olds – From Living at Home to Living Alone*, market analysts Datamonitor provide four reasons why companies should consider buying the report:

> *Understand* how living arrangements of young adults fundamentally impact their needs, lifestyles and consumption behaviour. *Determine* the type of households young adults reside in, how this differs significantly by country and how the pattern of living arrangements will develop in the future. *Achieve* a greater understanding of how to capitalize on certain anxieties experienced by young adults at home and recent nest leavers. *Refine and enhance* your marketing strategy to more effectively target young adults (Datamonitor, 2003: 1 – emphasis in original).

One of the key recommended action points of the report is to 'provide solutions for each domestic setting'. In the context of shared households, companies are urged amongst other strategies to 'target house sharers with similar products to those in single person households', 'reassess "multibuy" products and promotions', 'develop established home-care brand preferences' and 'broaden the appeal and usage of "sharer occasion" products'. Similarly, companies are urged to target the 'desires for convenience and indulgence' of the young person living alone. At a cost of over $4000 for the full report, Datamonitor clearly believe that a detailed knowledge of changing patterns of household formation will pay off in terms of profit maximisation – and they may well be right. Nonetheless, the development of loyalty to a particular brand of oven cleaner may be less pressing for most young people than the lack of purpose-built housing targeted at single young adults, particularly in the context of shared accommodation.

Commenting on the ways in which housing styles and room usage have changed over time to reflect the shifting needs, norms and expectations of society, Rapoport (2001) states that 'new values and norms result in new lifestyles affecting housing' (p. 154). This is an interesting comment in the light of Beck and Beck-Gernsheim's question, 'What architecture, what spatial planning...does a society need under the pressure of individualisation?' (1996: 43). With the shift away from family households as the immediate and obvious destination for all young adults, housing that caters specifically for groups of independent sharers may need to grow in importance and status in the future. The market has already begun to respond, albeit slowly, to the specific needs of single person households through the gradual provision of more 'new build' one and two bedroom apartment blocks. House sharers, however, are caught between two poles: they need access to larger properties, but not necessarily in the form of existing 'family housing', which tends to be designed to incorporate a series of bedrooms of varying size, from a large master bedroom at one extreme to a box room at the other. Such arrangements can make the allocation of rooms and the practicalities of living in them difficult for shared households which, in contrast to families, tend not to be characterised by pre-given status hierarchies. Although some households in our own research overcame this problem by drawing straws for rooms, household members were still aware of the uneven allocation of space and associated facilities. In some shared households, downstairs rooms are not uncommonly used as bedrooms due to insufficient upstairs space. In addition, kitchens designed for the preparation of family meals can be unsatisfactory for independent sharers who may choose on occasions to cook for each other as a group, but on other occasions may all decide to cook independently but at the same time.

Likewise, in planning new forms of housing it should be recognised that the boundaries of privacy and intimacy for adult sharers are rather different to those of cohabiting partners and households with children. An issue that has proved to be embarrassing for generations of parents and their children – the overhearing of couples having sex – can take on increasing significance if all adult members of a shared house are sexually active (Gurney, 2000). Similarly, bathrooms designed primarily for family life cannot necessarily support the various – and often simultaneous – needs of house sharers. Arguably, then, the challenge for planners and architects will be to create dwellings that can adapt to a diverse range of households. One potential solution to this conundrum, which embraces the British cultural preference for owner-occupation, yet challenges the privacy and potential loneliness that this can bring, is currently under construction in Stroud, Gloucestershire. The development is based on the clustering of private homes in a variety of sizes around a circular building and garden where neighbours will gather to share evening meals and other social activities. Interestingly, Cunningham (2001) reports that many of 'these prospective co-housers have tried an alternative lifestyle when younger and now have jobs in the professions' (p. 2). Perhaps, then, such developments pave the way for future housing which supports more flexible, individualised lifestyles. Two households involved in our own research had created their own version of this ideal, whereby two close friends had bought houses next-door to each other, had taken down the dividing fence and had keys to each other's houses.

Whilst only a minority of young adults appear able to contemplate and plan for a continuation of their independent living arrangements in the longer term, this should not detract from the fact that young people are spending increasing periods of their twenty-something years either in shared accommodation or in single person households. Moreover, the reality of their domestic lives once in their thirties may well turn out to be very different to the future scenarios which young people imagine whilst in their twenties. Many of our own respondents, for example, would not have predicted, when younger, that they would (still) be living in shared accommodation in their mid- to late twenties. One measure of the likelihood of ongoing independence is captured in statistics produced by Britain's largest mortgage lender, Halifax, which found that more than 40 per cent of all homebuyers are now single, rising to 50 per cent in London, compared with only 25 per cent in 1983 (Jones, 2002). A spokesperson for Halifax noted that 'these changes will impact planners and builders who will need to take account of these changes when designing the UK's future housing stock' (ibid.).

Future research agendas

A research focus on the architecture of individualisation is just one area which would contribute to a richer understanding of changing patterns of household formation amongst contemporary young adults and of the consequences of these changing patterns for the everyday lives and lifestyles of single young adults in particular. There are a number of other areas where greater research also needs to be conducted. First, there is a pressing need for research with an explicit focus on the experiences of household formation amongst young people from different ethnic minority backgrounds. Much of the existing research on changing patterns of household formation is largely quantitative in focus and, where ethnicity has been included as a variable, has been invaluable in highlighting broad differences in patterns of household formation amongst different ethnic groups (see, for example, Berrington, 1994; Heath and Dale, 1994; Goldscheider and Goldscheider, 1999; Berthoud, 2000). However, there is very little existing research, particularly of a qualitative nature, which has focused explicitly on 'youthful domesticity' amongst young people from different ethnic minority groups. Disappointingly, the limitations of our sampling strategy resulted in our own research proving not to be an exception to this trend. Available evidence nonetheless suggests that even amongst ethnic communities where more traditional patterns of family formation are still dominant there is a shift towards a diversification of household and family forms amongst younger generations (Berthoud, 2000).

Secondly, the experiences of young lesbians and gay men continue to remain largely invisible within most existing research on changing patterns of household formation. This is largely due to the assumptions of heterosexuality that underpin much research in this area and the consequent lack of fit between the lived experiences of non-heterosexuals and the dominant models of transition which continue to assume eventual progression to marriage and parenthood. When these possibilities are largely removed from the frame, notwithstanding the rise in 'pink parenting' over the last decade and the introduction of schemes for the registration of same-sex couples in some countries, some of the weaknesses of the youth transitions model become apparent. As Skelton (2002) has argued,

> The experiences of young lesbians and gay men means that we have to question the notion of transition and critically engage with a literature on young people which still ignores significant groupings of young people within its definition of youth (p. 102).

In much the same way that researchers such as Weston (1991) and Weeks *et al.* (2001) have redefined the scope of the sociology of the family through their work on the 'families of choice' of gay men and lesbians, a focus on the growth of independent living arrangements and on intimate relationships which are not based exclusively on the heterosexual couple relationship arguably provides an excellent starting point for the 'queering' of the study of changing patterns of intimacy and household formation amongst young adults.

Finally, there is a need for more comparative work to be done in the area of changing patterns of household formation. We have brought together a wide range of literature from Europe, Australia and the United States, and the weight of evidence suggests that in many respects we are witnessing a degree of convergence in outcomes. Nonetheless, it would be a mistake to assume that the processes underlying these outcomes are necessarily similar. Moreover, the extent to which these trends may be emergent in other nation states beyond Northern Europe, North America and Australasia remains to be seen. Fussell and Greene (2002) indicate, for example, that delayed transitions to adulthood are also found in East Asia. Moreover, in the European context there is some evidence to suggest that certain elements of the model are increasingly detectable in southern countries such as Italy where sociologists are seeking to explain the 'striking decrease in births' amongst southern Italian women (Leccardi, 2000).

Conclusion: Household formation, privilege and generational change

It would be fair to say that in recent years contemporary young adults have not had a good press. According to Howe and Strauss (1993), two writers who have devoted much energy to mapping out the characteristics of successive generations of young Americans, the generation born between the late 1960s and the early 1980s is without question 'a generation with a PR problem' (p. 9). Young people within this age group are often portrayed in confusing and contradictory ways. They are accused of being apathetic and lazy, fully deserving of the 'slacker' label, yet at the same time are, apparently, work-obsessed, over-ambitious and grasping. They are politically disengaged and individualistic in outlook, yet simultaneously are involved in the selfish pursuit of lifestyle-based identity politics or are naively pursuing lost causes such as the downfall of capitalism and the destruction of the free market. The promulgation of such contradictory generalisations about 'the youth of today' certainly highlights the absurdity of trying to attach a common set of character traits to an entire generation, and could be disregarded merely as a classic example of what Douglas Coupland, the erstwhile chronicler of Generation X, wryly refers to as the strategy of 'clique maintenance':

> the need of one generation to see the generation following it as deficient so as to bolster its collective ego: '*Kids today do nothing. They're so apathetic. We used to go out and protest. All they do is shop and complain*' (Coupland, 1991: 26, emphasis in original).

However, these contradictory representations are also suggestive of the increasingly fragmented nature of contemporary young adulthood. Today's young adults experience greater levels of risk and uncertainty in contrast with their parents' generation. For some, this has resulted in a proliferation of choices and options which, if successfully negotiated, tend to confer advantage; for others, this has resulted in a closing down of choices and the ever-present possibility of the reinforcement of disadvantage and social exclusion. Significantly, the expansion of further and higher education is exacerbating this divide: as Bynner *et al.* (2002) note, 'the continuing and growing disparity between those young people who gain access to and benefit from furthering their education and those who do not is disturbing' (p. xiii). The polarisation of young people's experiences has, then, continued apace, yet is often overlooked by those who trade in simplistic generational stereotyping. If there is any validity to some of the more extreme generalisations that are made about contemporary youth, it cannot be divorced from the uncertainty and risk which increasingly frame young adulthood as a life phase.

The realms of household formation, intimacy and youthful domesticity are equally subject to the effects of uncertainty and risk and are further areas where young people, particularly those who are single, have been portrayed in negative and sometimes contradictory ways in recent years. It is often claimed, for example, that they are outstaying their welcome in the family home, yet as a generation have no time for their families and wider kin. Contemporary young adults are labelled as relationship-rejecting singletons, yet are also in thrall to the constant search for Mr/Ms Right. They are, simultaneously, hopeless loners and prodigious social networkers. In this book, we have sought to interrogate some of these generalisations by focussing on the rise of independent living arrangements, the impact of this rise on the ways in which young people relate to their friends, housemates, partners and parents, and the effect of these changing relationships on present and future conceptualisations of home and family. We have brought together recent literature from a wide range of areas in order to highlight the experiences of young people from diverse social backgrounds, but in presenting our own research we have deliberately focused on the experiences of a group which consists largely, although not exclusively, of relatively privileged individuals.

We do not claim that the young people involved in our own research are representative of their generation as a whole, although their common experiences of shared housing shed light on an under-researched living arrangement that is experienced by a growing proportion of young adults from all social backgrounds. Nonetheless, as a group consisting largely of graduates and young professionals they are representative of one of the groups who appear to be very much in the vanguard of social change with respect to the transformation of intimacy and household formation. The financial advantage conferred on those who are able to attend university remains an important factor in determining the extent to which young people are, in the longer term, able to make genuine choices in their housing careers or are faced with restricted opportunities. Above and beyond the enhanced social status associated with being a graduate, however, the continuing expansion of the student lifestyle to an increasing proportion of the relevant age cohort in turn provides a greater proportion of young people than ever before with access to niche housing markets at a critical phase of their housing careers and exposure to forms of independent living that many continue to adopt well into their twenties, if not beyond.

In a period when normative scripts concerning leaving home, 'settling down' and 'adulthood' are in the process of being rewritten, single young adults appear, then, to be becoming increasingly adept at (re)negotiating intimate relationships both within and across a variety of domestic settings. Work mates may become best mates, strangers may become housemates, partners may be kept at a distance, friends may live together, family members may become friends, and friends may become 'like family'. Not all young people negotiate these relationships from a position of strength, and those with restricted resources and few realistic alternatives may feel that they are being forced into ways of relating to strangers, friends, parents and partners which are not of their choosing. For the post-adolescent elite, however, being young, free and single may represent a genuine preference during their twenty-something years. We are, then, witnessing a redefinition of the boundaries of adulthood, as we have similarly witnessed a redefinition of the boundaries of youth.

Appendix 1
The Young Adults and Shared Household Living Project

Choice of methods

The ESRC-funded Young Adults and Shared Household Living project was based around three strands of enquiry. The socio-demographic characteristics of individuals who live in shared households and the aggregate characteristics of those households were explored through analysis of a national-level subset of sharers and their households contained within the household file of the Samples of Anonymised Records from the 1991 Census. The main phase of the project was based on 25 semi-structured household interviews, involving 75 of the 81 residents in these households, and one-to-one biographical interviews with 63 individual household members from these households. Three pilot household interviews were conducted prior to the main phase, and one-to-one interviews were piloted with three individuals drawn from these households, which were accessed via 'room to let' adverts on the university's staff club notice board.

Establishing the boundaries of the research

Our primary focus was on non-student shared households, which we defined as 'households that are made up of individuals who are unconnected by marriage, cohabitation or by family'. We decided on an upper age limit of 35, but nonetheless included two households which each contained at least two older members. In one case, they were not only over 35, but turned out to be a cohabiting couple. However, we nonetheless included their household in the sample as their decision to share was based on an explicit commitment to communal living, rather than financial expediency (i.e. it did not appear to be a typical 'lodger' household). Apart from their own bedroom and a room they used for teaching yoga, the rest of the house was shared in common, and all (vegetarian) meals were shared, with food being prepared on a rota. We also included a student household consisting of mature undergraduates to explore the effect of age on student living arrangements and to see whether it might be more akin to a 'standard age' student household or to a non-student household. These households each provided thought-provoking variation to the broader sample.

Gaining access

The shared household as a collective entity was our initial contact point, providing an effective way of producing a data set consisting of household-level data with linked individual-level data: having already given their consent to group participation, individuals were generally disposed towards giving their consent for further involvement. If we had sampled individuals living in shared households in the first instance, we might have secured a broader range of individuals prepared to cooperate, yet there was no guarantee that we would then be able to recruit the entire household for a group interview, or to then secure individual interviews with each housemate, which would have left us with an unconnected set of interviews.

We adopted a variety of strategies for locating suitable households. The most successful strategies were (i) contacting individuals advertising 'rooms to let' in the local daily newspaper; (ii) contacting shared houses in the private rented sector via letting agents, who agreed to forward a copy of our introductory letter to shared households on their books whom they believed met our criteria; and (iii) personal contacts and snowball sampling. Other strategies included contacts via members of the local Landlords Association; placing an advert in the window of a local left-wing bookshop; a request for volunteers published in the local weekly free newspaper; leaving flyers in a city centre record shop; contacts via the warden of a block of local authority apartments earmarked for single young people; and using the city council's register of houses in multiple occupation to identify HMOs which had only one door bell rather than several, and were therefore likely to consist of shared households rather than bedsits.

Finding suitable households proved to be an extremely difficult, frustrating and time consuming task. The strategies listed above involved contacts with 195 gatekeepers and direct contact with 481 households. These households were sent an introductory letter which briefly explained the project, and a short questionnaire to be returned by interested households which solicited details such as of the number of tenants, their age and gender, their economic activity, their tenure, and, if tenants, the nature of their tenancy agreements. 51 households returned the questionnaire, but only 25 were suitable for inclusion. These 25 households were contacted by telephone or email to arrange a suitable date and time for a group interview.

Interview procedures

Household interviews

The group interviews were, with one exception, all conducted in a communal room of each shared household, usually the lounge, but occasionally the kitchen. In the exceptional case, the only communal space available was a kitchen that proved to be too small for the interview, so we adjourned to one of the bedrooms. Permission was sought, and in all cases given, to record the group interview on minidisc. All but one of these interviews were conducted jointly by both of us, partly for safety reasons, but also as a means of keeping track of the order of speech for later transcription. This was particularly important in single-sex households where it was very difficult otherwise to differentiate between voices on the recording.

The group interviews lasted an average of 95 minutes and covered a number of areas: (i) a discussion of the household's history; (ii) the organisation of the household, including ground rules, the organisation of household space and time, differing expectations of acceptable behaviour, social interaction, divisions of labour, household consumption and household finances; (iii) support and solace within the household, including emotional support and the negotiation of conflict and difference; (iv) processes of household reconstitution, and the role of non-household members in the household, including family members and partners; (v) negotiating privacy in shared households; (vi) a discussion of home, neighbourhood and the community; and (vii) an evaluation of the pros and cons of shared living. In most of these interviews we introduced each of these sections with an apposite video clip from *Friends*, *This Life* or the film *Shallow Grave*, as a way of breaking the ice and stimulating discussion. This technique worked well with households consisting of people in their early to mid-twenties, generating lively debate. It was less effective with older respondents, amongst whom we decided whether to use the clips on an *ad hoc* basis. In a small number of cases the decision was taken out of our hands due to a lack of a TV or working video player in the shared space, although on a number of occasions we took a VCR with us.

A number of interesting household-level narrative forms emerged during these interviews. Some households, for example, were eager to stress the similarities that existed between their own household and representations of shared households in programmes such as *Friends* and *This Life*, whilst others were at great pains to stress the opposite. Other households developed narratives based on shared housing as a normative expectation, whilst others developed defensive stories, as if they felt their arrangements needed to be justified. It may well be that sharers whose peers largely live in other household forms come to regard their arrangements as unconventional, and are used to developing justifications for their 'unusual' living arrangements.

In addition to the topics covered in interview, part way through the interview each participant was asked to complete a short questionnaire on their involvement in, and responsibility for, particular domestic tasks. At the end of the interview they were then asked to complete a second questionnaire which solicited personal details on their age, highest qualification, occupation, and their length of residency in Southampton and in their current household. They were also asked to complete a housing history form, detailing the nature and duration of each of the households they had lived in previously, and their reasons for moving in each case. Respondents were invited to indicate on this form whether they were willing to participate in an individual interview.

After each household interview we produced a spatial map of the communal space in which the interview was carried out, noting details of decor and furnishings, including ornaments and paintings, photographs, videos and books. The extent to which communal spaces drew on pooled items of this nature provided a useful indicator of the degree of intimacy that existed within each household, with almost totally bare rooms at one end of the spectrum, containing only items belonging to a non-resident owner, through to rooms which were bursting with pooled objects, including household photographs depicting events such as shared parties, holidays, and outings. In one house, for example, one wall was given over to a display of pictures of *Mr Men* characters, with the names of various household members and household friends attached to each picture.

As an experiment, we also gave disposable cameras to five households and asked them to produce a photographic record of shared household living. In the event, two households returned the cameras to us, and each produced a fascinating set of images. In each case, we then conducted a follow-up interview, with the household members taking us through each image and discussing its content. Given the limited amount of data collected in this manner we have not incorporated these images into our broader analysis, but nonetheless found it to be an invaluable experiment with a method which we hope to use more systematically in any future research (see Heath and Cleaver, forthcoming).

One-to-one interviews

The one-to-one interviews were mainly conducted in local bars. They lasted an average of 70 minutes and were based on an adaptation of biographical interviewing techniques. Using the previously completed housing history form as an *aide-memoire*, respondents were asked to respond to the following opening question: 'starting where you like, and in your own words, I'd like you to tell me about the places you've lived and the people you've lived with, and your experiences and memories of living in each of these places.' After the initial telling of their housing narrative, respondents were then invited to retell their story a number of times, changing the emphasis each time to explore – if not already covered – the quality of relationships in each household, including the impact of their housing decisions on current and past intimate partnerships, fluctuating notions of progress and regression, independence and freedom, choice and constraint, the meaning and relevance of the concept of 'home' over the course of the narrative, and changing relationships with parents and siblings at each point. Respondents were also asked about their future housing plans, and what 'settling down' meant to them. This method proved to be an extremely effective tool. In most cases, interviewees responded enthusiastically, and at great length, to the opening question, and developed idiosyncratic narrative forms which highlighted to us the strong link between housing decisions and ontological security at a variety of different levels (see Kenyon, 2003). In the context of a theoretical framework which sought to scrutinise Beck's ideas concerning the writing of subjective individualised biographies in late modernity, the biographical interview proved to be a highly appropriate method.

Sample characteristics

Our sample consisted of 25 households, containing a total of 81 individuals. Seventy five of these household members were present for the group interviews, 61 of whom subsequently agreed to be interviewed individually. In four households a partner was present for the group interview, and in one of these households two friends from next door, also a shared house, were also present. One of the three girlfriends and one of the two friends also completed housing history forms and agreed to take part in an individual interview. Data on the individual characteristics of our sample are derived, then, from the information provided in the housing history form by the 75 household members present for the group interviews, plus the neighbour and the girlfriend (77 in total). The tables below summarise some of the key characteristics of the individuals in our sample and of their households.

We were initially concerned that the self-selectivity of our sample introduced a bias towards relatively socially cohesive households. Our decision to place a greater emphasis on the narrative interview data than originally planned helped to redress this possible imbalance, as our respondents' experiences of 259 past shared households had by no means been entirely positive. This enhanced our understanding of the reasons why some households 'worked' while others did not, and of the reasons why shared living proved to be more or less attractive at different points in a young person's life.

Characteristics of the 25 households

Tenure of household	
Private rented sector (non-resident owner)	17
Resident owner plus tenants	6
Resident joint owners, no tenants	2
Dwelling type	
Flat/apartment	3
Terraced house	11
Semi-detached house	7
Detached house	4
Number of residents	
2 residents	7
3 residents	8
4 residents	7
5 residents	2
6 residents	1
Gender mix	
All female	7
All male	5
Mixed	13
Means of formation	
University-based friendship	8
Non-university friendship	8
Working for same employer	2
Tenants selected by advertising	7
Age mix	
All 18–25	11
All 26–30	2
All 31+	1
Mix of ages, maximum 30	7
Mix of ages, some aged 31+	4

Homogeneity of economic activity

All employed	20
All students	1
Employed/student mix	4

Time resident in current shared household

All less than or equal to one year	14
All more than one year	3
Mix of time periods	8

Characteristics of the individuals

Gender

Male	36
Female	41

Age	Male	Female
18–21	0	6
22–25	18	29
26–29	11	2
30–34	5	3
35+	2	1
Mean	26.9	24.3

Occupation		
Accountancy/finance	3	2
Computing	3	6
Engineering	7	0
Architecture/design	2	0
Business management	2	2
Teacher	3	2
Other professional/managerial	3	3
Nurse/paramedic	0	14
Development worker	1	0
Sales	1	2
Clerical/administration	3	2
Customer services	1	1
Other, skilled manual	2	1
Other, unskilled	1	2
Student	4	4

Highest qualification		
None	0	2
GCSE/GNVQ	2	7
BTEC/City & Guilds	2	1
A level	5	1
Diploma	2	12
Bachelors degree	14	13

Characteristics of the individuals

PGCE (teaching qualification)	1	1
Masters degree	10	4

Social class (based on current occupation of those in employment: excludes students)	Male	Female
I: Professional	13	3
II: Managerial & Technical	12	29
IIIN: Skilled non-manual	4	3
IIIM: Skilled manual	2	1
IV: Partly skilled	–	1
VI: Unskilled	1	–

Number of shared households ever lived in		
1	5	9
2	5	11
3	8	5
4	8	8
5	2	5
6	1	1
7	3	0
8+	4	2
Sum	155	129

Route to living in Southampton		
Grew up locally, have never moved away	6	4
Grew up locally, left and later returned	4	2
Current student in Southampton	4	4
Former student in Southampton, has never left	6	14
Former student in Southampton, left and later returned	4	1
First moved to Southampton for work-related reasons	12	13
Other	0	3

Ever returned to parental home since first leaving?		
Yes	11	11
No	25	30

Ever lived with a partner		
Yes	12	15
No	24	26

Ever lived alone?		
Yes	8	4
No	28	37

Appendix 2
Household Profiles

Household 1 ('the nurses') consisted of six newly qualified nurses renting a large semi-detached house in an area with a high density of bedsits and shared houses. The six women had lived there for three and a half years, since the second year of their nursing training, and planned to stay in the house for a further six months, at which point five of them were setting off together for a year of world travel. The sixth nurse was getting married at this point, and at the time of the interview had just moved out to live with her fiance.

Name	Age	Occupation	No. of moves since first leaving parental home
Liz	25	Nurse	4
Ray	24	Nurse	2
Jules	24	Nurse	2
Caitlin	24	Nurse	3
Jane	22	Nurse	2
Daisy	24	Nurse	3

Household 2 consisted of an owner occupier, Jackie, and her tenant, Cathy, sharing a four-bedroomed semi-detached house in a residential district of Southampton. Two other tenants had recently moved out together. Jackie had started renting out rooms as a way of financing her mortgage following her divorce several years earlier.

Name	Age	Occupation	No. of moves since first leaving parental home
Cathy	21	Factory worker	1
Jackie (owner)	34	Customer service manager	6

Household 3 ('the engineers') consisted of three young men who had first met as students in Southampton. Two of the three had left the city on graduating, but had later returned for work, and they had lived together in their current household for the last year. They rented a fashionable townhouse near the city centre, and collectively paid the highest monthly rental of all of the households.

Name	Age	Occupation	No. of moves since first leaving parental home
Huw	25	Electronic engineer	6
Jack	24	Research engineer	6
Mike	25	Software engineer	7

Household 4 consisted of a resident owner, and his two tenants. Robert's girlfriend was also a frequent visitor to the house, and participated in the interview, as did Stacy, a tenant from the shared house next door which was owned by Robert's best friend (who also joined in). The fence between the two properties had been removed to enable movement between the two terraced properties. Both owners rented rooms to cover their mortgage payments, and none of their tenants had been known to them before moving in.

Name	Age	Occupation	No. of moves since first leaving parental home
Nigel	29	Designer	5
Heather	22	Market researcher	5
Robert (owner)	29	Teacher	9
Stacy	18	Customer service coordinator	2

Household 5 ('the physios') consisted of three newly qualified physiotherapists, who had all lived together as students in the Midlands and had, more by chance than design, all ended up working in Southampton for their first posts. The three women had lived in their shared house, a spacious semi-detached property on a main road, for eight months at the time of our first contact with them.

Name	Age	Occupation	No. of moves since first leaving parental home
Julia	22	Physiotherapist	4
Dawn	22	Physiotherapist	5
Louise	22	Physiotherapist	5

Household 6 ('the computer analysts') consisted of four women, all working for the same company in the city centre, and living in a large detached property in an area with a high density of privately rented (including student) accommodation. Three of the four had first met as students at Southampton University, and had lived together in various combinations for the previous six years, whilst the fourth resident had met them through work, and had first lived with them in an earlier house. They had all moved to their current house seven months previously.

Name	Age	Occupation	No. of moves since first leaving parental home
Ellie	24	Computer programmer	10
Ella	24	Computer programmer	13
Justine	23	Computer programmer	7
Hilary	24	Computer programmer	7

Household 7 ('the chemists') consisted of four Oxbridge graduates who had first met as students. All four had joined the graduate training scheme of a major petrochemical company in the Southampton area, and after nine months living in lodgings and other shared houses had decided to rent a detached property together on a large housing estate near to their workplace. The four men had lived there for three months when we first met them.

Name	Age	Occupation	No. of moves since first leaving parental home
Mark	23	Chemical engineer	6
Paul	24	Design engineer	6
Piers	24	Chemical engineer	6
David	24	Chemical engineer	7

Household 8 ('Jamie's household') consisted of a resident owner, plus three tenants and, at the time of the interview, the girlfriend of one of the tenants who had recently moved to the area and was experiencing difficulties in finding somewhere suitable to live. Jamie had lived in his large, detached house for 12 years, originally with three co-mortgagee friends, each of whom had subsequently moved out. When we met him, Jamie was just about to take over legal responsibility for the full mortgage. The three other permanent residents had lived with Jamie for six years, two years and six weeks respectively.

Name	Age	Occupation	No. of moves since first leaving parental home
Jamie (owner)	33	Production engineer	5
Kim	25	Nurse	8
Sean	26	Transport manager	8
Carole	32	Teacher	6
Hattie	24	Trainee accountant	5

Household 9 consisted of four recent graduates from Southampton University, all of whom had lived together in halls of residences and other shared houses as students. The two men and two women had lived in their current house, a semi-detached property in a largely 'studenty' area, for the last four months.

Name	Age	Occupation	No. of moves since first leaving parental home
Roger	22	Student teacher	5
Sian	22	Nurse	5
Claire	22	Nurse	5
Brendan	22	Trainee accountant	5

Household 10 consisted of a resident owner, his best friend and a third tenant who had moved in two months earlier. Warren, the owner, had grown up in the Southampton area, had lived elsewhere as a student, but had moved back to his parents' home a year earlier on graduating. Rick, his best friend from university, had recently moved to Southampton, paving the way for Warren to buy a place of his own. Three months earlier they had moved into a Victorian terraced property in a popular residential area near the city centre.

Name	Age	Occupation	No. of moves since first leaving parental home
Warren (owner)	22	Business administrator	4
Rick	26	Research student	7
Martha (not interviewed)	24	Solicitor	6

Household 11 consisted of four tenants, although only two of the tenants participated in the research, Luke who had lived in the house for two years, Bobby who had lived there only six weeks, both on having moved to the city for work. They lived in the same street as household 6, in a large terraced house. We had expected to interview all four tenants. In the event, Barbara was working away from Southampton, whilst Allan had not been seen for seven days.

Name	Age	Occupation	No. of moves since first leaving parental home
Luke	28	Civil servant	6
Bobby	22	Business analyst	8
Barbara (not interviewed)	Late 20s	Barrister	Not known
Allan (not interviewed)	Late 20s	Barrister	Not known

Household 12 ('the other nurses') consisted of two women who had previously shared together in a house with two others. They had both lived in Southampton for four years, and had moved into their current property – a smart purpose-built flat in a quiet cul-de-sac – two months previously.

Name	Age	Occupation	No. of moves since first leaving parental home
Jill	22	Nurse	5
Lucy	22	Nurse	5

Household 13 ('the vegan household') consisted of four residents, one of whom was on an extended trip overseas at the time of the research. He and another resident co-owned the house, a large semi-detached property in the same street as households 6 and 11. The absent co-owner had lived in the house for many years, but none of the others had lived there for longer than six months. The house had a long history as a 'quasi-commune' committed to left-wing causes.

Name	Age	Occupation	No. of moves since first leaving parental home
Matt	34	Support worker	18
Holly	22	Student	7
Randall (co-owner)	37	Development worker	29
Jim (co-owner, not interviewed)	40s	Development worker	Not known

Household 14 consisted of four tenants, although we only met three of them. The fourth had become something of a recluse, with the other tenants only seeing her rarely. All had moved into the house, a terraced property in a rather run-down area, at different times, in two cases on first moving to Southampton for work. The longest-standing resident had lived there for 18 months, the others for four and five months respectively.

Name	Age	Occupation	No. of moves since first leaving parental home
Miles	30	Information officer	10
Steve	28	Surveyor	8
Nathan	29	PC support analyst	6
Lynn (not interviewed)	Not known	Not known	Not known

Household 15 ('the yoga household') consisted of five residents living in a large terraced house which doubled as a yoga school. The house was owned by two residents, both yoga teachers, who had lived in the house for 11 years and who turned out not only to be a couple, but also to be well outside of the age range of our research. Nonetheless, we decided to include the household as an interesting contrast to the younger households. The other residents were all mature overseas students who had lived in the house for only a few months. The owners had for many years rented rooms for additional income, but they all ate together regularly and were expected to take their turn in the kitchen on a rota basis.

Name	Age	Occupation	No. of moves since first leaving parental home
Patrick (co-owner)	43	Yoga teacher	14
Felicity (co-owner)	48	Yoga teacher	7
Anton	23	Mature student	3
Mica	28	Mature student	8
Hans (not interviewed)	Not known	Mature student	Not known

Household 16 ('the mature students') consisted of four mature students, three of whom had shared together for a year, the fourth for six months. They lived in a terraced property in an area dense with student housing and bedsits. They had all met in their first year at college.

Name	Age	Occupation	No. of moves since first leaving parental home
Tammy	21	Mature student	2
Richard	27	Mature student	5
Jack	24	Mature student	5
Natalie	25	Mature student	7

Household 17 (the self-styled 'birds behaving badly') consisted of three young women, two of whom had grown up in Southampton. The third had moved from London to move in with a partner, and had moved in with the others when her relationship had disintegrated. They lived in a terraced house in an older and rather run-down residential area.

Name	Age	Occupation	No. of moves since first leaving parental home
Viv	21	Bar supervisor	11
Angie	20	Traffic operator	2
Katie	20	Microfilm technician	4

Household 18 consisted of two brothers and the best friend of one of the brothers. The brothers had lived in the Southampton area all of their lives, the friend since the age of eight. They had lived in their current house, a terraced property, for the last two years.

Name	Age	Occupation	No. of moves since first leaving parental home
Nick	24	Bar supervisor	4
Simon	24	Accounts clerk	13
Jimmy	23	Welder	5

Household 19 consisted of two women who worked for the same company. Both had been looking for somewhere to live following their arrival in Southampton for work, and a mutual acquaintance at their workplace had suggested they consider finding a place together. They had lived in their shared house, a modern 'Barrett style' terraced house on a suburban housing estate for five months when we met them.

Name	Age	Occupation	No. of moves since first leaving parental home
Susan	25	Trainee management consultant	6
Paula	30	Account manager	8

Household 20 consisted of three residents, one of whom was the son of the no-longer-resident owner, another of whom was an old childhood friend of the son. The son had lived in the house for five years, initially with his father, whilst the friend had lived there for the last nine months. The third resident did not take part in the research.

Name	Age	Occupation	No. of moves since first leaving parental home
Michael	26	Computer engineer	1
Bev	24	Sales coordinator	8
Martin	Not known	Not known	Not known

Household 21 consisted of two friends, renting a purpose-built flat near the city centre. They had shared for the past nine months, prior to which Nell had shared the same flat with another woman for a similar period of time and had taken over the tenancy agreement from her when she had moved out. Nell was in the process of buying a flat of her own when we met.

Name	Age	Occupation	No. of moves since first leaving parental home
Nell	25	Sales consultant	7
Tanya	26	Systems manager	1

Household 22 consisted of three tenants who shared a terraced property in a quiet residential area. They knew each other via mutual friends and work contacts, and had moved in together five months previously. The boyfriend of one of the tenants was a frequent visitor and participated in the group interview.

Name	Age	Occupation	No. of moves since first leaving parental home
Jasper	27	Office worker	4
Ivan	25	Customer relations manager	11
Kath	24	Computer programmer	6

Household 23 consisted of two friends who had bought a house together seven years previously, as the only affordable way of leaving home. They had both lived in the Southampton area for most of their lives, and had known each other since childhood. They had been the first of their friends to leave home. Their house was a modern mid-terraced property on a suburban housing estate.

Name	Age	Occupation	No. of moves since first leaving parental home
Stewart (co-owner)	31	Salesman	1
Martin (co-owner)	31	Upholsterer	1

Household 24 consisted of a resident owner and a friend who had moved in to help him pay the mortgage. They lived in a modern terraced house in a popular residential area, and had been there for seven months.

Name	Age	Occupation	No. of moves since first leaving parental home
Sam	25	Accountant	6
Damien (owner)	27	Financial contoller	7

Household 25 consisted of two friends who had moved in together three months earlier. They shared an apartment in a sought-after marina development close to a large waterside leisure complex. They paid the highest individual rents of all our respondents.

Name	Age	Occupation	No. of moves since first leaving parental home
Scott	23	Trainee architect	7
Jade	22	Pay clerk	4

Bibliography

Abbott-Chapman, J. and Robertson, M. (1999) Home as a private space: some adolescent constructs, *Journal of Youth Studies*, **2**(1), 23–43.

Aggleton, P. (1987) *Rebels Without a Cause: Middle Class Youth and the Transition from School to Work* (Lewes: Falmer Press).

Ahier, J. and Moore, R. (1999) Post-16 education, semi-independent youth and the privatisation of inter-age transfers: re-theorising youth transition, *British Journal of Sociology of Education*, **20**(4), 515–30.

Ainley, P. (1991) *Young People Leaving Home* (London: Cassell).

Albrow, M. C. (1966) The influence of accommodation on 64 Reading University students, *British Journal of Sociology*, **17**, 403–15.

Allan, G. (1986) *Kinship and Friendship in Modern Britain* (Oxford: Oxford University Press).

Allan, G. and Crow, G. (1989) *Home and Family: Creating the Domestic Sphere* (Basingstoke: Macmillan).

Allan, G. and Crow, G. (2001) *Families, Households and Society* (Basingstoke: Palgrave).

Allatt, P. (1993) 'Becoming privileged: the role of family processes', in I. Bates and G. Riseborough (eds) *Youth and Inequality* (Buckingham: Open University Press).

Allatt, P. and Yeandle, S. (1992) *Youth and Unemployment: Voices of Disordered Times* (London: Routledge).

Anderson, I. (1999) 'Young single people and access to social housing', in J. Rugg (ed.) *Young People, Housing and Social Policy* (London: Routledge).

Anderson, M., Bechhofer, F., Jamieson, L., McCrone, D., Li, Y. and Stewart, R. (2002) Confidence amid Uncertainty: Ambitions and Plans in a Sample of Young Adults, *Sociological Research Online*, **6**(4): http://www. socresonline.org.uk/6/4/anderson.html.

Appleyard, D. (1979) Home, *Architectural Association Quarterly*, **11**(3), 4–20.

Arlidge, J. and Thorpe, V. (2000) They said they wanted a revolution. You want the money, *The Observer*, 19th November.

Arnot, M., David, M. and Weiner, G. (1999) *Closing the Gender Gap: Postwar Education and Social Change* (Cambridge: Polity Press).

Australian Bureau of Statistics (1997a) *Youth Australia: A Social Report* (Canberra: Australian Bureau of Statistics).

Australian Bureau of Statistics (1997b) *Australian Social Trends 1997* (Canberra: Australian Bureau of Statistics).

Australian Bureau of Statistics (2001) *Census of Population and Housing: Selected Social and Housing Characteristics, Australia, 2001* (Canberra: Australian Bureau of Statistics).

Australian Bureau of Statistics (2003) *Year Book, Australia, 2003* (Canberra: Australian Bureau of Statistics).

Avery, R., Goldscheider, F. and Speare, A. (1992) Feathered nest, gilded cage: parental income and leaving home in the transition to adulthood, *Demography*, **29**(3), 375–88.

Baird, L. L. (1969) The effects of college residence groups on students' self concepts, goals and achievements, *Personnel and Guidance*, **47**, 1015–21.

Baizan, P. and Lo Conte, M. (1995) A comparison of family and household classifications using intra-European data, Paper presented to the Workshop on European Family and Household Patterns, Luxembourg, 28th–29th January.

Baldasser, L. (1999) Marias and marriage: ethnicity, gender and sexuality among Italo-Australian youth in Perth, *Journal of Sociology*, **35**(1), 1–22.

Banks, M., Bates, I., Breakwell, G., Bynner, J., Emler, N., Jamieson, L. and Roberts, K. (1992) *Careers and Identities* (Buckingham: Open University Press).

Barber, L. (1998) *Demon Barber: Interviews* (London: Penguin).

Barnet, R. (1998) In and for the Learning Society, *Higher Education Quarterly*, **52**, 7–21.

Baum, F. (1986) Shared housing: making alternative lifestyles work, *Australian Journal of Social Issues*, **21**(3), 197–212.

Bauman, Z. (2001) *The Individualized Society* (Cambridge: Polity Press).

Bawin-Legros, B. and Gauthier, A. (2001) Regulation of intimacy and love semantics in couples living apart together, *International Review of Sociology*, **11**(1), 39–46.

Beck, U. (1992) *Risk Society: Towards a New Modernity* (Cambridge: Polity Press).

Beck, U. and Beck-Gernsheim, E. (1995) *The Normal Chaos of Love* (Cambridge: Polity Press).

Beck, U. and Beck-Gernsheim, E. (1996) 'Individualisation and precarious freedoms: perspectives and controversies of subject oriented sociology', in P. Heelas, S. Lash and P. Morris (eds) *Detraditionalisation* (Oxford: Blackwell).

Beck, U. and Beck-Gernsheim, E. (2002) *Individualization* (London: Sage).

Bell, R. and Jones, G. (1999) *Independent Living: Income and Housing* (Leicester: Youth Work Press).

Ben-Amos, I. (1994) *Adolescence and Youth in Early Modern England* (New Haven: Yale University Press).

Bennett, A. (1999) Subcultures or neo-tribes? Rethinking the relationship between youth, style and musical taste, *Sociology*, **33**(3), 599–618.

Bernstein, B. (1978) 'Class and pedagogies: visible and invisible', in J. Karabel and A. Halsey (eds) *Power and Ideology in Education* (Oxford: Oxford University Press).

Berrington, A. (1994) Marriage and family formation among the white and ethnic minority populations in Britain, *Ethnic and Racial Studies*, **17**(3), 517–46.

Berrington, A. and Murphy, M. (1994) Changes in the living arrangements of young adults in Britain during the 1980s, *European Sociological Review*, **10**(3), 235–57.

Berthoud, R. and Gershuny, J. (2000) *Seven Years in the Lives of British Families: Evidence on the Dynamics of Social Change from the British Household Panel Survey* (Bristol: The Policy Press).

Berthoud, R. (2000) Family formation in multicultural Britain: three patterns of diversity, *ISER Working Papers*, Paper 2000–34 (Colchester: University of Essex).

Bianchi, S. and Casper, L. (2000) American Families, *Population Bulletin*, **55**(4): http://www.prb.org/Content/NavigationMenu/PRB/AboutPRB/Population_Bulletin2/American_Families.htm.

Birdwell-Pheasant, D. and Lawrence-Zuniga, D. (1999) (eds) *House Life: Space, Place and Family in Europe* (Oxford: Berg).

Birmingham, J. (1997) *He Died with a Felafel in his Hand: Hilarious True Stories of House-sharing Hell* (London: Flamingo).

Blackwell, L. and Bynner, J. (2002) *Learning, Family Formation and Dissolution*, DfES Research Brief RCB08 (London: DfES/ Centre for Research on the Wider Benefits of Learning).

du Bois-Reymond, M. (1998) 'I don't want to commit myself yet': young people's life concepts, *Journal of Youth Studies*, 1(1), 63–79.

Boseley, S. (1999) Cheating, lying and sleeping with the boss: is this the young person's route to success?, *The Guardian*, 14th July.

Bourdieu, P. and Passeron, J. (1979) *The Inheritors: French Students and their Relation to Culture* (Chicago: University of Chicago Press).

Brooks, R. (2002) Friends and Futures: Young People, their Friends and their Higher Education Choices, Unpublished PhD thesis, University of Southampton.

Brothers, J. and Hatch, S. (1971) *Residence and Student Life: A Sociological Inquiry into Residence in Higher Education* (London: Tavistock).

Brown, P. (1995) Cultural capital and social exclusion: some observations on recent trends in education, employment and the labour market, *Work, Employment and Society*, 9(1), 29–51.

Brown, P. and Scase, R. (1994) *Higher Education and Corporate Realities: Class, Culture and the Decline of Graduate Careers* (London: UCL Press).

Brown, T. (1992) Inadequate homes for students, *Housing Review*, **41**, 100–1.

Browne, C. (2003) Two borrowers are better than one, *The Independent*, 15th January.

Brownell, G. (2002) Going back to school, *Newsweek*, 8th July, p. 25.

Brynin, M. (2002) Graduate density, gender and employment, *British Journal of Sociology*, **53**, 363–81.

Burrows, R., Ford, J., Quilgars, D. and Pearce, N. (1998) A place in the country? The housing circumstances of young people in rural England, *Journal of Youth Studies*, 1(2), 177–94.

Bynner, J. (2001) 'Critical discussion: empowerment or exclusion?', in H. Helve and C. Wallaced (eds) *Youth, Citizenship and Empowerment* (Aldershot: Ashgate).

Bynner, J. and Pan, H. (2002) 'Changes in pathways to employment and adult life', in J. Bynner, P. Elias, A. McKnight, H. Pan and G. Pierre (eds) *Young People's Changing Routes to Adulthood* (York: Joseph Rowntree Foundation/York Publishing Services).

Bynner, J., Ferrie, E. and Shepherd, P. (1997) *Twenty-something in the 1990s: Getting On, Getting By, Getting Nowhere* (Aldershot: Ashgate).

Bynner, J., Elias, P., McKnight, A., Pan, H. and Pierre, G. (2002) *Young People's Changing Routes to Adulthood* (York: Joseph Rowntree Foundation/York Publishing Services).

Calcutt, A. (1998) *Arrested Development: Popular Culture and the Erosion of Adulthood* (London: Cassell).

Callender, C. and Kemp, M. (2000) *Changing Student Finances*, Department for Education and Employment Research Report RR213 (London: HMSO).

Carlen, P. (1996) *Jigsaw: A Political Criminology of Youth Homelessness* (Buckingham: Open University Press).

Carolin, L. (1999) House and home, *Diva*, April 1999, 36–7.

Centrepoint (1996) *The New Picture of Youth Homelessness in Britain* (London: Centrepoint).

Chatterton, P. (1999) University students and city centres: the formation of exclusive geographies, *Geoforum*, **30**, 117–33.

Chatterton, P. and Hollands, R. (2002) Theorising urban playscapes: producing, regulating and consuming youthful nightlife city spaces, *Urban Studies*, **39**(1), 95–116.

Cherlin, A. (1978) Remarriage as an incomplete institution, *American Journal of Sociology*, **84**(3), 634–50.

Christie, H., Munro, M. and Rettig, H. (2001) Making ends meet: student incomes and student debt, *Studies in Higher Education*, **26**, 363–83.

Christie, H., Munro, M. and Rettig, H. (2002) Accommodating students, *Journal of Youth Studies*, **5**, 209–35.

Cieslik, M. (2001) Researching youth cultures: some problems with the cultural turn in British youth studies, *Scottish Youth Issues Journal*, **1**(2), 27–48.

Clarke, G. (1981) 'Defending ski-jumpers: a critique of theories of youth subcultures', in S. Frith and A. Goodwin (eds) *On Record* (London: Routledge).

Clarke, J., Hall, S., Jefferson, T. and Roberts, B. (1975) In S. Hall and T. Jefferson (eds) *Resistance through Rituals: Youth Subcultures in Post-war Britain* (London: Hutchinson University Library).

Coffield, F., Borrill, C. and Marshall, S. (1986) *Growing Up at the Margins* (Buckingham: Open University Press).

Cohen, P. and Ainley, P. (2000) In the country of the blind? Youth studies and cultural studies in Britain, *Journal of Youth Studies*, **3**(1), 79–86.

Coleman, J. and Hendry, L. (1999) *The Nature of Adolescence* (London: Routledge).

Coles, B. (1995) *Youth and Social Policy: Youth, Citizenship and Young Careers* (London: UCL Press).

Coles, B. (2000) *Joined Up Youth Research, Policy and Practice* (Leicester: Youth Work Press).

Coles, B., Rugg, J. and Seavers, J. (1999) 'Young adults living in the parental home: the implications of extended youth transitions for housing and social policy', in J. Rugg (ed.) *Young People, Housing and Social Policy* (London: Routledge).

Collinson, P. (2001) In search of bricks and mortarboard, *The Guardian*, 14th April.

Cooper, C. (1976) 'The house as a symbol of self', in H. Proshansky, W. Ittleson and L. Rivlin (eds) *Environmental Psychology: People and their Physical Settings* (New York: Holt, Rineheart and Winston).

Cooper-Marcus, C. (1995) *House as a Mirror of Self: Exploring the Deeper Meaning of Home* (York Beach: Conari Press).

Côté, J. (2000) *Arrested Adulthood: The Changing Nature of Maturity and Identity* (New York: New York University Press).

Côté, J. and Allahar, A. (1994) *Generation on Hold: Coming of Age in the Late Twentieth Century* (New York: New York University Press).

Coupland, D. (1991) *Generation X: Tales of an Accelerated Culture* (London: Abacus).

Csikszentmihalyi, M. and Rochberg-Halton, E. (1981) *The Meaning of Things: Domestic Symbols and the Self* (London: Cambridge University Press).

Cunningham, J. (2001) Pulling down the fences, *Guardian Society*, 25th July pp. 2–3.

Datamonitor (2003) *Young People's Living Arrangements*, Promotional brochure, www.datamonitor.com/consumer.

Dearing Report: National Committee of Inquiry into Higher Education (1997) *Higher Education in the Learning Society* (London: HMSO).

Dench, S., Aston, C., Meager, N., Williams, M. and Willison, R. (2002) *Key Indicators of Women's Position in Britain* (London: Women and Equality Unit).

Department for Education and Employment (1998) *Statistics of Education: Student Support England and Wales 1996/97* (London: The Stationery Office).

Department of the Environment, Transport and the Regions (1999) *English House Condition Survey 1996: Houses in Multiple Occupation in the Private Rented Sector* (London: DETR).

Desprès, C. (1993) 'A hybrid strategy in a study of shared housing', in E. Arias (ed.) *The Meaning and Use of Housing* (Aldershot: Avebury).

Dixon, I., Salvat, G. and Skeates, J. (1989) 'North London young lesbian group: specialist work within the youth service', in C. Jones and P. Mahoney (eds) *Learning Our Lines: Sexuality and Social Control in Education* (London: The Women's Press).

Dunne, G., Prendergast, S. and Telford, D. (2002) Young, gay, homeless and invisible: a growing population? *Culture, Health and Sexuality*, **4**(1), 103–15.

Dwyer, P. and Wyn, J. (2001) *Youth, Education and Risk: Facing the Future* (London: RoutledgeFalmer).

Eggars, D. (2000) *A Heartbreaking Work of Staggering Genius* (London: Picador).

Ellis, B. (1996) Leaving the nest, NOT! How young people, with parental support, are living at home longer, *Youth Studies Australia*, **15**(1), 34–36.

Epstein, D., Elwood, J., Hey, V. and Maw, J. (1998) *Failing Boys? Issues in Gender and Achievement* (Buckingham: Open University Press).

Ermisch, J. (2000) Personal relationships and marriage expectations: Evidence from the 1998 British Household Panel Survey, *ISER Working Papers*, Paper 2000–27 (Colchester: University of Essex).

Ermisch, J., Di Salvo, P. and Joshi, H. (1995) Household formation and housing tenure decisions of young people, *Occasional Paper 95-1* (Colchester: University of Essex).

Ermisch, J. and Francesconi, M. (2000) 'Patterns of household and family formation', in R. Berthoud and J. Gershuny (eds) *Seven Years in the Lives of British Families: Evidence on the Dynamics of Social Change from the British Household Panel Survey* (Bristol: The Policy Press).

European Commission (1997) *Youth in the European Union – From Education to Working Life* (Luxembourg: Office for Official Publications of the European Commission).

European Commission (2000) *The Social Situation in the European Union 2000* (Luxembourg: Office for Official Publications of the European Commission).

European Group for Integrated Social Research (2001) Misleading trajectories: transition dilemmas in young adults in Europe, *Journal of Youth Studies*, **4**(1), 101–18.

Fields, J. and Casper, L. (2001) America's families and living arrangements: March 2000, *Current Population Reports*, 20–537, Washington DC: US Census Bureau.

Finch, J. and Mason, J. (1993) *Negotiating Family Responsibilities* (London: Routledge).

Ford, J. (1999) 'Young adults and owner occupation: a changing goal?', in J. Rugg (ed.) *Young People, Housing and Social Policy* (London: Routledge).

Ford, J., Rugg, J. and Burrows, R. (2002) Conceptualising the contemporary role of housing in the transition to adult life in England, *Urban Studies*, **39**(13), 2455–67.

Forsyth, A. and Furlong, A. (2000) *Socio-Economic Disadvantage and Access to Higher Education* (Bristol: Policy Press).

Franks, S. (1999) *Having None of It: Women, Men and the Future of Work* (London: Granta Books).

Furlong, A. and Cartmel, F. (1997) *Young People and Social Change: Individualization and Risk in Late Modernity* (Buckingham: Open University Press).

Fussell, E. and Greene, M. (2002) 'Demographic trends affecting youth around the world', in B. Bradford Brown, R. Larson and T. Saraswathi (eds) *The World's Youth: Adolescence in Eight Regions of the Globe* (Cambridge: Cambridge University Press).

Gelder, K. and Thornton, S. (1997) *The Sub-cultures Reader* (London: Routledge).

Giddens, A. (1991) *Modernity and Self-identity: Self and Society in the Late Modern Age* (Cambridge: Polity Press).

Giddens, A. (1992) *The Transformation of Intimacy: Sexuality, Love and Eroticism in Modern Societies* (Cambridge: Polity Press).

Gilding, M. (2001) Changing families in Australia, 1901–2001, *Family Matters*, **60**, 6–11.

Gillies, V. (2000) Young people and family life: analysing and comparing disciplinary discourses, *Journal of Youth Studies*, 3(2), 211–28.

Gillies, V., Ribbons-McCarthy, J. and Holland, J. (2001) *Pulling Together, Pulling Apart: The Family Lives of Young People* (London: Joseph Rowntree Foundation/Family Policy Studies Centre).

Goldscheider, F. and Goldscheider, C. (1993) *Leaving Home before Marriage: Ethnicity, Familism and Generational Relationships* (Madison: University of Wisconsin Press).

Goldscheider, F. and Goldscheider, C. (1999) *The Changing Transition to Adulthood: Leaving and Returning Home* (Thousand Oaks: Sage).

Gordon, R. (2002) Should you buy with friends? *Money Guardian*, 8th May.

Griffin, C. (1985) *Typical Girls?* (London: Routledge).

Griffin, C. (2001) Imagining new narratives of youth: youth research, the 'new Europe' and global youth culture, *Childhood*, 8(2), 147–66.

Gurney, C. (1999) Lowering the drawbridge: a case study of analogy and metaphor in the social construction of home ownership, *Urban Studies*, **36**, 1705–22.

Gurney, C. (2000) Transgressing public/private boundaries in the home: a sociological analysis of the coital noise taboo, *Venereology*, **13**, 39–46.

Hall, R., Ogden, P. and Hill, C. (1997) The pattern and structure of one-person households in England and Wales and France, *International Journal of Population Geography*, **3**, 161–81.

Hall, R., Ogden, P. and Hill, C. (1999) 'Living alone: evidence from England and Wales and France over the last two decades', in S. McRae (ed.) *Changing Britain: Families and Households in the 1990s* (Oxford: Oxford University Press).

Hall, S. and Jefferson, T. (1975) *Resistance through Rituals: Youth Subcultures in Post-war Britain* (London: Hutchinson University Library).

Hands, J. (1971) Students in the housing market, *Housing Review*, **20**, 76–8.

Hatch, S. (1969) *Student Residence: A Discussion of the Literature*, Research into Higher Education Monograph No. 4 (London: SRHE).

Hayward, D. (1975) Home as an environmental and psychological concept, *Landscape*, **20**, 2–9.

Heath, S. (1997) *Preparation for Life? Vocationalism and the Equal Opportunities Challenge* (Aldershot: Ashgate).

Heath, S. (1999) Young adults and household formation in the 1990s, *British Journal of Sociology of Education*, **20**(4), 545–61.

Heath, S. (2002) 'Domestic and housing transitions and the negotiation of intimacy', in M. Cieslik and G. Pollock (eds) *Young People in Risk Society: The Restructuring of Youth Identities and Transitions in Late Modernity* (Aldershot: Ashgate).

Heath, S. and Cleaver, F. (forthcoming) 'Mapping the spatial in shared households: a missed opportunity?', in C. Knowles and P. Sweetman (eds) *Picturing the Social Landscape* (London: Routledge).

Heath, S. and Dale, A. (1994) Household and family formation in Great Britain: the ethnic dimension, *Population Trends*, **77**, 5–13.

Heath, S. and Kenyon, E. (2001) Single young professionals and shared household living, *Journal of Youth Studies*, **4**(1), 83–100.

Heath, S. and Miret, P. (1996) Living in and out of the parental home in Spain and Great Britain: a comparative approach, *Cambridge Group for the History of Population and Social Structure: Working Paper Series*, No. 2 (Cambridge: The Cambridge Group).

Heiman, R. (2001) The ironic contradictions in the discourse on Generation X or how 'slackers' are saving capitalism, *Childhood*, **8**(2), 275–93.

Hendy, N. and Pascall, G. (2002) *Disability and Transition to Adulthood: Achieving Independent Living* (Brighton: Pavilion Publishing/Joseph Rowntree Foundation).

Hetherington (2000) *New Age Travellers: Vanloads of Uproarious Humanity* (London: Continuum International Publishing Group).

Hewlett, S. (2002) *Baby Hunger: The New Battle for Motherhood* (London: Atlantic Books).

Higher Education Statistics Agency (2001) *Higher Education Statistics for the United Kingdom 1999/2000* (Cheltenham: HESA).

Higher Education Statistics Agency (2002) *Higher Education Statistics for the United Kingdom 2000/01* (Cheltenham: HESA).

Hillman, K. and Marks, G. (2002) *Becoming an Adult: Leaving Home, Relationships and Home Ownership among Australian Youth* (Camberwell: Australian Council for Educational Research).

Hine, T. (1999) *The Rise and Fall of the American Teenager* (New York: Avon Books).

Holdsworth, C. (2000) Leaving home in Britain and Spain, *European Sociological Review*, **16**(2), 201–22.

Hollands, B. (1990) *The Long Transition* (Basingstoke: Macmillan).

Holland, J., Ramazanoglu, C., Sharpe, S. and Thomson, R. (1998) *The Male in the Head: Young People, Heterosexuality and Power* (London: Tufnell Press).

Holloway, S. and Valentine, G. (2002) *Cyberkids: Youth Identities and Communities in an On-Line World* (London: RoutledgeFalmer).

Hopkins, S. (2002) *Girl Heroes: The New Force in Popular Culture* (Annandale: Pluto Press).

Howe, N. and Strauss, B. (1993) *13th Gen: Abort, Retry, Ignore, Fail?* (New York: Vintage Books).

Humphrey, R. and McCarthy, P. (1997) High debt and poor housing. *Youth and Policy*, **56**, 55–63.

Hunter, C. and Nixon, J. (1999) The discourse of housing debt: the social construction of landlords, lenders, borrowers and tenants. *Housing, Theory and Society*, 16, 165–78.

Hutson, S. and Jenkins, R. (1989) *Taking the Strain: Families, Unemployment and the Transition to Adulthood* (Buckingham: Open University Press).

Hutson, S. and Liddiard, M. (1994) *Youth Homelessness: The Construction of a Social Issue* (Basingstoke: Macmillan).

Iacovou, M. (1998) Young people in Europe: two models of household formation, *Working Papers of the ESRC Research Centre on Micro-Social Change*, Paper 98-13 (Colchester: University of Essex).

Irwin, S. (1995) *Rights of Passage: Social Change and the Transition from Youth to Adulthood* (Buckingham: Open University Press).

Jackson, S. and Scott, S. (1997) Gut reactions to matters of the heart: reflections on rationality, irrationality and sexuality, *Sociological Review*, 45(4), 551–75.

Jamieson, L., Stewart, R., Li, Y., Anderson, M., Bechhofer, F. and McCrone, D. (2003) 'Single, 20-something and seeking?', in G. Allan and G. Jones (eds) *Social Relations and the Life Course* (Basingstoke: Palgrave).

Jamieson, L. (1999) Intimacy transformed: a critical look at the 'pure relationship', *Sociology*, 33(3), 477–94.

Johnston, L., MacDonald, R., Mason, P., Ridley, L. and Webster, C. (2000) *Snakes & Ladders: Young People, Transitions and Social Exclusion* (Bristol: The Policy Press).

Jones, G. (1987) Leaving the parental home: an analysis of early housing careers, *Journal of Social Policy*, 16(1), 49–74.

Jones, G. (1992) Leaving home in rural Scotland, *Youth and Policy*, 32, 19–29.

Jones, G. (1995a) *Leaving Home* (Buckingham: Open University Press).

Jones, G. (1995b) *Family Support for Young People* (London: Family Policy Studies Centre).

Jones, G. (2000) Experimenting with households and inventing 'home', *International Social Science Journal*, 52(2), 183–94.

Jones, G. (2001) Fitting homes? Young people's housing and household strategies in rural Scotland, *Journal of Youth Studies*, 4(1), 41–62.

Jones, G. (2002) *The Youth Divide: Diverging Paths to Adulthood* (York: Joseph Rowntree Foundation/York Publishing Services).

Jones, G. and Wallace, C. (1992) *Youth, Family and Citizenship* (Buckingham: Open University Press).

Jones, R. (2002) Halifax warns on rise in single homebuyers, *The Guardian*, 22nd August.

de Jong-Gierveld, J., Liefbroer, A. and Beekink, E. (1991) The effect of parental resources on patterns of leaving home among young adults in the Netherlands, *European Sociological Review*, 7(1), 55–72.

Katz, A. (1997) *The 'Can Do' Girls: A Barometer of Social Change* (Oxford: Department of Applied Social Studies and Research/The Body Shop).

Kelly, J. (2001) Employers unlikely to value greatly a gap in experience (Weekend), *Financial Times*, 7th April.

Kemp, P. and Rugg, J. (1998) *The Single Room Rent: Its Impact on Young People* (York: Joseph Rowntree Foundation).

Kemp, P. and Ktoghan, M. (2001) Movement into and out of the private rental sector in England, *Housing Studies*, 16(1), 21–37.

Kemp, S. (2001) Personal Communication from Accommodation Research Officer, National Union of Students, 13th June 2001.

Kenyon, E. (1997) Seasonal sub-communities: the impact of student households on residential communities, *British Journal of Sociology*, **48**, 286–301.

Kenyon, E. (1998) A community within the community? An empirical exploration of the formation and constitution of 'student areas', Unpublished PhD thesis, Lancaster University.

Kenyon, E. (1999) 'A home from home: students' transitional experiences of home', in T. Chapman and J. Hockey (eds) *Ideal Homes? Social Change and Domestic Life* (London: Routledge).

Kenyon, E (2003) 'Young adults' household formation: individualisation, identity and home', in G. Allan and G. Jones (eds) *Social Relations and the Life Course* (Basingstoke: Palgrave).

Kenyon, E. and Heath, S. (2001) Choosing *This Life*: Narratives of choice amongst house sharers, *Housing Studies*, **16**(5), 619–35.

Kiernan, K. (1985) The departure of children: the timing of leaving home over the life cycle of parents and children, *CPS Research Paper 85-3* (London: Centre for Population Studies).

Kiernan, K. (1986) *Transitions in Young Adulthood*, National Child Development Study User Support Group, Working Paper No. 16.

Kiernan, K. (1992) The impact of family disruption in childhood on transitions made in adult life, *Population Studies*, **46**(2), 213–34.

Kilmartin, C. (2000) Young adult moves: leaving home, returning home, relationships, *Family Matters*, **55**, 36–40.

Klein, N. (2000) *No Logo* (London: Flamingo).

Kumar, K. (1995) *From Post-industrial to Post-modern Society* (Oxford: Blackwell).

Langford, W., Lewis, C., Solomon, Y. and Warin, J. (2001) *Family Understandings: Closeness, Authority and Independence in Families with Teenagers* (York: Joseph Rowntree Foundation).

La Valle, I., O'Regan, S. and Jackson, C. (2000) *The Art of Getting Started: Graduate Skills in a Fragmented Labour Market*, IES Report 364 (London: IES).

Leblanc, L. (1999) *Pretty in Punk* (London: Routledge).

Leccardi, C. (2000) 'Matters of identity: young women and birth control in Southern Italy', *NYRIS 7: Proceedings*, http://www.alli.fi/nyri/nyris/nyris7/papers/leccardi.htm.

Leonard, D. (1980) *Sex and Generation: A Study of Courtship and Weddings* (London: Tavistock).

Lesko, N. (2001) *Act Your Age! A Cultural Construction of Adolescence* (London: RoutledgeFalmer).

Ley, D. (1996) *The New Middle Class and the Remaking of the Central City* (Oxford: Oxford University Press).

Litwin, S. (1986) *The Postponed Generation: Why America's Grown Up Kids are Growing Up Later* (New York: William Morrow).

Lovatt, J. (2003) Home isn't where the heart is, *Observer Magazine*, 2nd February.

Lucas, R. and Lamont, N. (1998) Combining work and study: an empirical study of full-time students in school, college and university, *Journal of Education and Work*, **11**, 41–56.

MacDonald, R. (1997) *Youth, the Underclass and Social Exclusion* (London: Routledge).

MacDonald, R. (1998) Youth transitions and social exclusion: some issues for youth research in the UK, *Journal of Youth Studies*, **1**(2), 163–76.

MacDonald, R., Mason, P., Shildrick, T., Webster, C., Johnston, L. and Ridley, L. (2001) Snakes & Ladders: In Defence of Studies of Youth Transition, *Sociological Research On-line*, **5**(4), <http://www.socresonline.org.uk/5/4/macdonald.html>.

MacGregor-Wise, J. (2000) Home: territory and identity, *Cultural Studies*, **14**(2), 295–310.

Mackay, H. (1997) *Generations: Baby Boomers, their Parents and their Children* (Sydney: Macmillan).

Maffesoli, M. (1996) *The Time of the Tribes: The Decline of Individualism in Mass Society* (London: Sage).

Marris, P. (1963) Hall or digs for students? *New Society*, **1**(33), 8–10.

McGlone, F., Park, A. and Roberts, C. (1999) 'Kinship and friendship: attitudes and behaviour in Britain', in S. McRae (ed.) *Changing Britain: Families and Households in the 1990s* (Oxford: Oxford University Press).

McKay, G. (1998) *Diy Culture: Party and Protest in Nineties Britain* (London: Verso).

McKean, J. (1975) Do students need special housing? *Royal Institute of British Architects Journal*, **82**, 9–20.

McMinn, M. (2002) 'Friends united', *Observer Magazine*, 19th May.

McNamee, S. (1998) 'The home: youth, gender and video games: power and control in the home', in T. Skelton and G. Valentine (eds) *Cool Places: Geographies of Youth Cultures* (London: Routledge).

McRae, S. (1999) *Changing Britain: Families and Households in the 1990s* (Oxford: Oxford University Press).

Miles, S. (2000) *Youth Lifestyles in a Changing World* (Buckingham: Open University Press).

Mitterauer, M. (1992) *A History of Youth* (Oxford: Blackwell).

Moore, J. (2000) Placing home in context. *Journal of Environmental Psychology*, **20**, 207–17.

Morgan, D. (1996) *Family Connections* (Cambridge: Polity Press).

Morgan, D. and McDowell, L. (1979) *Pattern of Residence: Costs and Options in Student Housing* (Guildford: SRHE).

Mori (2001) *Student Living Report* (Bristol: Unite).

Morris, K. and Fuller, M. (1999) Heterosexual relationships of young women in a rural environment, *British Journal of Sociology of Education*, **20**(4), 531–43.

Morrison, P. and McMurray, S. (1999) The inner-city apartment versus the suburb: housing sub-markets in a New Zealand city, *Urban Studies*, **36**(2), 377–97.

Murphy, M. (1996) 'Family and household issues', in A. Dale (ed.), *Looking Towards the 2001 Census*, OPCS Occasional Paper 46 (London: OPCS).

Natalier, K. (2002) 'I'm not his wife': doing gender in share households, Unpublished PhD thesis, University of Queensland.

Niblett Report. University Grants Committee (1957) *Report of the Sub-committee on Halls of Residence* (London: HMSO).

Nudd, T. and Stier, D. (1969) Do you really want classes taught in your residence hall? *Journal of the National Association of Student Personnel Administrators*, **7**, 101–3.

Observer Life Magazine (2000) *The Singles Issue*, 5th November 2000.

O'Connor, P. (1992) *Friendships between Women: A Critical Review*, Hemel (Hempstead: Harvester Wheatsheaf).

Office of the Deputy Prime Minister (1999) *Housing Statistics: Projections of House-holds in England 2021* (London: Office of the Deputy Prime Minister).

Office for National Statistics (2000) *Social Trends 30* (London: ONS).

Office for National Statistics (2001a) *Social Trends 31* (London: ONS).

Office for National Statistics (2001b) *Social Focus on Men* (London: ONS).

Office for National Statistics (2002) *Social Trends 32* (London: ONS).

Office for National Statistics (2003) Marriage in decline, National Statistics Online, http://www.statistics.gov.uk/cci/nugget.asp?id=322, accessed 25th March 2003.

Pahl, R. (2000) *On Friendship* (Cambridge: Polity Press).

Perkins, H. and Thorns, D. (1999) House and home and their interaction with changes in New Zealand's urban system, households and family structures, *Housing, Theory and Society*, 16, 124–35.

Pilkington, H. (1994) *Russia's Youth and its Culture* (London: Routledge).

Pitcher, J. and Purcell, K. (1998) Diverse expectations and access to opportunities: is there a graduate labour market, *Higher Education Quarterly*, 52, 179–203.

Pooley, C. and Turnball, J. (1997) Leaving home: the experience of migration from the parental home in Britain since c.1770, *Journal of Family History*, 22(4), 390–424.

Population Reference Bureau (2003) *While U.S. Households Contract, Homes Expand* (Washington: Population Reference Bureau).

Prendergast, S., Dunne, G. and Telford, D. (2002) A light at the end of the tunnel? Experiences of leaving home for two contrasting groups of young lesbian, gay and bisexual people, *Youth and Policy*, 75, 42–62.

Procter, I. and Padfield, M. (1998) *Young Adult Women, Work and Family: Living a Contradiction* (London: Mansell).

Punch, M. (1967) The student ritual, *New Society*, 7th December, 811–13.

Purcell, K. and Rowley, G. (2000) *Higher Education Careers Services and Graduate Guidance Needs: The Evidence from Surveys of Users.* (Stage 1 Report to the Sub-Group of the HE Careers Advisory Service Review.) Bristol: University of the West of England, Employment Studies Research Unit.

Putnam, R. (2000) *Bowling Alone: The Collapse and Revival of American Community* (New York: Simon and Schuster).

Quilgars, D. and Pleace, N. (1999) 'Housing and support services for young people', in J. Rugg (ed.) *Young People, Housing and Social Policy* (London: Routledge).

Rapoport, A. (2001) Theory, culture and housing, *Housing theory and society*, 17, 145–65.

Ravanera, Z., Rajulton, F. and Burch, T. (1995) A cohort analysis of home-leaving in Canada, 1910–1975, *Journal of Comparative Family Studies*, 26(2), 179–93.

Ravetz, A. (1996) When parts of town rely on gown, *Town and Country Planning*, March, 72–3.

Raynor, J. (2000) We want to be alone, *The Observer Review*, 16th January.

Reay, D., Davies, J., David, M. and Ball, S. (2001) Choices of degree or degrees of choice? Class, 'race' and the higher education choice process, *Sociology*, 35(4), 855–74.

Reed, R. and Greenhalgh, E. (2002) Factors influencing the rent vs buy decision – implications for housing markets, Paper presented to 26th Australia and New Zealand Regional Science Association International Annual Conference, October 2002.

Rhodes, D. (1999) 'Students and housing: a testing time?', in J. Rugg (ed.) *Young People, Housing and Social Policy* (London: Routledge).

Rigby, A. (1974) *Alternative Realities: A Study of Communes and their Members* (London: Routledge and Kegan Paul).

Robbins Report. Committee on Higher Education (1963) *Higher Education* (Cmnd.2154) (London: HMSO).

Roberts, K. (1993) 'Career trajectories and the mirage of increased social mobility', in I. Bates and G. Riseborough (eds) *Youth and Inequality* (Buckingham: Open University Press).

Roberts, K. (1995) *Youth and Employment in Modern Britain* (Oxford: Oxford University Press).

Robson-Scott, M. (1999) This shared life, *You Magazine*, 9th May.

Rose, D. (1984) Rethinking gentrification: beyond the uneven development of Marxist urban theory, *Environment and Planning D*, **2**, 47–74.

Roseneil, S. (2000) Why we should care about friends: some thoughts about the ethics and practice of friendship, ESRC Research Group on Care, Values and the Future of Welfare, Workshop Paper No. 22, University of Leeds, http://www.leeds.ac.uk/cava/research/strand1/paper22Sasha.htm.

Rowlands, R. and Gurney, C. (2001) Young people's perceptions of housing tenure: a case study in the socialisation of tenure prejudice, *Housing, Theory and Society*, **17**, 121–30.

Rowley, G. and Purcell, K. (2001) Up to the job? Graduates' perceptions of the UK higher education careers service, *Higher Education Quarterly*, **55**, 416–35.

Rubin, L. (1985) *Just Friends: The Role of Friendship in Our Lives* (New York: Harper and Row).

Ruddick, S. (1996) *Young and Homeless in Hollywood* (London: Routledge).

Rugg, J. (1999a) *Young People, Housing and Social Policy* (London: Routledge).

Rugg, J. (1999b) 'The use and "abuse" of private renting and help with rental costs', in J. Rugg (ed.) *Young People, Housing and Social Policy* (London: Routledge).

Rugg, J., Rhodes, D. and Jones, A. (2000) *The Nature and Impact of Student Demand on Housing Markets* (York: Joseph Rowntree Foundation).

Saunders, P. (1990) *A Nation of Homeowners* (London: Unwin Hyman).

Savage, M., Barlow, J., Dickens, P. and Fielding, A. (1992) *Property, Bureaucracy and Culture: Middle Class Formation in Contemporary Britain* (London: Routledge).

Schneider, B. and Stevenson, D. (1999) *The Ambitious Generation* (New Haven: Yale University Press).

Scott, J. (1997) Changing households in Britain: do families still matter?, *Sociological Review*, **45**(4), 591–620.

Scott, J. (1999) 'Family change: revolution or backlash in attitudes?', in S. McRae (ed.) *Changing Britain: Families and Households in the 1990s* (Oxford: Oxford University Press).

Silver. H. and Silver, P. (1997) *Students: Changing Roles, Changing Lives* (Buckingham: SRHE and Open University Press).

Sixsmith, J. (1986) The meaning of home: an exploratory study of environmental experience, *Journal of Environmental Psychology*, **6**, 281–98.

Sixsmith, J. and Sixsmith, A. (1990) 'Places in Transition: the impact of life events on the experience of home', in T. Putnam and C. Newman (eds) *Household Choices* (London: Fortune Publications).

Skeggs, B. (1999) Matter out of place: visibility and sexualities in leisure spaces, *Leisure Studies*, **18**, 213–32.

Skelton, T. (2002) 'Research on youth transitions: some critical interventions', in M. Cieslik and G. Pollock (eds) *Young People in Risk Society: The Restructuring of Youth Identities and Transitions in Late Modernity* (Aldershot: Ashgate).

Smith, J. (1999) The power of one, *The Guardian*, 26th April.

Smith, N. (1996) *The New Urban Frontier: Gentrification and the Revanchist City* (London: Routledge).

Social Market Foundation (2002) *Lifelong Parenting: The Changing Shape of the British Way of Life* (London: Social Market Foundation).

Solomon, Y., Warin, J., Lewis, C. and Langford, W. (2002) Intimate talk between parents and their teenage children: democratic openness or covert control?, *Sociology*, **36**(4), 965–83.

Somerville, P. (1992) Homelessness and the meaning of home: rooflessness or rootlessness, *International Journal of Urban and regional studies*, **16**(4), 529–39.

Southampton City Council (1998) *Southampton's Housing Strategy 1998* (Southampton: Southampton City Council).

Stone, W. (1998) Young people's access to home ownership: chasing the great Australian dream, *Family Matters*, **49**, 38–43.

Stewart, G. and Stewart, J. (1988) 'Targeting' youth or how the state obstructs young people's independence, *Youth and Policy*, **25**, 19–24.

Sullivan, O. (2000) The division of domestic labour: twenty years of change?, *Sociology*, **34**(3), 437–56.

Swain, H. (2001) Does home work or is it better to break away? Times Higher Educational Supplement: Student Focus Supplement, 19th January, vi–vii.

Tapscott, D. (1998) *Growing Up Digital: The Rise of the Net Generation* (New York: McGraw-Hill).

Taulke-Johnson, R. and Rivers, I. (1999) Providing a safe environment for lesbian, gay and bisexual students living in university accommodation, *Youth and Policy*, **64**, 74–89.

Taylor, I., Evans, K. and Fraser, P. (1996) *A Tale of Two Cities: Global Change, Local Feeling and Everyday Life in the North of England* (London: Routledge).

Thomson, R., Bell, R., Holland, J., Henderson, S., McGrellis, S. and Sharpe, S. (2002) 'Critical moments: choice, chance and opportunity in young people's narratives of transition', *Sociology*, **36**(2), 335–54.

Thornton, S. (1997) 'Introduction to part 1', in K. Gelder and S. Thornton (eds) *The Subcultures Reader* (London: Routledge).

University Grants Committee (1968) *Returns from Universities and University Colleges 1965–1966* (Cmnd.3586) London: HMSO.

Valentine, G., Skelton, T. and Butler, R. (2002) The vulnerability and marginalisation of lesbian and gay youth: ways forward, *Youth and Policy*, **75**, 4–29.

Villeneuve-Gokalp, C. (1997) Living as a couple but living apart, *Population*, **52**(5), 1059–81.

Vipond, J., Castle, K. and Cardew, R. (1998) Revival in inner areas: young people and housing in Sydney, *Australian Planner*, **35**(4), 215–22.

Wallace, C. (1987) *For Richer, For Poorer: Growing Up in and out of Work* (London: Tavistock).

Wallace, C. (1995) Young people and families in Poland: changing times, changing dependencies? *Journal of European Social Policy*, **5**(2), 97–109.

Wallace, C. and Kovatcheva, S. (1998) *Youth in Society: The Construction and Deconstruction of Youth in East and West Europe* (Basingstoke: Macmillan).

Watling, R. (1999) 'The high life: the apartment boom in Melbourne', in K. O'Connor (ed.) *Houses and Jobs in Cities and Regions: Research in Honour of Chris Maher* (Brisbane: Australian Housing and Urban Research Institute).

Webster, C. (1975) 'Communes: a thematic typology', in S. Hall and T. Jefferson (eds) *Resistance through Rituals: Youth Subcultures in Post-war Britain* (London: Hutchinson University Library).

Weeks, J., Heaphy, B. and Donovan, C. (2001) *Same Sex Intimacies: Families of Choice and Other Life Experiments* (London: Routledge).

Weston, K. (1991) *Families We Choose; Lesbians, Gays, Kinship* (New York: Colombia University Press).

Weston, R., Stanton, D., Qu, L. and Soriano, G. (2001) Australian families in transition, *Family Matters*, **60**, 12–23.

Whelehan, A. (2000) *Overloaded: Popular Culture and the Future of Feminism* (London: The Women's Press).

Wilkinson, H. (1994) *No Turning Back: Generations and the Genderquake* (London: DEMOS).

Wilkinson, H. and Mulgan, G. (1995) *Freedom's Children: Work, Relationships and Politics for 18–34 Year Olds in Britain Today* (London: DEMOS).

Willmot, H. (2001) Young women and intimacy, Unpublished PhD thesis, University of Leeds.

Wolf, N. (1993) *Fire with Fire* (New York: Chatto and Windus).

Wulff, A. (2001) Growth and change in one-person households: implications for the housing market, *Urban Policy and Research*, **19**(4), 467–89.

Young, C. (1987) *Young People Leaving Home in Australia: The Trend Towards Independence*, Australian Family Formation Project Monograph No. 9 (Canberra: Australian Institute of Family Studies).

Young, L. (1997) Now we are one, *The Guardian*, 1st February.

Index